ARE YOU A WALK-IN?

A NEW FORM OF BENEVOLENT BIRTH IS NOW AVAILABLE ON EARTH

Zoosh, Isis, Reveals the Mysteries, and More
through **Robert Shapiro**

OTHER BOOKS BY ROBERT SHAPIRO

EXPLORER RACE SERIES

1. The Explorer Race
2. ETs and the Explorer Race
3. The Explorer Race: Origins and the Next 50 Years
4. The Explorer Race: Creators and Friends
5. The Explorer Race: Particle Personalities
6. The Explorer Race and Beyond
7. The Explorer Race: Council of Creators
8. The Explorer Race and Isis
9. The Explorer Race and Jesus
10. The Explorer Race: Earth History and Lost Civilizations
11. The Explorer Race: ET Visitors Speak Vol. 1
12. The Explorer Race: Techniques for Generating Safety
13. The Explorer Race: Animal Souls Speak
14. The Explorer Race: Astrology: Planet Personalities and Signs Speak
15. The Explorer Race: ET Visitors Speak Vol. 2
16. The Explorer Race: Plant Souls Speak
17. The Explorer Race: Time and the Transition to Natural Time
18. The Explorer Race: ETs on Earth Vol. 1
19. The Explorer Race: Walk-Ins
20. The Explorer Race: Totality and Beyond
21. The Explorer Race: ETs on Earth Vol. 2
22. The Explorer Race: ETs on Earth Vol. 3

SHAMANIC SECRETS SERIES

A. Shamanic Secrets for Material Mastery
B. Shamanic Secrets for Physical Mastery
C. Shamanic Secrets for Spiritual Mastery

SHINING THE LIGHT SERIES

Shining the Light I: The Battle Begins!
Shining the Light II: The Battle Continues
Shining the Light III: Humanity Gets a Second Chance
Shining the Light IV: Humanity's Greatest Challenge
Shining the Light V: Humanity Is Going to Make It!
Shining the Light VI: The End of What Was
Shining the Light VII: The First Alignment: World Peace

ULTIMATE UFO SERIES

Andromeda
The Zetas: History, Hybrids, and Human Contacts

SECRETS OF FEMININE SCIENCE SERIES

Transformation
Benevolent Magic & Living Prayer

SHIRT POCKET BOOKS SERIES

Touching Sedona
Feeling Sedona's ET Energies

THE EXPLORER
RACE SERIES

ARE YOU
A WALK-IN?

A NEW FORM OF BENEVOLENT BIRTH
IS NOW AVAILABLE ON EARTH

Zoosh, Isis, Reveals the Mysteries, and More
through **Robert Shapiro**

LIGHT
Technology
PUBLISHING

For more information about special discounts for bulk purchases, please contact Light Technology Publishing Special Sales at 1-800-450-0985 or publishing@LightTechnology.net.

ISBN-13: 978-1-891824-40-1

Published and printed in the United States of America by

PO Box 3540
Flagstaff, AZ 86003
1-800-450-0985 • 928-526-1345
www.LightTechnology.com

DEDICATION

I'd like to welcome all of you who are walk-ins or who may become walk-ins or might know walk-ins plus everyone else who is interested in this subject. I'm dedicating this book to you all for your benefit and well-being.

Goodlife,
Robert Shapiro
2-16-2016

FROM THE PUBLISHER:

I know that the walk-in phenomenon is real because I have experienced it. I am happily living in my body as a different personality than the memories I have of living previous to the walk-in. In fact, there was such a difference that I took the name Melody because I no longer identified with my legal name, O'Ryin Swanson. So to all those people in Miami and Sedona who knew me as O'Ryin, I am still here, in Flagstaff, looking the same but feeling better.

I know many people who are walk-ins, some who know they are and many who don't because there is no current awareness of the concept, and one cannot interfere in another person's life without being asked. We hope this book will change this lack of awareness of the walk-in as one of life's possibilities. This book is largely the result of the million questions I had about the process. I was fortunate because Robert Shapiro channels delightful spiritual teachers who answered my questions during regularly scheduled sessions for book and magazine material.

If you have questions or comments about your walk-in process, we are setting up a column in our monthly metaphysical magazine, the *Sedona Journal of Emergence!*, to feature your questions, and we will ask the channels who contribute to respond.

To all of you who come across this book,
birth soul or walk-in,
I hope you have a great and good life,
Melody O'Ryin Swanson
18 February 2016

Contents

Spirit Replacement

Isis

December 30, 2015

In these tumultuous times or just busy life, there's a form of birth going on that might surprise some of you, and includes (just slightly before it) a very safe, calm, and (frequently) completely pain-free form of death. This form of birth is spirit replacement. This is not something forced on you. It is something you have chosen on the soul level while guided by your teachers, angels, and Creator.

You might move away from life, let go, but in the split second (the same second, no more time than that; it usually takes a hundredth of a second) you step out and within the next hundredth of a second, a spirit will walk in. That, in this case, might be you. What I mean by that is it could be anyone. You step out, and your soul goes on. You go and visit Creator. You have your after-death experience, and instead of somebody having to be born physically to your mother (in that most time-honored way done on Earth and other places), you are born in an instant in a body that is totally attuned to who you are as a soul.

Your soul must be very close but not identical to the soul who stepped out. In this way, you are able to assume the person's life, but you will find you bring in new skills and new abilities. Occasionally there will be things the other soul did in that body that do not interest you, but it practically never affects relationships.

It can, briefly, sometimes confuse your dog or your cat, but you might still have a good relationship there because of your brotherhood or sisterhood with the previous soul. So spirit replacement is a benevolent function of the birth-death cycle that allows you to have a gentle death and a gentle birth with no violence at all.

Introduction

Zoosh

August 20, 2002

Zoosh here. I'd like to welcome you to the world of rapid transformation. Transformation for most of you is slow — step by step — and a "this way, not that way" experiment. That's good in its own way. "Walk-in" (the term has been coined by another, so we will use it as a common usage) simply means the transfer of one soul out of the human body followed by the welcoming of another soul meant to come into that physical body. It is not random. It is not done without permission. Everything is done with sacredness and with permission.

Usually when a soul leaves the body, the normal process follows through: The body dies in a death, and you carry on as you're used to. In the past, it was rare for a walk-in to occur, but now you're having something occur that requires more walk-ins.

You are all quite well aware that the population on Earth is becoming not exactly excessive but reaching certain boundaries given that you need to grow food and have fresh water to support and sustain all the human beings plus your animal population. So there are certain limits as to how many human beings can be here, yet there are more souls who need to come to Earth than there are means for you to be born here. Therefore, the walk-in circumstance has been allowed by Creator to take place much more often.

When a soul has finished its life here (say you were born here, go through the birth process, grow up as a youngster, and live your life normally), you simply have a natural death, or your life ends in the way your soul expected it to, given certain parameters. Things are not set in stone; there isn't fate as you

1

know it, but it's an interesting philosophy. I don't like to think about it or talk about it as fate because that sounds very much like it's predestined. I'd rather say that there are certain potentials. So normally, then, your soul would go on, as you are immortal in your personality — your immortal personality, the soul. You go on, but the body dies.

However, in the walk-in circumstance, instead of the body dying, another soul attuned to that specific body that the soul, for this example, is leaving will be welcomed by that body only if it is that specific soul. It's not random in any way. That soul knows it's going into a certain body in a certain place. Your body knows it's receiving that soul, and they will be compatible with each other. It's important to understand this so that you understand this is really another form of birth. It just eliminates the long process of childhood.

There are billions and billions of souls who need to come here, some of whom do not need to be here very long but need to create either resolution from previous experiences or have a great deal to offer to the population on Earth. Because what they have to offer needs to come from an articulate adult rather than a dependent child, walk-ins occur most often in an adult situation.

It is extremely rare (and will continue to be rare) for a walk-in to take place for a child. If it ever happens, which is occasional, it will happen most likely after the child has passed his or her twelfth birthday. I have known a few seven-year-olds to have walk-in experiences on Earth, but that's very unusual. I'm talking a few, and by a few, I mean you can count them on the fingers of your hand. In your time now, walk-ins are something that could be expected for people who are seventeen years old or older because of what is needed and what needs to be resolved.

Problem Solvers Will Walk In

Now, you might reasonably ask, "Why are these souls so needed now?" You know that you have a lot of problems socially — from human being to human being. You have a lot of problems that are the result of technology's best efforts. This does not mean that technology is going to create problems. But very often when technology is in transit (meaning you haven't achieved the zenith of that technology), all it has to offer (and you are involved in steps on the way to create it to be the best it can possibly offer, given its parameters) are leftovers — for example, atomic waste — that you don't really know what to do with.

There will be souls who will come in who have had prior experience on other planets or other existences and not only will know what to do with that atomic waste but also have greater avenues of inspiration open to them. So even if they don't know exactly what to do with atomic waste, they will be open to receiving the inspiration and acting on it to bring about — in the most benevolent way — resolution to the problem of atomic waste to society and how to apply it and build on it to turn that into an industry that actually supports Earth and its population. There are such technologies; you just don't have them right now, not in any major way. That is one example you can all appreciate, given your awareness of these overall pollutants.

You might be surprised to find out that a great many of the pollutants (they are pollutants because they are where they don't belong or they are where they are not serving humans, other societies — animals and so on) in the mixtures that you find them actually can be utilized constructively. But those who will receive and work on that inspiration to create an overall vision and then go from there (you understand, there are lots of different people involved here) into putting it into practical application are not here with you yet. You can't really wait, given the urgency of these problems, for them to arrive through the usual processes — being born, coming up as children, going through school, and so on. You can't wait; you need to have them here now to handle these and all kinds of other problems you are aware of.

There need to be very clear-cut, easy ways for all people globally to be able to, in a heart-centered way, communicate with each other to resolve problems in ways best for all people so that you don't always "have the poor with you" or "have the starving" or "have the suffering." These are not givens. The idea that such things would always be with you is a philosophy born of cynicism. You can't have cynicism; it doesn't work for you. It simply perpetuates the problems. So you need to have many different souls arrive.

No one is kicking any of you out. Understand that as many of you think about people in your society, many of you might feel as if you're at your wits end. You've gone as far in life as you possibly can go. That doesn't mean you're not having a good time and you won't be allowed to stay as long as your soul desires to stay. But some of you, maybe not even consciously in your mind, I'm not talking about suicide here, might genuinely be needed other places in lives that follow this life more than you are needed here, or some of you might feel complete. You are having a nice life; things are going along well for you, yet you feel as if there's something else. You don't know what that is. I'm trying to give you landmarks, or too many landmarks in this introduction.

I'm just trying to lay out for you the basic circumstances of "what" and "why" so that it will prepare you to read the more specific details of this book. Just know, for you the whole experience of the walk-in phenomenon is something that is intended by Creator to support the most benevolent outcome for all souls on Earth as it is now and as it is becoming.

So on that note, enjoy this book. I think you will find it very interesting. Many of you will identify personal qualities within that you didn't really have a finger on before. You will be surprised to come to the realization that perhaps you are a walk-in. If you are, the information within will help you understand why your life has changed and perhaps what the sudden change is about and so on. I just want you to know that this book is presented with love and encouragement, and we believe (speaking for our spirit in general) that it is timely and perhaps in your best interest to know now so that you can welcome the process, whether you're coming or going.

CHAPTER ONE

How the Body Prepares for a New Soul

Zoosh

August 20, 2002

I'd like to talk to you now about the welcoming process in your physical body. I think you have some ideas, and there's been some research and even books written about so-called after-death experiences, so there is information available to help you understand what happens when you exit the body. But I'm more interested in talking about what happens when a soul enters a body that has been occupied by a previous soul. There have been however many years that the previous soul, the birth soul, has been in that body. The body has adapted to that birth soul's needs and requirements, and the body is instantaneously responsive to the birth soul's circumstances moment to moment. Then that birth soul leaves on its journey to continue life elsewhere.

Before a soul leaves the body, it usually feels in danger, such as by some process that lasts more than an instantaneous death. With an instantaneous death, sometimes the body's in shock but not always. Generally, something unexpected happens, and the body will have had a few days of warning. But for a death brought about by a lingering disease or, in the case of a younger person, a military death (during which the body feels in danger and therefore the idea of death is not surprising), how does the body prepare itself to welcome another soul? Obviously, a destructive military death would not be a good example, but you might have a circumstance in which a physical body would have wounds that are not debilitating. One soul would leave for a walk-in situation. The heart does not have to stop. As a matter of fact, that is not typical.

What typically occurs is that the soul in the body — in this case we're talking about the birth soul — simply feels complete and usually leaves in a moment (perhaps during sleep or in transcendence) of physical energy that is usually benevolent or pleasant during which one feels a little sleepy. At the very least, it is a feeling of vagueness. That's how the transition takes place, so I'm not talking about something traumatic. I am using this example so that you understand the possibilities.

The Incoming Soul

How does the physical body actually mechanically welcome the new soul? For one thing, in the case of something that happens like that (where there is notice to the body well in advance), a walk-in circumstance might easily be a situation in which the physical body is a receptive mechanism. I'm not saying that your mouth gets bigger or your eyes get wider but rather the actual energy field of your body extends. This is often referred to as your auric field. Your auric field will get larger. When your auric field gets larger in a typical human life, it is usually because you are sensing something, meaning you are listening or you are trying to feel something — you are expanding your energy self for some purpose — if this is something that occurs when you are awake. This is something that occurs well before the birth soul departs and the walk-in is welcomed.

The energy body doesn't just expand in circumference. Each individual cell in the body will have something like a cord — minute, obviously, given the size of the cell. Each cell makes up a different tissue, and these cells — let's say these are skin cells — all go out to your auric field with an individual cord. This is not typical. Typically, there is more of a radiance that traverses from the cells to the auric field, but here is a situation in which there is actually an individual cord (granted minute) to the auric field as well as the radiance, so it gives more than one path to the auric field. The reason this occurs is not because the cells are reaching out to the auric field but rather that the auric field has expanded on its own to create a broader footprint of where, mechanically, the physical body is so that the soul coming in can find it.

This also occurs when the energy of the soul begins to drift into the auric field from wherever that soul is coming from (it could be far away), and that soul doesn't want to interfere with the soul that's in the body at that time. What happens is that a thin cord comes from the expanded auric field and puts minute quantities of the expanded auric energy with a light tint (to use the term from the painting world) of that arriving soul. It only comes in minute quantities from the auric field to each cell as the cells can accept it.

There are minute quantities that come in from time to time as the cell feels more comfortable with it. In short, it is a gradual process; it's not as sudden and instantaneous as it seems to be to the conscious self when the walk-in takes place. Understand that when the walk-in takes place, there is usually, as I say, a moment of transcendence if you are awake, which is often the case. There is a feeling of vagueness. What follows is almost immediately an attitudinal change, meaning with the birth soul (and it's immortal personality) you might have very specific likes and dislikes, as everyone does. In this moment of transcendence, you might feel a sense of physical energy — benevolent, you know, a good feeling — or you might feel a feeling of vagueness. There might even be a tingling. I grant the tingling takes place during other circumstances, but I'm trying to give you landmarks so that you might identify the process.

What invariably follows is an almost instantaneous, across-the-board impact of attitudinal change, meaning in the moments before the exit of the birth soul, you have your likes and dislikes and so on, but after this transcendence takes place, those things that seemed to be so very important to you before — things that you could put your finger on and say, "I like this; I don't like that," not "Well, I like this sometimes and other times I don't like it," not that, but things you can really put your finger on and say, "This is something I like, and this is something I don't like" — that literally changes out of the blue. Suddenly something that you could definitely say you liked before becomes something you're not sure of. That's the transcendence, all right? Or something that you didn't like again becomes something that you're not sure of, and as time goes on, your likes and dislikes may very well change radically.

I grant that this is not always going to have a benevolent impact in the sequence of the life, but you have to understand what is taking place is literally birth — not in the way you normally experience birth, not childbirth as a woman giving birth to a child, but a soul birth is taking place. As one soul personality leaves and another soul personality arrives, there will have to be certain compatibilities between the two soul personalities because it is not acceptable from Creator's point of view to have a radical change — so radical that the people, the soul personalities, are polar opposites. That's not acceptable. There needs to be a sense of familiarity, a significant feeling that if the two soul personalities were there in two different bodies, there would be a friendliness, an affinity. So there needs to be at the very least an affinity.

Soul personalities, or just personalities, being who and what you are, have differences, even if you have an affinity. You might have a best friend right now or a loved one with whom you have a great deal in common, and you often agree on things, but there are very specific differences. It would be something like that when the soul then enters.

What is typically the case is that the absolutes of likes and dislikes change to a transcendence, meaning that all absolutes of likes and dislikes are not present. Some likes and dislikes that were not present before become present, and things that you might have (or the body might have) expressed, certain likes and dislikes, before then become vague for a while, usually for a few weeks. Maybe things that weren't appealing to you at all before suddenly become possible or even desirable. Of course, the opposite is true too: Something that was very appealing before either becomes less so or really becomes something that the new soul personality doesn't like at all.

As I said, this can sometimes broaden a life. Someone living a very narrow life might suddenly begin expressing him- or herself in broader terms. Often this is welcomed by friends and family. However, there are some circumstances that cannot be ignored: Sometimes there will be a lack of compatibility with friends, family, and the circumstances in which the new soul arrives. If friends, family, and the circumstances can change to adapt to that new soul, then everything is fine. Very often, they will get along better with the new soul than with the previous soul because the previous soul was — though unconscious to the personality in your conscious state — getting ready to leave. When you're in that transitional state, as you might have noticed with the elderly sometimes, there is less interest in the life that is going on, sometimes less interest in family or friends or the circumstance of life — a detachment, you might say.

Life Adjustments of the New Soul

With the arrival of the new soul personality, there is much greater interest in what's going on with the family, the friends, the world, and so on. Family and friends might find this more desirable, more interesting. For example, "Oh, I feel as if you're more present now, and this is wonderful and — what? You want to go bowling? You never used to like that. That's great! I love to go bowling. This is something we can do together. Isn't that wonderful?" So things like that are very often the case, but we need to recognize the fact that sometimes — don't expect this as always — there will be enough difference with the new soul personality coming in that they might not feel attracted to the life that they find their bodies have been living.

Now, we need to talk about that in detail. You can understand how one personality might not be attracted to the same things as another personality; that's clear. But what about the circumstance in which a soul personality comes in and isn't happy being married to the person he or she is married to? This needs to be recognized, because that new soul personality is probably going to want to leave that marriage and might do so gradually or quickly. Now, if you're the one who is left, this can be devastating. But I want to tell you something: This never happens.

I don't often speak in absolutes, but this is an absolute. This never happens without there being someone better for the person who is left in the lurch, as it were. This never takes place if there isn't at least more than one — there needs to be something like a gift for you — ideal person for you to be with whom you will like and love better than the person you have been with, who will improve the quality of your life in many ways. Many of these ways you did not heretofore believe were possible for you. In short, Creator would not inflict a trauma like this on you without making certain that you would receive a gift as a result.

This does not mean you will not go through some grieving process if it happens to you. I'm saying these things because some of you might have experienced this already. If so, I want you to look back on your life over the years and pay attention. Who did you get involved with? Not immediately, but who did you wind up settling down with later? Some of you will clearly be able to say, "Wow, this next person was such a big improvement." Generally speaking (I'm going to give you a percentage so that you'll know what I'm talking about), when that takes place, say, you're with someone, you seem to be doing all right, and suddenly, boom, out of nowhere, that person leaves — and not because he or she falls in love with someone else. It's because he or she just feels different. That person doesn't seem to love you anymore. He or she is a little vague about it and can't really express him- or herself. "I don't know why," he or she says, "but I just feel like I have to go on. There's something I need to discover."

In short, you just feel as if you're in a science-fiction movie. But within a few years, you're with this marvelous, ideal person. If you can look back at your life and say, "This really happened to me," the chances of that circumstance having been that the person who left you was a walk-in are at least 80 percent — if those specific circumstances occurred in that way.

I'm not saying this is the source of all divorce. I am saying that if you can use those landmarks as I've delineated, then you can be pretty sure that was the case and that Creator made certain you would have a wonderful new person to be with who provided a relationship you enjoyed much more than the previous one.

This information needs to be put out for those on the receiving end of that experience, meaning you're in a relationship with or you're the son or daughter of such a person who leaves. What might you expect in your new father or mother? Do they simply come into your life like Simon Legree [the cruel slave-owner character in *Uncle Tom's Cabin*]? No. Creator would not allow that. The person would necessarily be someone you like better. Creator does not allow such things, nurture such things, or specifically create such things if the walk-in is not going to be an improvement for all concerned. Is that not fascinating?

There Is No Trauma

We're not talking about possession or something frightening or terrifying here. That is an entirely different situation. This is no possession. It is not some horrible, agonizing, miserable thing. I'm not saying that possession is all those things, but I am saying that this isn't possession and that, to the degree that possession exists, it is something entirely different. The person who is possessed can be healed from it, and the person who does the possessing can also be extracted and healed from that. That's something entirely different, but I need to mention it for those of you who feel that this walk-in thing sounds frighteningly like possession. It isn't. A Creator-engendered phenomenon is another form of birth.

In the past, in your now linear time — let's take your generally accepted business calendar time of the past few thousand years. Let's just go back and say that before 1870, it was very unusual. How unusual? It was something that would occur to perhaps 1,000 to 1,500 people on Earth per year. Let's go back before that, from about 1500: It would have occurred to perhaps 800, maybe 870 people per year. Let's go back to about 1300. (These are just markers; they're fairly arbitrary years.) This would have occurred to about 65 to 70 people per year. When we go back to about the year 800, it almost never occurred — one, maybe two per year.

Bringing it up to, say, 1940, it started to occur much more often, to maybe 20,000 people per year. Then we come up to, say, 1980 — and you understand how it's moving gradually up; it's not just jumping from one to another — and this is happening to about 80,000 to 90,000 people per year. Let's jump up to the year 2000. It was happening to about 300,000 or 400,000 people per year. So you can see the number is moving up precipitously; the rate is increasing, and that trend will continue.

This does not mean that you have to worry. Many of you out there said, "Oh, I'm going to die," or "Oh, I'm suddenly going to have a trauma." As I say, the typical way for a soul personality, a birth soul personality, to exit the body during a walk-in experience is very benevolently, either during sleep or a moment of transcendence, like energy that you might feel or a tingling. It's very benevolent. You leave; the other one arrives. When you, as the birth soul, leave, you experience that leaving in an identical fashion (in most ways) to the way you experience a typical stepping out from a body that is dying. The only difference is that there is no trauma involved, so your guide or angel who comes to get you does not have to soothe and nurture you because there has been some traumatic experience; rather, it is more like a welcoming. It is literally as if you step out through a door.

You get up out of your body, if you're lying down (this doesn't happen while you're driving or playing tennis, you understand; you'll be sitting down, reclining, lying down), and just move out like nothing happened. You will see yourself in an energy body, and you will see yourself very much like you are physically at that time. By the time your angel or guide gets there and you literally take what seems like a step or two, you will almost immediately see yourself. If you are an older person, for instance, you will see yourself as you looked when you were in your twenties, younger and more vigorous. Even if in your twenties you weren't vigorous, you will see yourself that way, nevertheless. Is that not interesting? You will be whole and complete. Say you're missing a limb; you will have all your limbs.

Then you will move on through the veils (as it is sometimes called) or through the tunnel (as it is sometimes seen). You will, in short, move beyond physical Earth life and proceed the way any soul proceeds after a typical death. There is almost no difference. The only difference is that there is no trauma associated with it. There are rare occurrences when there might be a trauma. I'll use an example of someone.

This actually occurred: I recall an incident a year or two ago when a person was riding along on a motorcycle. He didn't have a horrendous crash or anything, but he was on a good-sized motorcycle. He found himself coming to an intersection out in a country situation where it was a two-lane road, but the shoulder of the road was not paved. The shoulder of the road tapered toward a drainage ditch farther off the road. The person riding the motorcycle was not paying complete attention, and when he rolled to a stop at the stop sign, he rolled on to the dirt shoulder, and the motorcycle rolled over. It had bars that extended out from it, as you sometimes see on motorcycles, so there was no damage to his legs, but he hit his head — not enough to lose consciousness, but just enough to know that he had a bonk on the head. He was dazed for about a minute and a half.

People weren't on the scene immediately, but after a couple of minutes, a car came along. The people stopped to help the cyclist, who was then up. They helped him lift up the motorcycle. "Are you all right? Do you need help?" There was no apparent injury. "Do you want to go to see a doctor?" The motorcyclist felt as if he only had a bump on his head, so he said no. But he described that he felt funny, so the other people in the car kept him talking until he seemed to be more lucid. Then the helpers felt it was all right for him to leave, and the motorcyclist got up on his motorcycle and left.

Of course, the people in the car always wondered how that turned out. The circumstances are that the person drove down the road, out for a drive in the country, you understand, about seven or eight miles down to the next small town. Then he pulled over on the side of the road and just felt odd. For one thing, he was a man in his fifties. It is a curious thing: a person riding down a country road on a fairly large motorcycle pulling over in the next small town. He literally looked down at the motorcycle below him, and thought to himself, "What on Earth am I riding this motorcycle for? I'd much rather be in a pickup truck." Understand that the previous soul had scrimped and saved so that he could buy this lifelong dream, the motorcycle. He had always driven around in a family sedan before that.

To give you some idea of this person's life, his wife had passed away a few years before, and he had two grown children no longer living in the house. The idea of driving around and exploring the country on a motorcycle was very appealing to him. But for this person, there was a transcendence; that soul left. The new soul looked down at the motorcycle and felt no sense of that old (birth) soul's attraction to the motorcycle at all. He didn't feel crazy; he just said to himself, "I don't feel any great interest in this anymore. I don't know what happened, but I don't feel any sense of interest." There's that feeling of vagueness, you see.

The man drove around the town and stayed overnight because he felt a little funny. He got up in the morning and looked at the motorcycle the way you'd look at something that you're not sure of. He got on the motorcycle, and being fairly independent and not pressed to go back anywhere — no dogs or cats waiting — he drove to the town's used car lot. It was a big, very nice motorcycle — a desirable object as far as the car dealer was concerned. The man walked around, looked at pickup trucks, and traded the motorcycle (an expensive motorcycle, you understand) for a pickup truck. Then he got into the pickup truck and drove back to his house.

I won't go on with this story; I just want you to understand that it doesn't have to be traumatic. That is an example of something that has some slight trauma with it, but he still loved his grown-up children. He loved the grandchildren; he found them appealing.

The Walk-In Soul Might Be Better Suited for the Life It Assumes

One difference the motorcyclist experienced, though: Whereas before he was not very comfortable with little children (the grandchildren were very young, and the son and daughter lived at a distance), he was no longer happy being far away in another state. So he moved to that state to be closer to his children and have better access to their children, who were little children he really liked. He now loves little children. Is that not interesting? So it can be a shift for the better. The son and the daughter said, "Gosh, Dad, you're so much fun. What happened, and what happened to the motorcycle?" In short, things change, but they can change for the better, and most often that is the case.

In this case, he came in because he didn't have anything that was particularly needed by the planet. There had been some distance between the son and the daughter and the birth soul that the birth soul could not resolve. There was a barrier; he could not resolve it, and he missed his wife who had passed away. He felt he had gone as far as he could go on the soul level, not the conscious level. He parted and went on with his life.

The new soul came in and had skills that were needed on the planet. What were those skills? He didn't come in to resolve atomic waste. The skills that were needed were the skills to resolve differences in the relationship so that not only would the son and the daughter find the father to be loving now but also have a wonderful grandfather for their little children. That is a resolution — something that was needed on the planet, simply needed by a smaller group.

The soul that left hadn't been able to create a resolution and was missing the wife who had passed over so terribly that he really needed to go on to something else, and he did go on. The soul that came in was able to resolve all the family problems — not just resolve them but turn things into a wonderful, loving situation that served all the people in that family who could go on and have a wonderful time together.

This is a simple example, but you might equally have a circumstance in another example, such as a woman living with her husband as missionaries in Africa. Granted, they had come over to support a longstanding mission there. It was a Christian mission helping many people to help themselves, but her role as a physician and surgeon was not only to serve the people when they were sick or traumatized but also to train young women and men as nurses and physicians' aides.

She had the experience — one soul left; the new soul came in — and instead of being an authoritarian teacher (which is the way she was raised and the way she was taught medicine) and speaking in an abrupt fashion to the young people learning, she started talking to them in a very nurturing way. She was very patient. I might add that her husband found this a wonderful quality. She literally shifted from being a physician and surgeon to also being a nurturing teacher. She also became much more involved in the day-to-day religious practices of the mission itself, serving more as a lay preacher than she had before. So this circumstance benefited the immediate family, husband, students, and larger community in the capacity of the mission itself. So this is something that Creator would not only allow but also nurture because things are improved.

She fit in smoothly, and the existing life fit her better than the person (the birth soul) who was in there. The birth soul went off and continued her life elsewhere. The birth soul had been in that position, had become a physician and surgeon, because of pressures from her family. She was expected to do that, and she went off to join this mission because she was also pressured to do that. She didn't want to do either one, and she not only passed on medical training the way she was taught (in an authoritarian manner) but also really resented having to give medical training in the first place because she would have much rather been a pianist. She was stuck, and the idea of the whole possibility of moving off as a soul without a personal death was attractive to her. The new soul fit the situation much better.

Walk-ins do not bring with them the conditioning that the birth souls experienced in the body from the trauma of birth, which is somewhat traumatic — certainly for the mother and very often for the baby. They didn't get all the conditioning and experience, some of which is wonderful but a great deal of which is very challenging, of childhood and growing up through teenage years. In short, they arrive in a very benevolent manner. They have vehicles, physical bodies, that have learned the street smarts, so to speak, or the necessary knowledge. But they arrive in a nontraumatized state, so whatever feelings, attitudes, opinions, thoughts, and memories are in the physical body are there when they arrive.

Those feelings, thoughts, memories, and so on, become decreasingly dominant over time because they bring with them a nonconditioned circumstance. They're more receptive, more inclined to be open, to things that the birth souls were not open to based on the circumstances of their lives. The new souls come in, and they do not bring any of that baggage, and as they get more and more settled in the body over time, the expressions of their personalities through that body are much broader, generally, than those in the body from the previous personality.

Possible Changes

DNA is used to identify people. Does it change after a walk-in?

There needs to be compatibility. The DNA will not change *at all* — can't change. If it changes, you then become an anomaly, and it might be possible to discern that, which might very easily disrupt the life of that person in some way in your society, which is becoming more and more technological. Remember the whole purpose of the walk-in experience is to improve the quality of life for all souls involved and *not* to create a complication with a potential discomfort associated with it. So no, the DNA will be identical. After all, the *body* doesn't change per se; the body is a vessel for the souls. But the body itself is identical, the only change is that the new soul is more relaxed, shall we say, in the body.

It might be a little uncomfortable for the first few months, generally speaking, while the new soul personality is getting used to what it has found in this vessel. Provided the soul personality in that vessel is reasonably encouraged by those around him or her or has enough self-motivation, the new soul will begin to transform within the body and adapt to the body. Over time, the new soul's personality will become dominant, of course, and the residuals of the personality that imprinted on that physical body, so the cellular tissue of the body itself (incorporating the whole body) can be responsive to the soul's needs, gradually changes. It changes because it has been getting ready to welcome that new soul. It gradually changes over time to adapt and embrace that new soul; hence, the physical body, then, entirely becomes the vessel for that new soul. But there is a period of transcendence, meaning there is a period when the body transcends from one soul to another — a lag time.

Which could be from what to what?

It depends on the impact of the birth soul on the body. Say the experience happens late in life (say the person is fifty-five to sixty years old, for example), that birth soul would have had a tremendous impact on that physical body, and it is likely that the transcendence, or that lag time, will take a while for that physical body to be the vessel of the new soul — a few months, maybe a year or a year and a half if there is a reasonable life, not a chaotic life. If the life is chaotic or if you're a soldier in the middle of a war, it might take longer because you'll have to at least be experiencing some peacetime for that to become calm enough to get settled. But if, on the other hand, life is reasonably calm or at least well ordered, then probably the bulk of the lag time will be resolved over, say, two to four months.

In another context, you once said that unless you're going through the birth canal, you don't have the emotional capacity of those who did, that walk-ins don't have the ability to respond emotionally. Has something happened so that this has changed?

Yes, something has changed. But before that, the statement applied to the "you wouldn't have." In that previous circumstance, you wouldn't express the same kind of emotions because you wouldn't have that baggage; you come in baggage-free. You wouldn't be likely to express extreme rage or frustration or profound passion, but you might develop it in time, depending on the experiences you have in that body over time. You wouldn't come with it because you wouldn't be arriving with preconditioning. Now things have changed a little bit, and because of the needs of Earth, the needs of your society, you're going to arrive in a soul that has much broader expressive capabilities. Even so, you're not going to arrive in a state of biased passion. It's still going to take you awhile to become conditioned to expressing strong emotions, with the possible exception of arriving as a soul in a traumatic situation (say, a body diseased or injured or a soldier in a war). You might quickly but not immediately (it will take you a few days, maybe a few weeks) be able to express very strong feelings. You might, for example, walking into a soldier's body in a war, find it very difficult to shoot other people. It might be impossible, in which case they'd find something else for you to do, or you wouldn't last very long.

Prior Soul Experiences

Are these souls who have had experience on Earth before or on other planets? Or is it full spectrum?

Generally speaking, these are *not* souls who have lived on Earth before. However, there are a *few* exceptions. Most of the souls have had some experiences of physicality in their lives elsewhere, but with whatever is needed — skills. In the case of our motorcyclist story, the soul might have been a grandfather somewhere else and loved the experience.

So they are part of the Explorer Race but haven't been on Earth?

Well, you can't be rigid about that. The occasional person might have been part of the Explorer Race here or there. Generally speaking, they can't come to Earth unless they are joining the Explorer Race. The Explorer Race is on Earth, so if you come to Earth as a human being, you're going to be part of the Explorer Race.

This book is serving the broader community. For those who are interested in the Explorer Race, that can be looked up on our website ExplorerRace .com. Our main objective in this book is to talk about walk-ins: the walk-in phenomenon, what is experienced as a walk-in, what you might experience, and so on. We don't want to wander too far because this book serves a specific purpose. This is for people who might become a walk-in. It's for people who might be affected by the walk-in experience. It is for people who are walk-ins — period. While there might be other subjects that are of interest, that's the primary focus.

CHAPTER TWO

Walk-Ins Happen to Improve Your Life

Zoosh

August 28, 2002

Now that the walk-ins have walked in and are happy and healthy, do they want to change their names?

If I might be precise, the new souls might not feel a sense of identification to the names they have, but it won't occur to immediately change their names. It just won't feel right. You have to remember that these souls arrive without names; they don't bring names. The souls don't have another sense of personal identity when they arrive. What is a little odd for the souls is to be given names at all. Think of it this way: When a baby is born in the usual way and the parents have picked a name out for the child already and they call the child by that name, the child does not respond to it for a long time because the child, or the soul in that baby, does not identify with the name as having anything to do with him or her. It is very similar in this situation.

You land, as it were, as a walk-in, and people call you this name, and sometimes (this happens briefly) people call you by name, and you don't even turn around. Usually that will just be a pause, then that residual energy within you from the former soul will react, and you will turn around.

There isn't a sense of personal desire to change the name. However, I often recommend to those who ask to consider changing their names to something they feel comfortable with if they are not comfortable with the name they have. This is not always possible, of course, but if it is possible, then I feel it is worthwhile. By "changing the name," I mean the first name, the name that one is called. In some societies, it wouldn't be the first name, but for English-speaking people, it is normally the case.

Let's say that the walk-in has been there for a few years and maybe changed the situation or something, and the walk-in really wants to establish his or her own identity. Then would the walk-in choose a name?

In that case, walk-ins might wish to on their own or if guided by someone, like me perhaps. I might say, "This could be a good idea." But it is not something that is always given because if the walk-in soul has managed to engage well, is performing well within the body, and is functioning well, it's not what I'd call a necessary thing. But if there has been some difficulty in engaging in the body and acting out the personality (even though there are very significant similarities in the personalities so that you can land in the body and the body can accommodate you), that's when I recommend a name change. It can make all the difference as long as you choose your own name, though of course not something that might appeal to you from where you're from originally. Those names are not going to sound like names in your culture, but you could use them as nicknames. Still I normally recommend something that is culturally acceptable.

Pay Attention to the Sounds You Make

How do walk-ins go about choosing names that are vibrationally suitable? Maybe they want to connect to the land or the water, or maybe they want a certain feeling. Do the letters of the alphabet carry those vibrations or connotations?

They can. If walk-ins feel a sense of strength or inspiration by looking at a particular feature of the terrain — be it water or mountains or sky — then they could pick a sound that strikes them as being in accordance with this feature. It will not be a sound; that is strictly an analytical accordance, meaning that when your mind analyzes a mountain, it says, "mountain," so maybe you would have to use *m* and *t* and *n*. It's not about that. Rather it's an actual physical feeling.

Now, how might you know what sound would be involved? I'll show you how, beyond the research, that has been done by others. Say, you see a mountain for the first time as a walk-in. You look at it, and you gasp. You make a sound, "Oh, it's so beautiful," or you look at the sea. Or you see a particularly beautiful sky, and you make a sound. Pay attention to the sound you make. That sound is likely to have letters in it. If you are able to, write it down. That is a sound that your physical body and your self, your soul, in harmony — in conjunction — identify as associated with that particular feature. In which case, if you wanted to, you could create a name for yourself that would support your connection to that particular feature.

I'm not saying this is the only thing to do, but I recommend it because it gives you a physical connection. It supports a long-range physical connection to that particular feature and allows you as an individual to engage more in physical reality and in the physical body in which you find yourself.

So, for instance, it's not like a particular letter is connected to the land, or whatever.

It's not fixed. Also, you might say a word when you see something, such as, "Wow, that's beautiful." However, that's not a real physical response. Say, you see it, you go [rapid intake of breath], and then you say, "Wow, that's beautiful." Try to write down, if you possibly can, the spelling of [rapid intake of breath]. It's not going to be easy, but try.

You can be pretty sure *h* is involved, among other letters. It won't be fun, but it's not a fixed thing. There might be *h*'s involved there, and there might be silent *c*'s. There could be various letters depending on how you interpret that sound. You might have to listen to it over and over and over again to get a spelling — at least one that would pass as a spelling for that, including possibly putting a little accent mark here and there. But it could be worthwhile. It is really a means of sound graphing, which is much more akin to what a musician might do. I don't want to get too technical here.

So there are no vowels that mean certain things or have a certain vibrational connection?

I'd rather not say there are, because if I do, then people will say, "Oh, that's how it is for me too." Maybe it isn't. There might be some groups of people who find that certain things apply to them in some ways as a shared experience, but I can't put it out and say, "Well, 'this' might be 'this' way" or "'This' might be 'that' way," because it might be a hundred different groups. What's the point? It's much easier just to take note of your experience.

Also, if you realize that you're a walk-in, taking note of your experience and your reaction to things is valuable, as it helps you to engage in the process of becoming physical. It isn't just about being the outsider, the observer, "Oh, I'm seeing a tree for the first time; isn't it marvelous." What does it look like? What does it smell like? That's analytical. What does a baby do when it can get up and move around? The baby doesn't think, "Oh, tree." The baby goes up and touches the tree because the baby does in physical form what it does not do in spirit form. In spirit form, the baby might go sit in the tree, but it does not feel the tree physically the same way. The baby goes over (to the best of the baby's ability) and touches the tree.

The next best thing for you to touch is sound. Since we're talking about that, sound is physical. So pay attention to the sounds you make that are not produced by a thought. A gasp in that sense doesn't come from your mind. Your mind is not structured as words connected to imply a meaning. It is a sound based on feeling.

How the Walk-In Assimilates to Physical Life

When the birth soul starts out, of course it doesn't have residual experience from the previous soul in the body. It imitates the people around it to learn how to fit into the culture, right?

That's right.

Now what about the walk-in? Is it going to be more susceptible to what's going on around it than an original, mature soul would be?

The question could be phrased this way: If a walk-in in an adult body comes into physical contact with people much the same way (or perhaps in some similar sense of physical contact as a baby might be contacted by the parents, touching and so on), is there a tendency by that walk-in to reproduce physically in the image of those people touching him or her? Perhaps it could be condensed, but that's the meaning of that question. The simple answer is yes.

Now, I grant that there are variables, but if you are just recently aware of being a walk-in and you touch a person or a person touches you, you are probably going to be more sensitive to that touch. How do you feel when you're being touched, or more importantly, how does the human being feel when you touch him or her? How does the actual arm feel, or how does the back feel? Whatever the feeling is, you have to understand that during the first few months, you will be highly receptive. You're going to tend to try to imitate that in your body if that is appropriate.

This is an expectation not based on rational, mental analysis but rather you would feel, "This is a human being," especially if you don't normally touch people as an adult, which happens in some Western cultures, yes? If you don't normally have much sense of touch and you aren't in a relationship or you don't have any kids running around and so on, then, on the physiological level as well as on the subconscious level, assume that this is the way you are intended to feel physically. "Feel," meaning you touch someone, he or she feels a certain way, and your mind says, "Doesn't it follow?" But your physical body would say, "Oh, this is how it's supposed to be," and then you might transform your body into that. If that's the question, that's a possibility. It doesn't mean that it will happen, but it could. The question is very technical.

It's also not clear to me. Are you saying the word "feel" as if the other person is feeling sad, then you'll feel sad?

No, I'm talking about physical touch. I'm not referring to emotional feeling but to the way a person feels physically. You pick up a ball; it's round. You pick up a cube; it's square, and it's angular. You touch a human being, and he or she is soft, resilient, firm, yes? Touch, feeling. You touch a person;

you don't reach back and touch yourself and say, "Oh, I should feel like this." When is the last time you did that? You don't do that. You touch, and it might go into you as a feeling, "Oh, this is how I am" or "This is how I might be" or something. It is not a thought. I'm trying to put feelings into words, which is a very poor means of defining a feeling, but for the sake of our purpose here, that's what we must do.

Life on Earth Is Trial and Error

I will say goodnight, and we'll see what others have to say. I'll just say this in closing: The walk-in process is intended to improve the quality of lives for all beings, including the soul that leaves, departs, without having to suffer. There's no suffering when you step out of the physical body in this way, such as there can be with a natural death, so walking out is fine. It's like that's it; you're gone. You go through the same or very similar processes that you normally do with a natural death or even an unexpected death — "death" as you understand it. So there is no terrible thing going on there.

It's not that another soul comes knocking on the door of your body, saying, "Hey you, get out." It's not like that, so don't be concerned about that. It's also a way to allow souls whose skills, abilities, capabilities, personalities, and attitudes quickly develop, because the personalities (the attitude for example) are able to come in and produce what they're going to produce and be able to do what they have the capability of doing without having to wait fifteen, eighteen, or twenty years (to be born and grow up). You often find that the walk-in phenomenon happens quite a bit more when urgent changes are needed, and there is no particular means to bring about those urgent changes other than some great event or catastrophic situation. But Creator does not like to create catastrophic situations if at all possible, although sometimes they naturally occur.

With most of the people on Earth now being anchored to the past timeline, walk-ins who come in are not automatically anchored to the future timeline. [At this time (2016) 45 percent of people are still anchored to the past timeline, and 23 percent are in flux between the past timeline and the future timeline. The rest of the people are tentatively connected to the future timeline.] However, they are much more amenable to anchoring to the future timeline, and this helps to support Earth and its peoples, including the animals and the plants, to be able to move onto that future timeline with less struggle. It is about the amenability, the acceptable experience of being connected to the future timeline.

But you cannot have souls come in who are already attached to the future timeline because that's almost like interference. They need to be amenable, accepting, of the idea of connecting to a future timeline that is more benevolent so that Earth and all her people can shift onto that and achieve that more benevolent existence quicker than they all are now.

Has this happened in the past?

That's right. In the past when there needed to be a change, this has been tried, but it hasn't always been successful. So that's the reason I'm not going into it. As a matter of fact, it has been unsuccessful more often than successful. This is one of the times I feel it will be successful, but we'll see. By "successful," I mean that it will allow Earth and all Earth's people to be connected to that future timeline more easily to achieve a benevolent society.

You understand, of course, that the animals and the plants are totally amenable to connecting to the future anchored timeline. It is only human beings who struggle with it. That's because human beings are here to learn. You arrive with the gift of ignorance, as I like to call it, so you can create reality. You can re-create your reality. In short, you can learn new things, do new things. You don't constantly reproduce what you've always done in other lives because that's what you know how to do. You essentially refresh that.

The point is that in order to move forward, you need some help without interference. This is a way. But to refer to things that have happened in the past, it won't help you very much. It might, in fact, cause you to feel intimidated because you might feel like, "They did it. What's wrong with us that we can't?" Maybe you'll be able to do it, and maybe you won't. This can help you to achieve the future anchored timeline more easily and more benevolently or at least before things of a major nature take place, such as conflict between one group of humans and another, which might create problems and certainly create delays. You might just feel bad, "What's wrong with us?" I want to avoid that. I don't want to go into what was done in the past.

What about in the past one hundred years? Have any people who have really helped the planet been walk-ins?

Lots.

Can you name names?

No, but others might. I do not choose to, but you can ask the others. Don't just assume that the people who are walk-ins are just mental or technical or scientific. Don't assume that at all. It's not all right to feel intimidated and shy about experiencing something simply because it's been successful in the past or has failed in the past. After all, I don't really have a lack of faith in humanity like that. You have experiences all the time in every life in which you try something and you fail; something doesn't work. You try it again in a different circumstance or perhaps in another way, maybe with new knowledge or new physical skills, and it works better. Maybe it takes quite a few tries to make it work the way you want. Just that, that's all.

Maybe you go to Las Vegas, you roll the dice, and on your first roll, "bing!" You win. Does that mean every roll after that's going to be a winner? Conversely, you go to Vegas and drop in your dollar coin in the slot machine, pull the arm, and nothing happens. You walk down the road, drop a coin into another machine, then bingo! You win $25.00. I'm not saying Las Vegas is an analogy to all existence, but I am suggesting that many different factors have to align to achieve success. Chance isn't one of them, although I realize that is one of the advertising pitches of the gambling industry.

✳   ✳   ✳

Your Heart Purpose

Isis

Can you comment about walk-ins?

Say there is a desire by a heart or an energy of the heart to accomplish a purpose. You can call this a line from the heart and the key is the purpose. One soul in one body cannot accomplish that purpose, but it can make a significant contribution toward that purpose until it's time for it to go on. In that case, you might have two souls. One goes up, and another one comes in. That single body accomplishes its contribution toward that heart purpose while requiring more than one soul to do so.

You might even, in other cases, have more than one walk-in but still function on that same purpose, perhaps having other things that the soul brings in that it wants to do. The second soul might very easily be able to accomplish that heart purpose where the first soul wasn't able to do it and struggled. Still, it was able to set up circumstances to achieve that loving purpose but the second soul was able to accomplish the purpose. It wouldn't have been able to set up the circumstances, however. So it's like a team effort within one physical body. I'm not saying this is the only situation in walk-ins, but it is a starting point as you learn.

It certainly is because that means that need of what the birth soul wants would draw that second soul in, right?

No. Things like that are usually set up beforehand, meaning the soul who goes into the body goes in with an awareness that it will be in that body. It doesn't know all it will be doing, but it will be in that body until it achieves its intentions. Once it has achieved its intentions, it could go on living, might even establish new intentions — which is less likely but possible — or simply return. Souls do not ever really consider that a death takes place because souls are immortal. As such, a soul occupies a body for a time. It doesn't think of itself as dying. It just thinks of itself as moving from one form to another; that's how it considers its existence. That soul moves out of that form, and if there is some ongoing purpose, a walk-in might take place. But normally when a soul walks out of a body, it is a death.

When that walk-in takes place, the soul that comes in, if there is an overall heart purpose going on for the planet, for the beings, for the immediate environment, for the family, whatever is going on, the soul that walks in is fully aware that it does not have to start from number one all the way up to whatever digits you want to apply to the heart purpose. It comes in with the awareness that things are already in place for it, and it only has to be itself. The heart purpose will be fulfilled just by you being yourself. This is why beings often say when talking to humans through a channel, "Just be yourself."

By just being yourself in that sense, you will fulfill not only your own purpose but possibly your portion of some other purpose that you may or may not even need to know. You might need to know, and you might not need to know. You might find out it is to your advantage. You might even find out it's to your disadvantage, and there's something you can do about it. The whole point is that you may or may not know while you are in the physical body, but when you leave, you will know.

Does this happen in a large percentage of cases, that it's set up before the birth soul comes in?

In a large percentage of the cases of walk-ins, that's right. It isn't always, but it is usually. A definition of "usually" on a percentage basis will be 70 to 80 percent of the time, meaning that it is usually the case that the soul, by living its life, actually sets up the circumstances for a heart purpose. Even the soul coming in will have set up the circumstances so that it doesn't have to go through all of this stuff and can land in the life that is already in existence, and because of what is going on in that life, that's the body the soul goes to — not having to take over that life as a burden and struggle through that previous individual's creations, but to land in the life and perform. Not just end that previous soul's existence by some benevolent means (you don't just wrap things up so that it can go on and do what it wants to do), but come into that body because of what is there. You are going to conduct your life with your talents and your abilities and do that job, let's call it, of living that life in a different way, which is usually going to be 70 to 80 percent more benevolent for that physical body and all the lives that body touches.

So you are going to do a more benevolent job. You might not feel for a while that you're doing a better job. You might feel grossly incapable because maybe the other soul had a more technical nature, and you arrive with less technical nature, even though your body can do all these technical things. Still, what evolves over time is you have other people do those technical things for you, or if you're in a job, other people take over those duties because you will be exhibiting skills and abilities your boss or the circumstances of your job might find more appealing. Your boss might say, "Oh, I didn't know you were good at that. Let's get you out of what you're into now and get you into that because you're obviously much better at that." In short, you are likely to do the work in a different way, just as you are likely to do the life in a different way. Usually this has a more benevolent impact for you and those around you.

For instance, in the case of people who have jobs in which many people depend on them, perhaps the owner of a company or a manager, you might find yourself doing things differently. You might suggest to other people that they do "this," or you might delegate differently. You will do things differently, but not because you can't do certain things. It's because you're not inclined to doing them, even though you know how. You're not inclined to doing them because your inclinations are different, some of which you haven't even discovered yet. But you discover them. Why do you discover them, and why do you discover them easily? You discover them because you've arrived in a life already created that has many things going on in it, and even though there are many things you will need to do based on your soul's desire, those things will in some way already be incorporated or connected to that life. So you don't have to start from scratch or square one.

The connections might not even be the life itself. It might be someone that person previously interacted with or sees, or it might be an old friend or a family member, something like that. It might be someone who comes and goes, it might be the location of the home, and it might be the location of the office. Something in the life is there that will trigger some activity, ability, propensity, capacity, and so on, that you have and that you can do easily — perhaps it's even fun to do — which might have taken you years and years, if ever, to run across if the previous soul in the body hadn't already set up those arrangements for you. That's why you go into that body — not just because of what you can do, but because of what the previous soul set up for you.

Because there is no time, is there some communication with the walk-in soul in which maybe new things are started or certain things are set up for that soul?

No. The soul that is originally in there in our example here will, on its own, have the desire. Remember I said that the walk-in soul has to have a lot of similarities. That's been established. Well, in this situation, you have the similarities in personality to achieve that. The middle ground, or let's say the meeting ground, between the two souls is that these things have been set up already because of the souls being so much alike. The original soul, having been in the body longer, in the case of the recent walk-in, all right, has already had an opportunity to at least feel out these particular areas to see whether they are something the souls will want to pursue. If they're not, then they don't do that. But the situations or connections are already in place.

The new soul arrives, and it's like, "Oh, I can do that. I already have the ability to do that" or "My body knows how to do 50 percent of what I want to do, so I already have the basic skills. I already know how to drive. So if I want to learn how to drive a speedboat and I already know how to drive a car, it's very similar. It has a steering wheel and pedals," says the new soul. You don't think like that; you just notice it. That's just a simple example. I'm not saying all walk-ins ought to drive speedboats, but if you think you might like it, then try it.

Famous Walk-Ins

Are you interested in telling us about any famous people who were walk-ins in the past one hundred years? Not necessarily famous, but people who have contributed to the ...

Ask me, and I'll say no comment or I'll say yes or I'll say no.

Tesla?

No. Always had scientific interests. How can you tell a walk-in? Remember, similarities but a tendency to strike out in new directions. There was a United States president about sixty or seventy years ago. He made quite a radical shift in his life in general. It started out that he would have gone into the family business. He even did so for a time. Then he took another direction. Good thing for the United States that he did. He literally, let's say, kept the country from reverting to a different system of government.

Well, have there been a lot?

Most of the time, walk-ins do not come to public prominence, but sometimes they do. It's not typical for them to come to public prominence.

So they might create an invention, change the way a company is run, run for office, or as Zoosh said, be a more benevolent father or grandfather.

That's right. They might just improve the quality of life in the family. They might even be in a tribal council, or they might get off the tribal council and make room for someone else who might be better. It's not just doing; it might be stepping away from something that one has done but has not done in a way that actually needs to be done by others. Someone is right there ready to take over the position and perhaps do it in a way that is better for the people at large, even though that is not always obvious but becomes obvious later.

So looking forward, will there be people in government and people who are famous? The whole spectrum of people on the planet are going to be doing things a little differently, have more ... ?

Yes. Walk-ins will become much more frequent, and I feel this is actually to your advantage right now. There are a lot of souls on the planet who really do not want to go the duration of the physical body's life capabilities, and this is one of the reasons you find so much unnecessary risk-taking going on. It isn't always the case. As you look back on other cultures, you do not typically find people jumping off bridges attached to stretching chords, like that. If they do something along those lines, it is a test. It is not something they volunteer to do, doing it for fun or like that, doing risky things with the idea of tempting fate, otherwise known as tempting death. When you see that kind of thing coming up a lot, that's a real landmark that there are many souls who really don't want to stay.

Don't assume because you're a risk-taker you're prepared to exit, but it is a sign in a society. Even in societies that don't have time for such activities, you might see risks that are unnecessary. That is something you see globally in some way — not in all societies, but you see it. When things like that happen, you can pretty well say, "Well, this is a landmark," to suggest not just that there's more population than people feel comfortable with in some places but also it's because it's happening in other places where there isn't so much population. You can't really say that. You have to say, "This is one of the landmarks suggesting that there's going to be a changeover in the soul structure of human societies at large." It's not going to happen suddenly for everybody at the same time. It has to happen gradually and slowly so that there is no disruption of your society. The whole point is to help and support you in your ventures to create, not to interfere and create something for you. That is certainly possible, but it's not going to be done.

Even if you're traveling in a societal basis toward something self-destructive, the interference won't be there to stop you. If it were, then you wouldn't be creating it yourself. You're in Creation School; you have to be allowed to create even if you make a mistake. That's how you learn. It might take a while, but you learn. It doesn't always take a while, but it might.

Sometimes Special Skills Are Needed

There's something we've never had before, and that's extreme sports. Everything is being taken to an extreme level.

Yes, there have been sports in the past that people might have identified as extreme. There was a time when skiing was considered to be an extreme sport, not just a sport of those who have leisure time, but a risky sport and so on. Now skiing is considered a winter activity, a pleasure for people. There are some hazards built in, but they are usually not life threatening. Now there are sports that people are not only exposed to, through media resources and whatnot, but actually encouraged to participate in that are very reckless and dangerous, and it is appealing to people now.

In time as walk-ins become more of a factor of existence — I'm not going to say when but well into the future — you will see such extreme sports and such extreme risk-taking fall away. You will still have sports, but it will tend to be ventures that are more cooperative rather than vindictive competitions. I'm not saying all sports are vindictive competitions, but there are some that are, and some of it is fostered. You will see that fall away.

Walk-ins might have a great love for Earth. They might want to encourage things on Earth to be done differently, but don't assume that they'll all be nice. Some of them might be adventurers. That doesn't mean that adventurers aren't nice, but they might land in jobs or occupations or lives that do not allow them to be just nice, in which case they'll have to adapt to taking over the dramatic life of the person they find themselves in. Maybe they'll be more pleasant, but that's not always the case.

Say you have a life established as a soldier, for example, and you're not a very successful soldier. Maybe your job is to train the troops that come in, and you're not very good at it; you don't relate very well to them. Maybe, according to your bosses, you're too friendly and too nice. A soul comes in, and the soul can be more abstract, not as friendly. Your bosses tell you, "That's the way to do it." I'm not saying that one thing is good or bad. What I'm saying is the new soul actually creates a more benevolent situation because the soldier, in that sense, is trained. The whole point from the military point of view, as I understand it, is that soldiers are trained to follow orders and not because they like the person giving them.

This new soul has an ability that could save a soldier's life.

It might save his or her life, and it might save the lives of the soldier's companions. So, you see, the soul who comes in actually can do more benevolent work in that position, which you might not normally think of as something spiritual, but it's more benevolent for the task at hand.

Walk-Ins in Potentially Dangerous People

What about people who are criminals or sadistic or dictators? They're going to be walked into also?

Most likely.

Then how do you see that? There's going to have to be an attraction in the person coming in for that kind of life?

Probably some aspect of the life, not necessarily mayhem or murder or other things, but there might be things that person does for which the soul coming in has a similarity. Let's pick something less horrific. Let's use the military again. Let's say that someone in the military is a sniper — a tough job. You don't often feel part of the rest of the team. You're a single individual, and the job you're doing is nasty. It's tough. There's not a lot of nurturing. There are not a lot of nights in the canteen with your fellow soldiers. It's kind of an isolated job. Say there's a walk-in, and the new individual is still a good soldier but isn't as good at sniping. Then the sergeant or the lieutenant or whoever notices this. "You can still shoot. I can tell you can still shoot straight, but you're not doing your job." That doesn't necessarily mean he'll be promoted to something else. He might be demoted because that's his job. But he might be able to find his way into some other thing to do.

Your question is in the case of, say, a dictator who is doing terrible things. Is the new soul going to be a dictator and do more terrible things in a more efficient manner or less terrible things and so on? What I'm trying to say is that there will be similarities, but by and large, the souls coming in will generally (you understand, I'm trying to create generalities here that do not cover all situations) be more benign than the soul that was in there because it is not arriving to a lifetime of conditioning and experience that allowed or nurtured or created or generated that soul to become that job or that personality. The new soul arrives and doesn't have that personality. It finds itself in that job and might not want to do it and might not be very good at it as a direct result. The new soul might make mistakes that are not necessarily consciously created but might be urged on by the subconscious self, which is really trying to suggest that the feelings are no longer present to do that.

Return to our sniper: Maybe the soul's feelings now are to not shoot that person at that distance, but the new soul still has that sense to do it, so he or she shoots and misses. Then the person shoots the sniper, and the sniper dies. Maybe the walk-in survives in the body. We can't assume that a walk-in will necessarily live on indefinitely.

You might walk in and be in the body for a couple days or even less time — not just be in the body for years and years. It depends on what you're doing. If you're doing a high-risk job in a combat situation, since I'm using that as an example, you might experience life for a day or two but maybe that was your intent. Maybe, "I want to try life. I want to have the experience of life, but I don't want to do it for years and years and years."

You're saving that first soul the pain and suffering of what is known as death.

That's right. The first soul gets to exit without suffering death and without suffering something terrible. Maybe that soul feared capture and what would happen to it because being captured is not fun. So that soul exits and is able to escape that terrible fear, and the next soul comes in and either inherits the fear or does not last very long.

So in both of those instances, that might happen to the dictator also.

It could as well as many other things. I'm not going to name names, but there was a dictator in your recent history of the past fifty to sixty years who had a walk-in, and here's what that dictator did: That dictator was pretty ruthless before the other soul walked out, and when the new one walked in, well, it's like when you wake from a dream. The soul noticed that he or she had a lot of money, was living in this country where most people hated him or her, and even those people who were close to the new soul were quite obviously suspicious. The new soul doesn't think, "I'm new, and I know this." Maybe there are a few people you feel good about. Maybe you feel good about your wife and your kids. You realize you're rich, and you have a lot of money, so instead of going on being a dictator, as the previous soul would have done, you simply take your money, leave the country, and go off somewhere else where you're safe, and that's it.

I'm not going to say who that was, but that happened as a result of the walk in. Then the person who succeeded was not as ruthless; there was an election, and the government changed. So it led, ultimately, to a better situation for all the people.

I can see all the little paths to a more benign life on Earth in whatever way.

Very much like capillaries or tributaries leading into a river.

The river is going to be a more loving way. That is wonderful.

Sometimes things change, and you get mad. You say, "Oh that dictator looted the treasury, and he left. This is a terrible thing." But down the road, the situation gets better.

I wish we could talk about real people.

Let's be careful because we often do not have permission to talk about real people and real names because they are still alive or, more likely, their descendants are, and it could make trouble for them. It could complicate their lives, or it could hurt them.

Benevolence for People Who Are Suffering

Where do all these souls come from? You don't have 2 million souls just standing at the gate, do you?

They are everywhere, well beyond your capacity to account for in your number system.

That many who want to get in and experience Earth before it's too late, before it's over?

You mean you want specifics. If you're talking about souls who want to get here … ?

Where are these souls coming from who are going to become walk-ins?

All points. Some of them want to come. Some of them might be making themselves available to come. They could go other places, but they're okay coming here. All of them want to come; no one is drafted. But as I say, the ones who, for instance, are "okay" to come, usually those will not stay very long, meaning from their point of view, it's all right to have a visit here. A "visit" from their point of view might not last very long, so you might have a walk-in situation near the end of that body's life.

But as you said, that's an incredible gift because the birth soul can go out without the fear of pain.

That's right. The birth soul gets to exit gently and comfortably with all of the loving tenderness the guides and angels can provide, and the other one coming in takes over for the duration.

We have souls on the planet who are more negative than they need to be. Is that one way that some of those negative souls are going to exit?

No. People who are more unhappy or suffering and so on, as you say, more than is good for the people around them or for their society are never doing so more than they need to be. They are doing so as much as they actually feel they need to even though others might not always understand why. So it isn't like that, but it might be more benevolent for the planet and all other people here if that soul is suffering and would be much happier elsewhere. Then that is done, and the walk-in comes in for the usual reasons, but it's not done to elevate consciousness, so to speak. (When I say "people," it always includes animals and plants, all of the species. Although, I don't like to say "species" because it sounds technical. "People" sounds more heart centered.) So it might be better for those who are suffering, but that would be interference, and that is not allowed. If that happens, that's nice. It's a pleasant side effect, but that's not the purpose.

Learning You're a Walk-In

In your book, The Explorer Race and Isis *[Light Technology Publishing], you talked about a group of souls (I thought it had something to do with a blue light) who were waiting to come in. Are these souls going to be walking in now?*

Not yet.

But they're still waiting? They're not part of the initial group of walk-ins coming now?

Correct.

Okay, we want to make this book a manual for walk-ins and their ...

Their needs so that their issues can be addressed. The main thing is this will be useful for people who are walk-ins and for people who work with walk-ins to help them understand the intricacies of the full experience. It's less important for those people, whatever position they have, to know about the technical aspects of the soul walking in and walking out. It's much more important for them to know, "Well, what about this? How will I feel when 'this' happens? How do I feel when 'that' happens? What do I do when 'this' happens? What do I do when 'that' happens?" That's an actual manual for experience.

The most extreme example is someone I heard from who was told he is a walk-in by a channel in a guidance session ...

Not having had any inkling before?

Yes. The person had no clue whatsoever, and he said he felt rage and a feeling that some- one had stolen his life and many very wild emotions about that. What's the best way for a person to deal with that?

For one thing, it is not likely that people would be told that if they're going to be enraged to the point of becoming violent. They might be told that because of their question, as they have been going to a being because of their confusion, doubt, and general lack of ability to proceed smoothly with their lives. In short, they might be told they are walk-ins to benefit them and help them to feel better, even though in the beginning they might say, "Well, what happened to my life?" meaning they wouldn't have had a chance to grieve the loss of the previous soul but, in fact, since they are not that soul, any spirit worth its salt will be able to tell them, "That's not you."

To the degree that you feel upset about that, you do not have to be upset. You can. I don't want to prevent you from being upset. Feel free to go out in the hall and be as upset as you want but not here. What I am saying is that these situations are not going to descend on people as a rule. Would you say in your example here that it is typical to feel enraged when you are informed that you are a walk-in? Or, for the individual you are asking about, did that individual feel enraged?

Yes, that individual did.

Why was that, if you can put it into words?

He had a sense of a life plan, and it wasn't complete. Then suddenly he wasn't there anymore.

But he is there quite obviously because he is present. The thing that's needed is to make the shift into being who you are. It's like when you are trained to drive a tractor, then your soul leaves and the new person who arrives knows how to operate the tractor because those skills are left in the body, but a problem comes up. There's something you need to do with the tractor. You might not know how to do it, and you won't have the finesse that the previous soul had. You'll wonder why, and you might be mad at yourself, "What's wrong with me? I've always been able to do this. I've always been able to move the blade just slightly, so why do I move it jerky now? I can't do it with finesse." It's because the new soul does not have the desire to be a good tractor operator and to move the blade just so. The new soul doesn't get pleasure out of that and might move around the blade of the tractor in such a way as to catch your attention, not the attention of others, but your attention that this is not something that you want to do.

A lot of the rage comes from finding yourself in a position, in a life, doing things in that life that you don't really want to do. So where the rage really comes from is that the spirit coming through the channel tells you something and the rage comes because you feel that you've been given a job for which you're not prepared. At the same time, you feel that the lines you've been given and the script you were handed when you showed up is not your script. You are angry because you are trying to fulfill a role placed on you by others, meaning the script they gave you: This is what you are. This is what you're supposed to say. This is what you're supposed to do. You suddenly realize that script is not your own script, so you're angry about the circumstances.

In general, the chances of you getting angry and that anger lasting a long time are very slim. It is rather typical in most situations to breathe a mighty sigh of relief and say, "You mean I don't have to do that stuff anymore?" That's the typical reaction 90 percent of the time. It is only the rare case in which the individual gets enraged because he or she is attached to the previous life — what the previous life was going to do, what the previous life intended to do — and the person is afraid of freedom, because he or she hasn't been conditioned (the body had never been conditioned) to be free. The body was conditioned to follow the voice of authority until the voice of authority was no longer present but was playing inside the mind.

Let's just say this: Rage passes. The rage comes from socialization, culturalization, of the individual. It does not come because the person is angry about being a walk-in. That point has to be made clear. Being a walk-in almost invariably produces the reaction of feeling liberated.

What is the general feeling? You said it's as if you wake up out of a dream. Is that how most people begin to experience that they're different from the previous soul? So mostly the situation is that a person suddenly feels different?

You feel different. That's the main thing, and you're aware of feeling different. Initially there might be some confusion, but it doesn't last long. The feeling that follows right on the heels of that initial confusion — and that's only for some people; for the majority of people, there's no confusion — is sometimes even greater clarity. The clarity, the thing you're quite sure of, is that you feel different. It is, in some cases, like waking from a dream. It's like, "Oh, all right. Now I see what I'm doing. What am I doing here?"

Maybe you find yourself in a job (it's probably not going to happen while you're on the job; that would be pretty hazardous). You wake up in the morning, get ready to go to work, and you say, "What in the world am I doing this job for? I really don't enjoy it much," and then you start making plans to change your job. Maybe you can do it immediately, or maybe it takes time and training, but you make plans to change your job and change your life.

This doesn't always mean you're a walk-in; it is rather the other way. This is typical for walk-ins. It is not always the case. Maybe you like your job. If you like your job, then you do it. Or maybe you add things to your job. Maybe you like your job, but it's not broad enough, so you add other things to it. There are choices and possibilities. You might even add things to your personal life and so on. Things are often added rather than subtracted.

But on the feeling level, what is the general feeling? This is going to happen to so many people who have never heard of walk-ins, and they're going to say, "What's wrong with me? I feel different."

They might not begin with, "What's wrong with me?" They might feel different. They might state that they feel different, but most likely they will say, "I feel better." For the people who say, "What's wrong with me?" it might be, in some cases, because they have landed in jobs with overwhelming, burdening responsibilities that the previous souls took on because of their conditioning and training in life. People sometimes have been conditioned that they must take on way more than is practical or even possible or very often necessary. Think of the conditioning this country is known for, as well as other countries, such as the rugged individualist. You do things yourself rather than having help from another so that you don't have to feel obligated to another, which is very anticommunity, antisocial, and even antifamily in some ways.

Life Is a Gift

You discuss in The Explorer Race and Isis *[Light Technology Publishing] that many people in America are trained to believe in sacrifice and discipline, which is really self-destructive.*

It can be because it's important to be taught that life is a gift. It might not last as long as you'd like it to sometimes, but it's a gift. If people are taught that, then they can experience the pleasures of little things or experience the challenge of learning things that they might need to learn simply to survive. Most people are not taught that life is a gift, but you'd be surprised how that is permeated in other cultures, that life has gift-like qualities — not always, not in all parts of the world. You don't always hear from those cultures because they're not producing as much history or drama, but it's happening. Now, I'm not trying to tell you how to live. I don't want to get into that, but what I will say is that there are situations and there are circumstances that are much more benevolent to your soul.

Your physical body has been established by Creator to do many things. One of those things, for example, is to enjoy sexuality, but look at your cultures. How many of your cultures, religions, and philosophies narrow down the possibilities so that you can't really get much fun out of that unless it's a guilty pleasure? But your body is that way. Are you going to say the Creator is bad for making your body like that? No religion would say Creator is bad, but religions almost say this by saying you're bad for being sexual.

You're going to want to say, "But that's how I am. That's my physical body. I want that. I need that." I grant that religion and philosophy are needed so that you will be sexual in a responsible way to others and treat them kindly while you are treated kindly and all that. Religion and philosophy do a good job that way, but if they're going to tell (train) you that having sex is bad, by the time you're ready to be sexual, even in an approved situation, it's drummed into you that it's bad.

So that too will change as souls come in with more benevolent, natural attitudes without the conditioning that Earth souls have now?

No. You will have to intentionally change it. Walk-ins cannot change things for you. I want to make it crystal clear (even though what you say might be partially true): Walk-ins are not here to save you as a culture, as a society. This is not about the Messiah. Recognize that it is deep in your religion and philosophies, of which you are a member — having been raised in such a society — even though you yourself are more interested in a broader outlook. Still, it is in there deep down.

"When are they coming to save us? How are we going to be saved?" The reason it's deep in there (of course I recognize you are also asking questions for the reader) is not only a reflection of cultural conditioning but, on other planets, in other societies when things go wrong, it is typical that someone comes to save you or lead you out of the mess. But this is Creator School. You are expected to create ways to lead yourselves out of the mess. You can't bring anybody here who is going to make it all better. That's why it's over and over again in your religions and stories and so on that someone comes to save you — the knight in shining armor coming to rescue you or the warrior with his or her great abilities or the leader or the seer or the visionary, no matter. It's always someone coming to save you.

This is something different; this is Creator School. You're here to learn how to create individually, but more importantly and more universally, you're here to create together. You have to create together just to be here, and you are taught how to create together when you arrive here as a baby, but you are also taught how to create individually. **Everything you do in every moment is always about creation.** I won't say never forget that, but if Zoosh were here, he would.

What we create, we have to take responsibility for the consequences.

Yes, but you can't think that way all the time; otherwise it will interfere with your life. You need to take note of the consequences and work with them in an attempt to improve them for yourself and others or to take note of their consequences, and say, "Hey, all right. Well done." How many people do you know who look at the consequences of something they created themselves (or at least participated in that creation) and say, "Hey, well done. Pat yourself on the back." Do you do that? When was the last time you did that? It's important to take note of that. When was the last time you said, "Hey, well done"? Very often you're inclined to say, "I did that again. I messed up." I'd really like to at least hear you say in an equal amount, "Hey, I did a good thing. Look how it turned out. All right! Well done, me."

A New Understanding

Let's look at walk-ins. They wake up or feel elated or have more clarity than what? In many cases, they are not going to know they are walk-ins.

In most cases, they're not going to know they're walk-ins, but even if you as an individual don't have a walk-in and you suddenly wake up and have more clarity — which often happens after sleep, a deep dream, a talk with your teacher — act on the clarity, especially if it's benevolent for you and others around you. Act on it. Don't just say, "Oh, I understand that now." What are you going to do now that you understand it? You see it clearly. You feel it. It makes so much sense. You know it's good for you, and you consider it. You think about it. Is it good for others? Once you determine that, then do something with it, or at least write it down, and say, "I now realize and understand this in a new way."

Maybe it was something your partner or a friend or someone was trying to tell you, and before this, nothing; you couldn't get it. It wasn't clear. You woke up in the morning after some explanation from your teacher, you finally got it, and it lasted in your life. "I get it. I completely understand it." Make a note because you know when you wake up from a dream that there's a progression of consciousness. Sometimes by the time you get fully conscious in your personality, you've already let it go, it's not as clear, or you have drawn the line in the sand and are determined to defend it even if you understand the other position very well.

You're saying it's not important for people to know they're walk-ins?

No. It's just important to take actions that support you and others based on your feelings and what you want to do. What I'm saying is that this book might be helpful to people who are aware they are walk-ins or people who might consider that they could be walk-ins. It is also filled with advice that would be good for people in general who simply become aware of a skill or talent, and by George, they might even be good at it. This often happens in a life as you discover your talents and abilities. So in that way, this book is intended to be life affirming and to help you to discover who and what you are so that you can live more easily. If there are things you don't do easily, you know other people who can, and you say, "Maybe I don't have to go into this as a career."

That's true. Many, many people fall into lives and never check out what their talents and abilities are.

Yes, because of the circumstances. Maybe your father was "this" or your mother was "this," and a business is waiting for you. It's being handed down to you. Often you feel ungrateful if you don't take it up, and it's true that sometimes you do take it up or you feel you have to take it up or there are other reasons you take it up, but even if you do that, still be open to exploring what other talents and abilities you have, even if it's just a part-time activity. If you feel the desire to paint pictures but you have to work in a plant, okay. If you really have to work at the plant, then go work at the plant, but get yourself a paint set. Learn about it. Go take a night course, or watch a video that teaches. In short, do it. Do something else that you like to do if you can. Of course, if it's radically different — you want to go to sea — then you'll have to make a decision.

So a person should be open to the possibilities even if he or she is not a walk-in? If you want to change your life, then have the courage to do it.

I'd rather say that if you feel a talent ... you might not know it's a talent. You're probably going to feel it as an interest. It's going to be hard for you to tell the difference between an interest and a talent until you pursue that interest. If it's easy for you to do, and you will know because other people around you (if you're pursuing it with others in a class) are going to be struggling, but for you it comes easily. Then you'll know you have a talent for that. That's the advantage of doing something in a class even though that's not always available. I'm not saying you should sign up for four years of education on that. Just see whether you can do it for one night, an afternoon, or a weekend. You'll know after that whether you have a talent. If you don't have the talent, that doesn't mean don't do it if you still have an interest. Stay with it. But if you have a talent, take note that maybe this is something that would be good for you to do if you like doing it.

I grant that does not always lead to good things. For example, you might have a talent for being a good safecracker, so I'm not talking about that. Generally, I'm talking about things that you know are benevolent, but I also recognize you might have the talent to be a safecracker. Maybe you can be a locksmith because you have a talent for opening locks.

When people feel different, their lives seem different. When would you advise people who think they might be walk-ins to look for professional help?

If they're aware that they are walk-ins and if they're aware of someone who works with walk-ins, then it's beneficial to those people, by all means. But as Zoosh said about this book, we are attempting to nurture a cottage industry, some of which might have already begun, to support people who are or think they might be walk-ins, and some people who think they might be but aren't. We're trying to provide a means and more depth so that that can be done.

When to Share with Others

People feel different; they don't know how to describe it, but they feel different. Should they talk about this to their coworkers and friends?

No, not unless you know they are comfortable with New Age phenomena or the metaphysical. In short, don't bring up the idea to your friends and say, "Gosh, I think I might be a walk-in," and they say, "What?" Obviously, be circumspect unless you feel people are open to discussing it, even if they are New Agers, but they don't identify you as a walk-in. If you feel they are New Agers or embrace the metaphysical or are even open philosophically to discussing such things, you can mention this, and you can talk it out. It might be helpful, obviously, to talk about it to people who have some knowledge of it or who are open to pursuing some knowledge of it.

But this answer is given in August 2002 ...

Then there might be more awareness of it in later years. For instance, you could say that thirty years ago people wouldn't be likely to say on the street corner, "Do you believe in flying saucers? Do you think they exist?" Nowadays someone might say that without fear of being laughed at or made to feel crazy. When the walk-in phenomenon becomes more generally accepted as a possibility and as a way of arriving as a soul and expressing the personality ... I don't like to use the term "birthing" even though I understand your use of it.

This doesn't mean that in five years there won't be more people interested to know about it, but it might not be at that point in comparison to the flying saucer situation, say, in 1972. People wouldn't have been as quick to say, "Oh, flying saucers. Sure, they could exist" or "They absolutely exist" or "Gosh, I saw something strange; it could have been one." Go back another thirty or forty years when people wouldn't talk about it in the open at all, unless they're at a convention or in a circumstance where people might be open to talking about it, at least as a fictional possibility.

What I'm saying is that even ideas, philosophies, or general beliefs take a while to be accepted as possible, to say nothing of being true.

CHAPTER THREE

The Physical Effects of the Walk-In Experience

Zoosh

August 30, 2002

I'd like to know whether each of the following is a function of the physical body that changes with the walk-in phenomenon, or does the soul regulate it? The first one is metabolism.

Metabolism, to a minor degree, especially in the beginning, is very unlikely to be affected much more than 2 to 3 percent, but over time, it might experience as much as a 10 percent impact. This is not directly associated with the change of soul but rather your own physical body is able to respond to you in ways that, for various reasons, it didn't respond to the previous soul. For instance, the previous soul might have been distrustful of the physical self or unhappy or frightened in many possible situations, which tends to make the body not shut down but sort of clamp down a bit. As you feel comfortable in your body or begin to do things — maybe for all you know your body's always wanted to do certain sports or activities or interactions with other people, in short have fun — then your body begins to open up more. As your activities increase — safely, of course, for older people or those who have certain health problems, then one proceeds cautiously. Nevertheless, the metabolism might improve to the degree of functioning better by as much as 10 percent, which is a significant difference.

Now, would that be the same as energy levels?

No.

Would energy levels change, like the amount of light-force energy available to the walk-in? Would that change after the walk-in is in?

It takes awhile. First it takes time to build up trust; the physical body will have a wait-and-see attitude. It will notice immediately, of course, a big difference, but it will take a wait-and-see attitude to know whether you are going to carry on in step with the previous soul or unfold into being your true self, which the physical body might actually be interested in or want to feel what that's like. So as that unfolding takes place over time, it is possible that the energy levels can increase. But what will ultimately increase the energy levels, especially in an older person since an older person is asking the questions, is greater physical activity done carefully and gently so as to invigorate the body in a safe way.

With a younger person, a more vigorous person, the energy levels might go up quite a bit if he or she has been suppressed. Equally, perhaps you have a person who is overly energetic, meaning that he or she has more energy than he or she knows what to do with. The person has difficulty relaxing — the previous soul, you understand. The parting soul is edgy and nervous and agitated all the time. The new soul that comes in may not be like that at all, so over time what occurs eventually is balance.

The whole point is balance. You want to have enough energy so that you can do what you would like to do given your stage of life, meaning young, middle-aged, elderly, and so on. You also want to be able to relax and be calm so that your sleep states are not disturbed by excessive, agitated energy, meaning you only nap instead of sleep deeply.

Allergies

Are allergies a function of the soul in its lessons or of the body?

Allergies are usually a function of the body in reflection to growth, you understand, to the soul's desires. So it is true that, if there's a walk-in situation in which the previous soul has left and the body has been created by that previous soul (let's just say that's how it worked), then the body is literally functioning as a creation with certain biological factors going on that would tend to create sensitivities. However, it is possible that within three or five or no more than seven years, the allergies might moderate, meaning not be as severe, or perhaps a change in location would be beneficial or perceived as beneficial.

It might be something worth checking up on scientifically to notice whether the physical body reacts differently. I might add that there's been some scientific research about this in the past, not based on the walk-in phenomenon, but how the body reacts over time and in different stages of life to allergy tests. I'm not trying to create an allied arrangement between those who study or experience walk-ins and those who practice the science of allergy study and so on. If you have allergies, don't assume that you don't have them after the walk-in takes place, but pay attention. See whether things improve. Don't expect the improvement right away; it may or may not improve.

What about sleep cycles and biorhythms? Should they be dealt with separately, or are they one thing?

Separately.

What about sleep cycles?

Sleep cycles are bound to change, very often radically. You have to understand you have what amounts to a soul being born. You have a soul being born into an adult body, or a mature body in most cases, and it's going to be excited. It wants to go here, go there, do things, and think differently. It's feeling feelings it hasn't felt before. In short, pretty exciting stuff. So you might have a sleep cycle that flip-flops or becomes difficult. It might take a while to create a practical sleep cycle. If your schedule for your life is flexible, allow your sleep to take place when it does. If your schedule is not flexible, then you might have to do things to support sleep.

I recommend aromatherapy because you can set this up for when you sleep. I think you can get good advice on that from aromatherapists, and I won't go into that. I would recommend some kind of a consultation to learn about certain fragrances to smell in your bedchamber at night. This might be more beneficial for some, less so for others. It is useful. I don't recommend sleeping pills unless your previous soul took them. If so, you may not be able to stop taking something, especially if there's a dependency on them. Don't do anything radical as far as altering medications. Keep up things pretty steadily, but take note of what you need. Expect your sleep cycles to be interfered with. It is likely. It might take as much as six months to calm down. During times of exploring, looking into things, inquiring, or perhaps being exposed to a great deal of energy (attending a channeling for instance) might tend to stimulate that circumstance again, but it will calm down.

Confusion with Other Medical Issues

How do people know they're walk-ins, and especially when they don't know, how can we train the doctors not to misdiagnose them?

You can't train the doctors. They're going to think New Age stuff is baloney. You have to be crystal clear and realistic. Not all doctors think that, obviously. The people you're going to train or the people you're going to support to work with walk-ins are probably not going to be MDs. Possibly not even naturopathic doctors. There are going to be other people.

Well, I didn't ask my question right. What can we do to keep walk-ins from being misdiagnosed? What can walk-ins do if they're aware? How can they be protected from being given pills for something that's a natural change for the new soul?

Well, you have to keep in mind that if you're experiencing a symptom that is uncomfortable or even a dangerous symptom and you go to see a medical doctor who puts you on a prescription, it is not for me to say you shouldn't take it. But you ought to be aware that if you're taking something on your own or because of a recommendation, it never hurts to check to see whether you don't need it anymore or perhaps reduce the amount you're taking. Is that what you're asking? Rephrase your question if you need to.

I'm concerned that when a walk-in comes in and the pattern of the person's life changes, if the person doesn't know what happened and the doctor doesn't know, there could be a possible misdiagnosis.

I appreciate your concern, and that's why it's valuable to work together to put out this book. That's all you can do and hope that it will broaden interest in the subject for others in their fields, including some metaphysically oriented physicians, who might be inspired to write articles or even channel. Some do, and they might be able to contribute in a way that could be read by others or absorbed by others. In short, it is our job with these books to influence and educate those who read them or hear about them — or get snippets in this way or that or even read an excerpt. It is not our job to change the world all by ourselves, so I appreciate your concern. Know that the book will (for our and other spirit beings and you, if I can speak for you at this moment) contribute our part to bringing about a greater awareness of this situation and that we invite others who channel and who are inspired to write about this situation if they feel the desire or the call to do so.

Could loss of memory, when the walk-in loses a large percent of the memory that was in the body due to the exiting soul taking it with itself, be mistaken as symptoms of amnesia? Is there a danger of the walk-in being diagnosed with Alzheimer's?

No, because Alzheimer's has other qualities, other symptoms. I grant that in the past there was a lot of confusion about that as the syndrome was being isolated from other things. But, no, I think as an individual concourse (shall we say) of symptoms, which vary a bit in that particular syndrome, that as time goes on, more and more is understood that it is a disease exacerbated by heavy metal pollution. It isn't the cause, but it is exacerbated in some people, especially those who have been exposed to levels of microwave energy. Just being around microwave energy doesn't do more than lower your immune system. But consider there are so many things in your culture nowadays, your technological culture, in your modern society that lower your immune system that you can't really say that one thing is the cause. Many things are creating susceptibility in people.

This is the challenge for doctors because a blanket cure is not always available. It works for some and not others, and there's not much you can do about that for now. In time, you will not use microwaves for anything, including cooking food. It will take a while to develop further and perfect other means to communicate effectively and economically and do all the other things you are using microwaves for now.

I think that these developments will happen in a less restricted fashion in other countries since there is a certain bias as technologies become established within industries to perpetuate them. In other countries, this will develop. There will be at first a competing system, and then in time, you'll replace microwaves. That will help.

If you measure the heart rate of a person, will that change with a walk-in?

No. It might at the moment of the walk in, but as far as the overall heart rate, no. The basic physiology of the body performs and functions rather like it did before. However, the motivations, the personal motivations, might change. Thus, you might develop a difference in your body but only based on what you change — exercise, diet, and so on. This is not a direct cause of the walk-in but rather the interests that the new soul has.

What about the immune system? Is that part of the physiology?

Yes.

Same-Sex Relationships

Is there anything else that the soul actually might cause to change in the bodily functions?

It is possible that the new soul might have a different sexual bias because nowadays you have a circumstance that didn't exist forty, fifty, or sixty years ago. Forty, fifty, or sixty years ago, people were talking about the population explosion, and now you're living it. As a result, as more people are living in a single place, meaning a single planet, you're going to develop — and many of you have seen the results and some of you are more comfortable with it than others — a greater sense with the sexes. You will have more bisexuality or more homosexuality and lesbianism simply as a result of necessity. Some social institutions and even governments are trying to make it difficult or impossible to do this, but realistically speaking, people's sexuality is a drive. It's not a drive to re-create the species contrary to what you think.

In the beginning, when humans were populating Earth, that was unconsciously part of the motivation. But for the vast majority, 99.9 percent — let's be specific, roughly 99.87 to 99.99 percent (in that range most of the time), with a few exceptions in places where there have been vast catastrophic situations, but I don't think that is really a factor for most continents except occasionally for island populations — the desire to have sex for the sake of having sex or love, demonstrated love between people, is because it's fun or at least intended to be fun. So since this drive is realistic for most people (not all), then you have to recognize it is only typical, to be expected, given the state of the world population and Mother Earth, you understand? Your bodies are made of Mother Earth, and if she is uncomfortable with more and more and more people, she would much rather you not produce as many children. Of course, this is one of the simplest ways to help her, and she doesn't manipulate you this way. It just happens on the basis of creation. Creation can be very practical.

As I've said in the past and continue to say and will say more so in the future, expect to see more same-sex relationships. I would appreciate it, my friends, if you would be more comfortable with that. You don't have to participate in it yourself; you don't have to. Just be open to it when you see it. You don't have to blow kisses to couples like that, but at least tolerate it. In time, consider that if these couples are not producing children (which they could do of course, through various means, especially technical means available to people these days, to say nothing of adoption) as in a male-female relationship in a marriage and so on, this is actually perhaps to your advantage because of the population.

It is much better to reduce the population lovingly than to have it reduced by catastrophic means. Don't take this as a threat. I'm just talking about reality. When planets (or let's say people) have felt overwhelmed by the population in the past, they have often produced some kind of event that would simply reduce that population. The Great Flood was a reality, all right, and it happened more than once. That's why scientists have been able to find physical evidence — because it existed. Such a thing existed. Don't be caught up, scientists, in the idea that this is some kind of a biblical story and doesn't bear researching. I think many people have researched it and found physical evidence. It's true. So those kinds of floods are almost always caused because Earth says, "Okay, too much," or too much of something extreme was going on in the population. Though flooding has been used as a weapon in the past, it hasn't been used that way in your time. Well, not particularly, just a little bit.

So sexuality as far as the walk-in goes, the souls being born now (in the usual way through mothers) are going to be open, not biased, to the degree of about 50 percent more. This goes for walk-ins and births and babies and so on; all of these souls are going to be about 50 percent more open to experiencing — when they grow up (in the case of babies) or as they become more comfortable in the physical bodies where they find themselves (in the case of walk-ins) — some form of same-sex sexuality or in being completely accepting of other people doing that. That's perhaps the most significant change you'll note.

Of course, it would be very easy to say that this is to be expected, given that the population of Earth is way more than many of you ever dreamed it would become, and it will continue to grow. People have to live somewhere, and food has to be grown. So at some point (obviously and quite clearly this has occurred already in some places) governments are going to have to step in and say to male-female couples, "I'm sorry. You're not going to be able to have more than two children." Then the time will come when, "I'm sorry. You're not going to be able to have more than one child."

For those of you who want big families, it doesn't have to mean that you won't have many children around. There are cultures even today on Earth, perhaps to a lesser degree, where children are somewhat shared. There will be couples who for one reason or another can't have children, but you might have friends in the neighborhood, and the kids come over and hang out with you for a while. The traditional side of that is that if children needed supervision, any adult who is responsible and could offer supervision might do so. Certainly, you have that now with babysitters and childcare. So recognize that adults also like to be around children simply because they're fun and so forth. Grandparents often are not exactly blood-related, like "Uncle" or "Auntie" or something like that, so you can share children to a degree. So for those of you who would like to have ten children in the future, maybe the neighborhood will have ten children you can get together sometimes.

I think when it goes to one child only, it probably won't have to go to the point where governments say, "I'm sorry, but you can't have any children." But at the point where they start saying, not universally but frequently and commonly, "No more than two children," you will already have more homosexual couples than you do now, especially if children are raised where they hear, "If you feel like this — if you feel attracted to the same sex — that's all right."

Right now, many of your cultures do not say that and might force such a child into a relationship with the opposite sex. That almost always turns out to be problematic for the person and creates a lot of unhappiness as time evolves. But if you know, if you are forewarned that same-sex attractions are going to become more and more common, then just know it is intended not only to give you the option of having such a circumstance (which is universal on other planets of course, that option) but also, in a loving way, reduce the population gradually over time in the most generous, kind, and nurturing way.

How to Tell Others You Are a Walk-In

Now let's look at the walk-in from the point of view of significant others. Do you have advice for when a partner suddenly changes, has different ideas, and seems different?

Yes. This can be a challenge for the lover and even other family members. It can be very challenging — if you come to believe and are able to pick up on the various signs from your lover, your brother or sister, your mother or father, or even (rarely) your child — to realize you are living with someone who is a walk-in. Don't just tell them they are. If you notice it, you notice it. If, on the other hand, they tell you they are, you can (with the assistance of this book and others) observe the traits and features that might help you to see whether or not that's true.

The main thing that will be required of you (for your own sake as well as for the sake of the walk-in soul) is patience. Don't assume that anything will happen or that the soul will be "this" way or "that" way. Try to avoid jumping to conclusions one way or another. There is no hard and fast rule for how walk-ins might express themselves in a physical body. They might change in some way that is significant. As long as it is benevolent, just be willing to go along with it.

You can look for signs, though. Don't assume, and don't bring it up if the other party hasn't, but if you are living in a metaphysically aware or New Age aware or even holistically aware family or relationship (a situation like that), you can gently broach the topic if you feel it's possible. You can even bring it up and talk about it as a phenomenon, meaning, "I've read this book about walk-ins. It's interesting and fascinating. There are characteristics associated with walk-ins," and so on. If the person is interested or if you feel the person is in any way involved in that, you can always leave the book around and hope he or she will read it. The person might or might not. There are other books that touch on the subject, so you can leave one of those around too. The main thing is that there will be changes, and you might not like all the changes. Just try to go with it as best you can.

That's where the significant other initiates or recognizes the process. But what if some-one just comes and says, "I'm a walk-in," and it's not even in your belief system?

There's not much we can do to make a change in that. If someone tells you he or she is a walk-in for various reasons and you don't think much of it or you feel bad about it, don't assume the person is crazy. Find some information, such as this book, in which we give you very specific details to understand that. Just because someone thinks he or she is a walk-in doesn't mean that person is soulless or that the soul who left the body didn't love him or her dearly.

After all, when people die in the traditional sense, it's not that they don't love the people they are with; it's just their time. It's no different when a soul exits the body in a walk-in situation, the soul exiting and walking out in that sense. It is just time. Instead of the body dying, the body remains alive and another soul walks in. Before arriving, souls are aware that the relationship you are in — family or friend or lover — exists. Souls might very well find that they want to continue the relationship, but they might want it to change. If the souls feel a change needs to be involved in such a way as to bring up the idea of walk-in and want to talk about it (and if you don't feel comfortable talking about it in that sense), please tell them so. Advise them to look in the place in the book where it says don't talk about being a walk-in if your mate, loved one, brother, sister, family member, friend, and so on, isn't comfortable with it. Feel free to say, "I feel a sense of personal change in me. I have certain attitudes that are changing, certain things I'd like to try. Maybe I'd like to go play golf or tennis; it looks interesting. Maybe it's time to go out in the park and throw around a Frisbee. I know you've been asking me to do that for twenty years, but it's not too late. Let's go. Let's have a little fun." It's all right, walk-in, to talk about how you feel different and how you've changed, but if the person you're with isn't comfortable with the idea of you saying you're a walk-in, be a little kind, be a little patient. Don't say it.

Then that same advice would be even more applicable at the office or work — or what-ever the person's profession is.

Definitely, unless you're working for a metaphysical magazine like the *Sedona Journal of Emergence!*, it is not acceptable to say that at the office because when you say, "I'm a walk-in," you are really asking people to believe in your beliefs. It is better to simply say, "I've had this big change in my life. I feel more open to certain things." You don't have to say this to people randomly. You can say it to your friends at work (if you want to continue that work), and you might very well, then you stay there. You might find that certain things on the job are much easier than they used to be.

Conversely, you might find that some things on the job, even though your body knows how to do them, might be more difficult to do because you have no personal interest in them, or you begin to lose interest because of that personal feeling. That would be a good time to try to move up in the company, if that's your desire, or to even look around for something else so that you don't have to do that and can maybe do something else. That's the reality.

Equally, you might find certain things that were boring, tedious, challenging, or difficult for the previous soul suddenly become much easier to do, and things that were hard to learn are suddenly easier to learn. Even social interactions might become much easier and smoother for various reasons. It is possible. But don't go into work and give out announcements and pass around balloons saying, "I'm a walk-in. Welcome me." It is not a good idea to do that, but by all means, if you have open-minded friends, you can say, "Wow. I feel so different these days. I want to try new things." It's all right.

Be careful, though, if your friend says, "Gosh, you never came out to the bar with us before. How about coming out for a couple of drinks?" and you've never had alcohol but decide to go. Then start out with a light beer or something like that. Have something with the least amount of alcohol possible. If that bar carries near beer, fine.

I'll tell you what. To be on the safe side, if you're not sure, for instance, about your medication — it might clash with alcohol, but it never came up since the previous soul didn't drink alcohol — check with your doctor or your pharmacist to see whether there's any problem. That's important to do. Honor your body and its needs. But if it turns out that it's okay, the best thing to start off with is a nonalcoholic beer because it actually has a little alcohol in it. If it feels okay, then if you want to have a regular beer, you can. But don't jump into alcohol. Go slowly, and make sure the first time you have it that somebody drives you home, even if you have a nonalcoholic beer.

You might be very sensitive. When walk-ins first come in, the sensitivity in the body is greatly increased. Babies are very sensitive. Walk-ins, as souls coming into adult bodies, even if you were Mr. Insensitive or Mrs. Insensitive before, you will suddenly become much more sensitive, so you have to be careful.

How long does it last?

It can be permanent, and you can use that to your advantage. You might become much more sensitive in conversing and communicating with others. You might find that certain things that were not appealing to you become more so. Perhaps your friend or family you're living with or someone you visit has a garden that previously was just a mass of color or a place to sit and chat or have tea or coffee, and now suddenly the flowers look wonderful. You want to run over and smell them. In short, you might very well find that there are ways to be sensitive and to experience sensitivity that is wonderful and enjoyable, so don't assume that being sensitive simply means that you'll fly off the handle every time someone looks at you funny.

Walk-In Celebration

There seem to be two flows with the walk-ins: (1) The life doesn't change much; it just goes on in a more benevolent, maybe happier, way, and (2) there seem to be extreme changes. In the case of extreme changes, would you recommend the person actually have a closing ceremony to say goodbye to the old soul and a party for the new one?

Well, let's define an extreme change. Let's establish a situation. I'm not saying this will happen, but this would be an example of a situation that could happen. Say there is a couple who has been living together for thirty years. They both have an interest in metaphysical and New Age things, and they feel, being of a certain generation and a little older, that they ought to stay together, but they're not happy. Still, they have certain shared interests. They go to the astrology meeting together, and they go to the Unitarian Church together. In other words, they have a life. They perhaps have children, and the children wouldn't understand if they were to go their separate ways. So there is a desire by both parties to go off and do other things separately. There's a lot of incompatibility in the relationship, but external reasons have been keeping them together, meaning their position in the community, their children, even grandchildren, like that.

Then all of a sudden, one of them has a walk-in. Now, this is an extreme situation, although I've set it up in a pretty benign way. There could be other variations, but this is the one I'm using. One of the people has a walk-in. The other is pretty sensitive and can tell something is quite different. Because the couple is of a New Age demeanor, perhaps there is an understanding of what one has experienced. The couple talks about walk-ins and the walk-in person gradually, perhaps even fairly quickly (over three to six weeks), realizes that the relationship is not working for either of them. Even though all the externals are the same — what the people at church expect, what the walk-in person expects of the church from all the meetings and groups he or she belongs to, what the children and grandchildren and so on expect of the walk-in person — still the walk-in feels very distinctly that he or she needs to go off and explore the world.

The walk-in person needs to go out and find him- or herself. The other party, while being a little nervous and upset about being left behind to face all of the external people who want things to remain status quo also feels like, "Well, this could be wonderful. I'd like to do different things. I'd like to try different things. I wouldn't mind going to 'this' club or 'that' place and trying out things I've never been able to do before with my mate because my mate wasn't comfortable with it." In short, let's say the relationship changes. They go their separate ways. They remain friends, most likely. That is typical, but they go their separate ways. That would be an extreme case, yes?

I'm not saying it would call for a party, nor do I recommend one, but if the walk-in person wanted to do a closing ceremony, I see no reason not to. However, it is not necessary. The walk-in, when he or she first comes in, is most likely going to want to act when "first coming in," meaning the first three to six weeks or so. They're not going to be interested in doing a ceremony. The thing in our example is that the people are relatively conscious and aware or at least expansive. You don't have to be a New Ager to be expansive and conscious. You might be intellectually conscious. You might even have psychological interests, but of course psychology might tend to create symptoms out of things that are simply personality traits. No offense to psychologists, but you know what I'm talking about.

So I'd say that you might have a circumstance where a closing ceremony would be beneficial, but it won't change anything. There has already been closure. The soul has walked out and another soul has come in, so closure is fait accompli, and there's no real point other than a personal desire to do so. If you find that it will make you feel better, go ahead. Or if you want to try it, something like a closing — what you call closure — ceremony, go ahead.

How long before the change of personalities is seen as a normal, everyday change to be adapted to? I mean, how long before this is taken as just another way that humans are born?

As long as it takes for information like this to get out and be accepted. You want a number, but that would be entirely arbitrary.

CHAPTER FOUR

Communication between the Exiting Soul and the Walk-In

Zoosh

September 14, 2002

Greetings. Zoosh here. Well, let's proceed. What do you want to ask?

How are the various bodies of the human being created? Does the soul come in like a dot of light through the veils? How does the soul come in through the veils?

The soul comes in on feeling. It has been explained in the past as a dot of light because that is something that people in your cultures tend to identify, especially in Western cultures, as being spiritual, you know, rather than to say that the soul comes in through mental intent. Obviously, you're past that point of analysis in terms of spirituality, so if you say "a point of light," well then, you know people can accept that. If you were able to actually see beyond the physical, functional, and even subtle spiritual and elemental influence on Earth, if you were able to feel a change — you wouldn't see it (which obviously on Earth might be defined as sense, "sense" means that there is some sense of change, all right) — how would a person sense that there's a change?

Say you were in a room, and there is nobody else in that room. You feel completely safe in that room. Then you turn off the light, and it is pitch dark in that room. You have your friend in the other room (also dark) whose purpose is to walk in and out of that room very quietly. It is your job, first, to feel the way you feel alone in the room. So you're in there quite awhile, and your sense of feeling completely radiates and fills that room.

When your friend, at some point, creeps into the room quietly so that he or she is not detectable by any sound, it is your job to notice how you feel within your energy, within your physical feelings. It's not something separate from your physical self. It's your instinct, you understand. What feels different about that room knowing that your friend is there? Same thing.

Now, if you were out in space, for the sake of your safety, you would be able to transfer a certain sense of feeling to that space, and you might say, "I request to be in space that is near," (you don't want to be where a soul passes right by you but is near) "where a soul will pass by in, say, a half-hour of my time." Not within, *in* a half-hour. So you go out there, and you set yourself so that you can feel the feelings that your body physically reacts to. Understand this is kind of a long touch [see Appendix A] experience. Your physical body is reacting to the feelings in this space, so of course the space and the physical room in which you sit must have a constant, meaning quiet, calm. It doesn't have to be dark but quiet and calm without any chance for stimulation. There are no sounds floating in from outside and so forth. Then you can feel space.

If you're feeling the space well enough, you will feel — in the time that you've requested (it won't be on the dot, but it'll be close) — a change in the space. That's all. It won't be lingering, but there will be a momentary change, and then it will be gone. That will have been the soul passing by.

You will not have seen anything, most likely. There is an outside chance that somebody might. But I don't want you to envision space. I want you to feel it. The whole point of your spiritual and physical growth on Earth, as it is now in these times of material mastery, requires your participation in a physical sense. The way you do that is to use your feelings. If you were to feel that soul going by, there would be a definite difference in the way you feel in that space. Do you understand?

That is what happens. So that is my explanation that allows you to participate. If we simply say the soul comes in as a point of light, we are talking to people who are not participating but would like to have a mental (intellectual) concept of the soul coming in. I feel you are ready to go to the next level, which allows you to have a remote, physical experience of a soul coming in. You will not be affected because you won't be there physically. All right? But even if you were able to be there physically, you still wouldn't be affected because you and the soul are not the same being.

Okay, so this is the part of the immortal personality that comes into the — what do you want to call it? — level, dimension, density, place, reality?

Experience.

It is the part of the immortal personality that comes into this experience, all right.

The Roles of the Lightbody and the Physical Body

We humans have a lightbody. Does the soul create that?

What did I tell you? What if we expand on what I said before, all right? What if I tell you that, yes, you have a lightbody. But the lightbody is not *in any way* greater than the feeling body. The lightbody is the one who comes to learn, not to teach. Why does the lightbody come here? The lightbody experiences itself here so that it can learn all these lessons you are learning. It can learn all these lessons in the Explorer Race, specifically material applications, physical experience, sense, and instinct — all of these things — which are not necessary in terms of physical application where the lightbody exists. Now, I'm not saying the lightbody comes; rather, what I'm saying is that the lightbody *forms*. And the teacher of the lightbody is your physical body, which forms as a result of the lightbody and soul essence and Mother Earth's cooperation in this experience that you exist in while you're here.

This is important because in the spiritual community, you have been taught about the lightbody. "This is the lightbody" and "this is the desire we need to be the lightbody" and all of that is complete baloney. The lightbody is the student. The physical body is the teacher because the physical body is made up of Mother Earth, and it is your personal, physical representative of what you came here to learn. Aside from your personal lessons, you all have overall lessons, and the overall lessons have to do, very specifically, with physical reality. Not just what can be gained from physical reality, not just how we can see the world differently as immortal personalities by interacting with physical reality, but how we can understand creation and its application in an advanced world. This is the advanced world, my dears; this world is the advanced world because it *demands*. It places demands on you to grow.

There are beautiful worlds in space with beautiful beings, and one might reasonably say these people are very advanced, but I am telling you they only appear to be advanced because they have not a trace of conflict; in short, nothing challenges them whatsoever. This is the advanced world because you are expected to grow. In fact, you are required to grow. That is why your lightbody, which appears to be on the outside, is also on the inside of your physical body, embracing and loving and hugging its teacher.

I am talking to the soul researcher. Do you know what every single walk-in wants to know? "Where am I from? How did I get here? What's all this about that I'm experiencing?" Many walk-ins will experience that in the beginning as confusion. Sound familiar? So the point is to readily have available a book so that you can create clarity and not build your new life on confusion [laughs] and also to remind you of that confusion so that you can create a thread back to the past of your moment of coming in as the walk-in.

This way you can build from your present to the past with clarity as to create a solid foundation for your being here, which will immediately give you a physical feeling of welcome and self-confidence. This will encourage you to embrace your physical world that you find yourself in, not just run into the mind to define things for you while you maintain and keep the physical world at a distance — which is a typical response from many walk-ins. Walk-ins are all soul researchers, and I am speaking to them inclusively.

Join with Teacher

What's your understanding of the teacher-student relationship? Would you not say that the teacher exists somewhere? Either you go to the teacher or, if you're fortunate, the teacher comes to you. But (we're talking about separate beings) would you not say that?

Here's a situation in which you have these beings, part of the Explorer Race, yes, souls. They have been through *so* much in their education process to come here, and as far as they have been able to get in this process is "this" teacher talking to them, "that" teacher talking to them. It has always been that no matter how advanced the teacher or how quickly the student learned whatever was needed to be learned, before the student was allowed to come to this place of advanced training (which *always* involves highly complex challenges), he or she had to talk to someone, no matter how wise the student was and no matter how wise the teacher was. It didn't make any difference. The connection was always someone talking or interacting with you. Even when giving you moments of spiritual insight, it was from them to you. Do you understand?

Now Teacher says, "You have learned well, student. You are prepared to go to the next step in learning." Then you eagerly jump up and down, metaphorically speaking, we will say, "Oh boy, oh boy, I can't wait to do that! What's the next step?"

Teacher says, "The next step is to join with Teacher inside its body. I want you to think about that for a moment: Join with Teacher."

"How can … ? Do you mean come into your body, Teacher?"

"No, no," Teacher says, "you need to be inside Teacher's body, to join with a teacher who can teach you all that you have not learned yet and help you to differentiate between what works on these levels that we are on now and what works on other levels, where you will find that some day, as a creator, you might be responsible for beings at this level."

"What level is that, Teacher?"

The teacher then reveals to you that there is a level where people are learning things on their own without any sense of constant external teaching guidance. Here in this place with teacher and student, all right, before you come to Earth, there is always a teacher present — if not your teacher, somebody else's teacher. You are never without guidance from moment to moment. No matter what questions you have, they will always easily and fully be explained to you in such a way as you completely understand them. As good as that might sound, it is not the experience of the understanding. It is as close to the experience as you can get because it is not just with words. It is with feeling. It is with many other levels, and if you are going to be responsible for beings who are in the advanced training process, you must experience a teacher who has complete experience with this process. Therefore, "Your next step," Teacher says to the student, "is to join with Teacher."

"How can I do that, my great Teacher?" asks the student.

"You will emigrate — temporarily."

"Away from you, Teacher? I don't want to leave you."

"Oh no, no. It's only for a short time, and there will be times that occur when you and I will still be able to talk on a regular basis, but the rest of the moments, you will be fully engaged within Teacher. You will be in the teacher, and the teacher will be wrapped around you. You will be able to learn what Teacher offers, but the challenges will be much greater."

"But what will I do?" says the student. "How can I ask questions?"

"Well, we will be available regularly for you to ask questions, but you won't remember it all. You will have to feel your way around and call on your knowledge and wisdom through the manner and means that is most available on this advanced plane of teaching."

"What is that, Teacher?" asks the student.

"That is feeling, of which you have only been slightly exposed to here."

"But I have feelings. I can touch you. I can touch 'this.'" The student touches various things.

The teacher says, "Yes, yes, but everything here feels very good to you, does it not?"

"Well, yes." Then with the great knowledge of a student, the student says, "But everything always feels good."

"Where you're going, you will have to learn what feels good to you as an individual, what doesn't feel good to you as an individual, and what feels good only sometimes as an individual."

The student misses the whole point, which is typical of students who have never lived on Earth, and asks, "What's an individual?"

[Chuckles.] You see, the student is missing the whole point about feelings and being within, experiencing the teacher as a personal experience. So the teacher tries to explain what an individual is to a being who is used to being fully interactive with all life around. In short, it can't be done; rather, it can only be experienced to understand it.

That's why the student is so desirous of coming to the planet you find yourself on and the energy you find yourself in. The student desires to come because the student knows this is the next level. The student isn't coming to save the world; the student is coming to experience the privilege of the next level of learning — in which the student is fully engaged with the teacher.

Of course, that's what you do when you experience your physical body, which is made up of Mother Earth's body. We know that Mother Earth is a spiritual master, a physical master, all right, a master of the physical world — knowing how to function in harmony in the physical world, knowing how to function in harmony in the spiritual world, yes? She is also a teaching master, knowing how to function in harmony within all levels of teaching that might be applied anywhere in any one of her existences between herself and all other beings or from all other beings to her, should that ever occur.

We also know that she is a dimensional master, meaning that she is able to function in harmony in all dimensions that she may ever be exposed to or that might wish to expose themselves to her. We also know that she is a quantum master, meaning she can function in harmony no matter what the consequence. You find yourself enveloped and embraced, and you embrace back this wonderful, experiential teacher made up of Mother Earth's being that you call your physical body.

The Exiting Soul versus the Walk-In Soul

How does the entry of the birth soul compare to the entry of the walk-in soul?

All right, now it is possible to understand your past from your present. That is vital if you want to understand the whole point of the walk-in process in this moment of the teaching. The walk-in does not have the advantage, or any particular interest, in understanding the physiology and spiritual engagement of the birth soul process. Do you know why the walk-in does not need to know that? The walk-in does not need to know that because that soul is gone! The walk-in is entirely engaged in what's going on with him- or herself now so that the walk-in can function here.

While I appreciate your desire to create a linear progression from the birth soul — "We understand how the birth soul works so that we can understand ..." — the whole point I'm trying to make is that it doesn't make any difference how the birth soul works. What makes the difference is how the walk-in soul works so that we can appreciate that. This book is about walk-ins. I appreciate your interest in explaining how the birth soul works, and we'll get around to that. The whole point now is that this is a personal situation for people who are walk-ins. That's why I explained that if, when the walk-ins come in, they are not supported in their immediate society by people who understand they might be walk-ins (which is typical), then when the walk-ins become aware of who and what they might be, they can then create a bridge to the past moment of their walking in to create clarity from the present to the past.

You understand that now. But I recognize that what you are trying to say is that if the walk-in and the general public can understand the spiritual process of the soul coming in on the birth level, they will then see how the differences exist when the walk-in comes in. But I am saying that is not what I wish to put my energy into now.

When the birth soul leaves, does it take ... ?

When the birth soul leaves, we are saying simply that the soul that leaves is the birth soul, and that the walk-in comes in and is essentially the second soul to occupy the body. All right? The number one feeling you experienced when you came in was an overwhelming feeling of total and complete confusion. But let's define confusion. Confusion means everything you understood to be so is no longer so, meaning your birth soul had a complete understanding of how the world was according to her up to that point in time and suddenly nothing made sense anymore. So if you could visualize that, it's like walking through a door, and what happens? You're suddenly in a room that you can't get out of, and nothing makes sense any more. We need to address that and work with that. To do that, I'm trying to bring that up in you personally to remind you of that feeling of confusion so that you ask questions based on that immediate urgency: "I've got to know right now."

In short, everything your civilization is going through now on Earth has everything to do with feelings. You watch the news sometimes or read about it. Why do you think that, no matter who's on what side of the issue, everybody is so wound up? You even have a president [George W. Bush], all right — this is important — who's wound up all the time, who's excitedly saying "this" and "that." He's not Mr. Calm, saying, "This is what we feel, and this is what ..." blah, blah, blah. He doesn't drone on. He's known for being excitable. In short, he is the ideal president right now because everybody else is just as excitable, and that level of being excitable, which is annoying to the mental, all right, because the mental says, "Well, if there's too much excitement going on and too much agitation going on, we can never sit down and talk about this reasonably. We can't do anything that makes the mental feel safe."

But I'm not saying it is a good thing. What I am saying is that it is a necessary thing so that people will recognize the very next step — after this physical agitation, which is only slightly understandable mentally — is the embracement of physical feelings, the understanding of physical feelings, and the incorporation of the physical feelings you actually want to feel and you want to feel from others.

This book, from my point of view, is intended to support that, acknowledge that, and salute the fact that world leaders and the people in the world are having such a difficult time truly communicating, meaning "I understand what you're saying, and you understand what I'm saying. I know this because of the way we're talking and communicating, not just that I understand your words, but you can feel what I'm talking about." Why do you think people like to talk to their peers, to others like them? Because you don't have to explain how you feel very much. Your peer completely understands it because he or she has had enough similar experiences to have the same, what? Thoughts? No, they don't have the same thoughts, because people are different. They are individuals. They have the same feelings, the same passions, and the same desires.

Why do you think that the United States, for instance, finds itself now in a battle with people who have minds, who can think, but who have given up trying to communicate with you mentally because you can't understand why they are so upset and agitated? I'm trying to put this in contemporary terms. The whole problem is that these people are communicating with their feelings, and you are trying to get them to slow down and talk in words so that you can put it in a mental construct. But it is not a mental construct. Once you can feel their feelings, you will understand what is going on.

I'm not trying to say good guys, bad guys, none of that. I'm not trying to say it's terrorism, okay. It certainly isn't. Never. But until you can move beyond the slowness of mentality to the immediacy of feeling communication, you will remain — what? Confused. And now we come back to the whole point.

Confusion is often based, all right — what do the walk-ins feel? They feel confused. That's because the mental construct that they understood life by is suddenly whisked away, and they find themselves in a world in which they only have their physical feelings, their physical bodies, and they can't remember who they were when they came in, right? So they find themselves in a world in which they can relate to physically, and therefore the best way for them to relate is to use their feelings.

The confusion that all walk-ins feel when they come in is because they are not surrounded by others who can help them (though this book will help and stimulate others to help). The confusion is that the complete mental construct (which is torn away because the birth soul leaves) falls away, leaving only vestigial remains of its existence, which is not enough to support the new soul who does not personally identify with those vestigial remains. Therefore, it is just like any other idea, even though it has been a personal experience for that physical body functioning with the birth soul. So the walk-ins feel confusion for however long they feel it, and sometimes it goes on for years and years. That is the whole purpose of this book, so that doesn't continue.

The walk-in feels this confusion, which is essentially a difference between the physical (also represented by the feelings) and the mental. Therefore many walk-ins remain confused because they do not build, not that they do not desire to build, their personalities on a mental construct. When they try to do that, they pull themselves back to the way the birth soul was in the body, and that birth soul doesn't want that to happen. Thus you have a conflict between the birth soul (who's gone on) and the vestigial remains of the body streaming from that birth soul having to do a complete identity on the mental construct and the mental discipline on the physical body because you are living in a society that caters to mental constructs.

The walk-in is forced to fall back on something for which the physical body does not really want you to do. It has those mental constructs from the former soul, but it would prefer that you communicate with the physical body — your physical world, the physical makeup of all things, physically. But the physical body does not have the means to communicate with you, the new walk-in soul, through any other means than by the most direct — through feelings. That's why it is essential for walk-ins to begin experimenting with their feelings when they come in: "What is this feeling? You know, what is it about? What do I want? This feels good." I don't just mean contact, touching something. I mean the feelings you have in your body. You have to have a bedrock of feelings that you choose to use and function with and embrace.

Remember, you are inside your teacher. Your teacher is going to communicate in the universal language of all beings, no matter what his or her language and culture is, and that universal language is feelings. It can't be pictures, because in other societies, on other planets, and so on, pictures might not relate to your society on Earth at all, so it can only be something that is bedrock. And bedrock is feelings. All feelings are felt the same way everywhere. The feeling of love is felt on Arcturus the same way you have the feeling of love here, and I'm talking about the physical feeling in your body. I'm not talking about making love. I'm talking about feeling love.

Walk-In Difficulties

One of the most vital and difficult communications to understand that takes place when the walk-in arrives is the communication of feelings, yet it is the most direct communication. This compares differently to the arrival of the birth soul. [Chuckles.] (I told you I'd get there.) The birth soul is fully conditioned and trained by — what? — the time that the body has to grow. Slowly and gradually, the body — the sperm, the egg, all that business — has time to grow, and the soul can jump in anytime during the time of that gestation period in the mother. Nine months is quite awhile. The soul can jump in, experience the body, experience what's going on for it, experience (to a degree) feelings. The mother is feeling this, "Oooh," feeling that little bit as baby [grows], and the baby then reacts with its own feelings and all of this going on inside the mother. Then the soul jumps out and goes and talks to its teacher. This doesn't mean babies are soulless. It means that the soul is intermittently present while the communication with teachers and angels and other beings is going on.

The walk-in does not have that. The walk-in doesn't have the gestation period. It doesn't have the learning. It doesn't have the means to adapt to physical feelings and be prepared for physical feelings. It is just one moment: this thing, and then the next moment — boom! It finds itself in a world. If there was no confusion at that moment, I would be very surprised indeed, given the state of consciousness on your planet at this time. This does not mean that the state of consciousness is some lowly thing on your planet but rather that in an advanced school, students — the moment they walk in the door — are expected to be exposed to, and react to, advanced lessons. The minute that occurs, you walk in the school, no orientation day, nothing — "bang!" Here you are in school, lessons are flying around like crazy, you have to interact with other beings, and you don't even know what to do. Would it not be strange if you were not confused?

The difference between that and the birth soul's having this long time of training to talk to teachers and angels and Creator Itself, all of these things, is that does not take place, and that's the essential difference that needs to be known and understood. You need to have this basic difference, because you can identify with that as an individual.

How many times have you, as an individual reading this book right now, found yourself in a situation for which you had absolutely no preparation? Did you not feel totally ill at ease? What did you do? What could you do? Sometimes you faked it, smiling and nodding, "Oh yes, absolutely, I agree with you completely" or "Oh yes, isn't that terrible" and so on. You faked it, without having a clue as to what was going on. That can work in some social situations, but when it's a matter of life and death, when it's a matter of urgency, when it's a matter of knowing where to go and what to do, and when it has to do with the nuances of a relationship between you and many other people, it is overwhelmingly challenging. So what I'm telling you is this: In the past, very few souls chose to walk in because it is so difficult, it is so challenging, and it is so overwhelming, as you yourself know very well.

It is so challenging, but as you well know, in the future, being a walk-in is going to become more normal. Why is that? How could it be possible? Are there suddenly all these souls who are willing to be overwhelmingly challenged? No. It's that your world is beginning to go through the changes it needs to go through to make it easier for beings to come in and walk in. And what is a perfect example of that? The perfect example of that is the one I already used, which is that people seem to be more excitable these days, even people who are publicly out there, speaking to you and for you, as your representatives, such as your president. Your president in the United States is a passionate man, and he cannot really deliver a talk without getting passionate. But that's good! In that way, he reminds you that is the way things are right now and you should be a feeling person, passionate about something.

I'm not saying that he is better than. I'm simply saying that he is a perfect example for you in that way right now, because to be passionate is the gateway, a gate that has big openings, not a big lock of a gate. It's like a gateway that is open, not closed, to feeling the feelings and to want to enjoy those feelings, to welcome the world of benevolent magic (see Appendix B and C) that you are being taught, and to embrace the idea that life can be better here based on what you do spiritually for yourselves, what you do on a physical feeling level for yourselves — the love, warmth, benevolent magic, the experience of benevolent magic. This is not something foreign. It is something fully engaged with Creator, the angels, and the wonderful teachers, and with yourselves. It is completely done to support and maintain the life of beauty, or the path of beauty, as native people might say sometimes, in other words, physical life.

For you to have the world you want, you need to be able to move past the intellectual model that you used as a transition. You need to be able to move past that, the intellectual model functioning not only on the individual level but also on a global level. You need to be able to move past that into a world by which you can practice feelings not simply as reactive feelings but also as feelings that you experience and naturally emote. You do not have to send them out; just experience feelings that are benevolent for you and benevolent for others. It is in the very nature of such things, the very nature of such existence and being, that prompts others to be stimulated to have those feelings themselves.

In the heart-warmth teaching (see Appendix D), the first level is to learn it for yourself. The second level is to go out and experience it with another being. The teaching is usually to go out and experience it with some natural being, such as a tree, which naturally does that, or an animal, perhaps, who naturally does that. Usually it's done with a tree, because they're easy to find — at least in your society in the United States.

You go out and experience it, and you discover that you experience the warmth to a greater degree. In short, you prompt each other — you and the tree — to feel the warmth in a greater way by being the warmth. What you are working toward, then, through this time of reactive passion is preparing yourself to desire and strive toward feelings that feel good in you and naturally prompt the same feelings in others. Then you will feel this wonderful feeling in a greater way, and it will prompt others to do the same thing. The feeling is that of beauty, warmth, love, and life, holding all life together because it wants to be together, not commanding all life to be together because the mental construct says you must be here.

Walk-Ins Can Connect with the Feeling Self of the Body

Are the birth soul and the walk-in soul ever in the body at the same time? Is it always that one walks out and then the other one comes in?

There has to be a gap because the physical body needs to know when it needs to be highly receptive. It is not typical for the birth soul to leave in that way when it is in the physical body. Even when the sleep state occurs, there is always a connection, even though the birth soul might be wandering around the universe, so to speak, in communication.

When the birth soul leaves entirely and unexpectedly — and it would normally leave like that only at the moment of death (the body knows it is still all right) — the body is suddenly alerted, knowing that this only occurs in this situation. If another soul is going to be arriving, it is at a heightened state of receptivity. When that soul arrives, it can welcome it and embrace it. No, there has to be a slight gap.

How slight?

I don't think I'm going to reveal that. Just take my word for it. It's not very long.

So the soul leaves, and the new soul walks in. And it doesn't know anything. But does it come in ... ?

It knows something. It has enough residual awareness of itself and the depth of its capacity. That's why souls have to have at least spiritual mastery before they come here, including walk-ins, because they have that depth to fall back on even if they cannot remember in their usual ways. Here's the issue: You have, until recently, on this planet, been using exclusively the linear mind. And most people are still attached to that which they personally identify. But the vertical mind — where you know things when you need to know them and don't necessarily retain that knowledge after that point — is your nature. So when that walk-in soul is whizzing in, its natural access to the mental is entirely vertical. It comes into a world where that is not as welcome. In the past, it used to be that it simply didn't function as part of the world, all right. But now it is changing.

The vertical mind is coming in a bit more, or being more accessible to those who are prepared to engage it, and the walk-in soul suddenly finds itself in a place where it does not have access to vertical wisdom. It must adapt to the linear world, so it's not that it doesn't know. It's that it has to fall back on its greater depth of learning, which can only come from some level of spiritual mastery, in this case, because it is a soul, and it is completely foreign to its — up to that point in time — surroundings, and it has to fall back on something. It can fall back on the feeling self of the body.

The body's mastery level is representative of Earth, and that body is filled with vestigial remains of the former personality based on the body's necessary reaction to that personality and the common ground that they had to share in order to live life. It doesn't always find that the soul, the walk-in soul, and the body's communication is fathomable. Therefore, it invariably falls back on its spiritual mastery wisdom, which may not apply, given that is usually learned on some other planet. Thus, it does not apply directly to Earth and the culture in which the walk-in finds him- or herself. But it may provide the depth and the underpinnings so that the soul can get along during this period of confusion and reorientation.

CHAPTER FIVE

Walk-In or Soul Braid

Isis

September 16, 2002

The walk-in experience feels as if you are here one day, then the soul exits and another soul walks in, and in the day-to-day life, you as the walk-in still feel the same. The sense of identity is complex, confusing. It seems to remain in the body, not with the soul who left or the one who came in.

That's why a lot of talk went on about the means to know certain things. It's one thing to just lose interest in a friend, but if you suddenly, out of the blue, find that your interests are changing across the board over a period of, say, two or three days — suddenly you don't like certain foods any more, suddenly you're not interested in certain people any more, and suddenly your attitudes are changing across the board about almost everything in your life — then whether you have a walk-in is something to consider.

But it doesn't necessarily mean that you will be entirely confused. You have to be open to the possibility that this attitudinal change, across the board, could be something to honor, not something to just ignore and ask, "What's wrong with me? Am I crazy?"

But it can happen as fast as two or three days?

It is typical to happen that way.

So in the people this happens for that quickly, there's a new sense of identity almost right away?

There's not necessarily a new sense of identity, because first, there's the shock and surprise of these attitudinal changes, and the person wonders what's going on. Sometimes people think they're depressed or they're upset. A lot of this is confused with depression, and of course, depression isn't really a factor. It's just that people are used to being a certain way — very often for a lifetime. Then suddenly they're another way, and they're not sure what it's about. Many of their friends try to talk them out of it, or they just say, "Oh, well, you're just tired; that's all," you know, like that. So, what's your question again?

Oh! I guess how to know.

Now, you understand, that is how to know. It's not going to be a flash of light for most people. It's not going to be a vision in the sky, nothing like that. It is subtle for most people. Some people who are sensitive to energies might feel a distinct change in a moment or a tingling or something like that. There might very well be something like that, but it's not always the case. It's actually not common, but it can happen.

Other people might feel a distinct physical change going on after which there is this attitudinal change. It doesn't mean you've had a walk-in, but the whole purpose of this book is to look at yourself or others around you — if you're living with people like that — to see whether maybe it's worth looking into. Is it a possibility?

Have they had any of these experiences that might relate to what you are talking about.

That's right, and just because people change doesn't mean that they're crazy. You'd be surprised how often in the past when people changed, particularly in certain societies where change is not easily dealt with, they were considered crazy or sick or something. In some societies, change is not acceptable. Granted it was more so in the past, but even these days you find that quite often, certainly in personal situations, to say nothing of, say, business or career situations or scholastic situations and so on.

So the point of the book is to say, "Look, it might not be so bad. Maybe it's just something like this, and you can get on with your life. But you need to explore what you are interested in, what you feel good about, and what you're drawn to. It doesn't mean you have to abandon everything you've ever done or everyone you've ever known or interacted with. But at least if you can acknowledge that things have changed, then you might find that the people you know or your family members might have interest."

You might even find that you'll suddenly be very interested in people in your family or in your group of friends whom you've spent time with and never really broached certain topics or subjects with. Or you might also find that the hobbies that these people have that you never participated in are suddenly very attractive to you. In short, you might change your way of relating to people or things in your life, but it doesn't mean you have to dump them and just go on.

The main thing is to acknowledge there's been a change within you, but it doesn't have to be a bad thing. It doesn't have to destroy your life or the lives of people around you. It very often brings people closer together because there's a sense of newness, and as you know, children are very interested in exploring their worlds. In the case of an adult with a walk-in, that same desire occurs, so there might be a tendency to ask about things. Maybe you were never interested in what your wife or husband was reading, and now suddenly you are interested: "What are you reading? Gee, that's interesting. Tell me more about it," and so on. Or another example, "What do you do when you go to your sewing group?"

Things like that might come up. So if you're living with someone who is a walk-in and you notice these things, don't automatically be frightened. It might just be that this person is going to take a greater interest in you or that his or her interest in you will come from a different approach. It might free you up and bring the two of you closer together, so don't let this frighten you.

Soul Braids

Can you discuss the difference between a soul braid and a walk-in?

A soul braid is a situation in which another portion of you that would have otherwise incarnated some place else, some other dimension, some other time, some other existence, or even is in existence there, might simply cease its existence and join you if you and your soul, your portion of your soul, have a need related to or interest in the community around you or what is expected of you or what you might wish to create or deliver to the world at large in the future. Then what might occur rather than a walk-in situation — with an exiting soul, of course — is that another portion of you might enter. In a case like this, you know, none of this happens without your soul's permission, so don't ever worry about that.

There is a similarity to the walk-in experience, but it's not as extreme. You aren't likely to experience a loss of interest in what you are doing, who you know, or how you do things, all right? But you might experience something more. Again, you might relate to the people, places, and things in your life differently, meaning you will have more interest or you will be interested in a different way as well as the way you've always been interested.

You might find that certain foods, for example, suddenly are more attractive, meaning perhaps you and your mate regularly go out Friday night to the Chinese food restaurant or the Italian food restaurant, or what have you, and you usually order one or two or three of the same things. So the next time you go, you will experiment. You order something completely different. Now, that might not seem very adventurous to some, but to others, it might be. Maybe when you play sports, perhaps you've always played tennis and enjoyed that, and you don't stop playing tennis but discover that you find golf interesting. Or you discover that swimming looks very attractive and the idea of swimming laps in the pool and seeing how many you can swim, in a gradual increase day to day, looks very attractive.

In short, you begin to see and experience and acquire new things associated with what you already do. You might also suddenly find that social things look more interesting, or in the opposite sense, you might find that while you've never been particularly interested in reading or doing things that you do on your own, it looks more attractive. You don't lose interest in what you are doing, but you might change.

There's another important aspect of the soul that is very distinct. Things that might have been hard for you in the past — challenging or difficult — not just that you weren't interested in, but things that you could never really do, are suddenly (not everything, now, but certain things) much easier or easy for you to do without having any training to speak of or anything extra. Maybe you had extra training in the past, but it just didn't take. You just didn't get it, and you couldn't apply it no matter how much training went on. Not because you're slow, but it just wasn't a talent that you had. However, out of the blue ...

You can do it.

... you can do it for no reasonable explanation. That's another real mark of a soul braid.

So a soul braid is part of your immortal personality?

Yes, that's right. It's a part of your overall being. For those who see lives in a linear sense, which is most everybody on Earth, although philosophically, you might see it differently, let's just say that lives have been that way for the sake of this discussion. This would be, say, a past or a future life that incarnated, not unlike yours, but you decided that your purpose, your function, whatever you were doing, was either more important or more attractive, but you didn't decide that on your own.

The signal really comes from your soul, saying, "I want to stay, but is there some other part of me that can join me and allow my life to be more full so that I can do more, be more, and experience more in some benevolent way for others and myself?" Now the words don't go out like that, but the feeling goes out, and those words help to identify that feeling for you to understand.

Is there a way to get a relationship or a percentage, like for every hundred walk-ins, there's how many soul braids? Is there a relationship?

There isn't a mathematical one, but I will say that in the past, counting, say, forty to forty-five years back, it was much more typical to have soul braids. Let's say in the past, there would have been two and a half to three and a half soul braids (trying to be mathematical here, all right?) for every walk-in, meaning not particularly common. Soul braids are more common than walk-ins. However, that's changed. Now you have something like one and a half to two soul braids for every walk-in. That's going to change in the future. Within the next ten years, it will even out to being like one soul braid to every walk-in, and it will stay about like that.

That's interesting. So in one way, you feel exactly the same — who you have been but just more. There's more interest in new experiences, a sense of being, just there's more of you, right?

Yes, there's literally more of you on the soul level, and more experience, more full experience of yourself, you might say. There's no real change in energy, because it is a portion of your greater soul or your immortal personality, as Zoosh calls it. But the soul that comes in has wishes, hopes, dreams, desires, and talents, as any soul might.

That's what occurs, pretty much what you've said. Yet you'll need to acknowledge that and apply it. Don't try to control it or suppress it. It will invariably, in the case of the soul braid, all right, add to your life and cause your life to be better.

Almost along the same trajectory but with a richer, more complete experience, whereas the walk-in might go in a different direction, right?

That's right, the walk-in could go in a different direction. It doesn't always, but it could. With the soul braid, you don't necessarily change what your life is about, but you could add things to your life, or you'll find that things are easier. The soul braid allows for an ongoing, continuing familiarity, and the walk-in doesn't allow that. The walk-in is likely to be more different from the soul braid, and a person occasionally has more than one soul braid. You might have two — on very rare occasions, three. You still remain yourself, but you will find, over time, different aspects coming in. Braids never come in two at the same time because that would be too overwhelming. Over time, sometimes more than one come in. Once you've had the experience — if you know it and understand what it was — when it happens again, it's not so surprising. You can adapt to it more easily and perhaps welcome it.

Soul Affinity

You can't come to Earth as a walk-in without going through the veil, right? I mean, the same rules apply as for a birth soul? You can't come in with your memories?

Well, that's not exactly right. You can come, but you can't incarnate. You can't enter a human being. Souls often travel about, certainly on the dream level and so on, but for the sake of this book, no.

Can you talk more about the affinity that brings in a walk-in? There has to be compatibility in the energy and in, I understand, some of the attitudes, so that the new soul can enter the body.

Yes.

Does the call go out and the soul responds because it kind of fits, kind of like they both have type O blood?

Well, aside from the obvious [laughs], of course the physiology of the body is going to stay the same for the most part, but there has to be enough similarity so that if the two actually met in separate bodies, they would be instantaneous best friends, like that. So there is a great degree of common ground. It can't be radically different because that would be traumatic for an individual, the physical body. The point is to improve the quality of life in general while allowing the soul in the body to move on without any suffering, which is very nice. So there has to be, as you say, affinity, but it doesn't have to be an identical situation; that's not required.

There has to be significant affinity so that there can be a gradual transition, but like the creation of personality in any baby into a young child and then a young adult, what happens is that the walk-in is very much the same way. The personality as it was with the previous soul in it remains, but it gradually diminishes as the new personality with the new soul begins to feel more self-assured in the body and more comfortable. By orienting itself to its surroundings, it begins to, over time, assert itself and its personality in the body. And the old personality, which was familiar and comfortable to the physical body, is no longer (how can we say?) like a crutch that the physical body leans on because it is familiar. The physical body and the new soul become friends, and the physical body does not put up physical barriers or resistance against allowing this new being to express itself, especially since that expression from the new soul might be different, in some ways, from the previous personality.

This all happens, in some cases, over a few days and in other cases, more often, over a few months. So the personality change might be noticeable instantaneously by those around you by the attitudinal changes. But as far as the actual presentation of one's personality to the outside world, meaning other people or your pets, this takes time to emerge just exactly the same way as it is with a baby. When a baby is born, there's sometimes a distinct personality that's shown. But more often, the personality emerges gradually over time as the baby begins to open his or her eyes and looks at you and smiles and shows certain feelings and certain actions and reactions. It's very much the same in a walk-in when a soul comes into the body.

That's wonderful. That's even better than I asked for. What I was actually wondering about is, do walk-in souls look for potentials or for talents or for possibilities within that body that will allow them to do what they came to do, even though maybe those potentialities or possibilities hadn't been expressed by the previous soul?

No. Actually, that does not take place. The walk-in soul understands that the body must feel at ease with it, so it's quite patient. It's only when the body feels familiar with it and relaxed that the walk-in begins to demonstrate it's personality. The body has been prepared somewhat to expect the exit of the soul that was in the body and the arrival of the new soul. But even so, there's a get-acquainted period, and during this get-acquainted period, the new soul does not make much effort to demonstrate its personality. Rather, its perfectly inclined to go along, allowing the old personality to largely be seen, but over time, that changes.

So there's not a tendency to become radically different overnight, so to speak. And I'm allowing overnight to be, say, for the first week or two. A person doesn't suddenly go from day to night, so to speak. But over time, there will be distinctly noticeable differences.

All right. Now I'll say good night.

CHAPTER SIX

Walking in, a Benevolent Birth Process

Speaks of Many Truths

October 28, 2002

This is Speaks of Many Truths. What do you wish to talk about today?

Your perspective on the walk-in process.

It's not that complicated. It is essentially an avenue of creation that works very similar to the birth process. Do you know that in civilizations on other planets, where the creation of a body, whether it is physical or something more (say condensed light), very often (especially with condensed lightbodies) would not — even if you were present — appear physical but rather would appear as light? Quite visual.

These bodies are essentially, with upkeep, you might say, immortal. There is no need for one personality to be in residence in such an immortal body indefinitely. So the process that is used to transfer one personality into a body is what is called here the walk-in process. This is not something unique to Earth. It is a process that essentially would be referred to as a higher-dimensional process that has been adapted to physical bodies of Earth human beings to accomplish the same goal, that is, to get greater use out of an already created body that would otherwise simply be unused. In the case of a human body, you cannot allow it to just remain in a dormant state; it will change.

Atrophy.

I'd say atrophy. It would essentially die. With a condensed lightbody, you could, you know, let it sit for a time if no one was in it, and that would be all right.

To allow life to take place, here, to change and adapt your current needs on Earth now, the walk-in process is actually becoming more common. It also allows the souls who've been in occupation in the bodies to depart along their natural lines of the passage through the veils. So death takes place in an entirely pain-free situation, for the most part. Granted, some walk-ins take place during traumatic events, but that is rare. Most of them are very benign and gentle. It can happen while you are asleep, but that is not typical. It often happens while you are awake; perhaps you will feel that you need to go to sleep suddenly as you are, maybe, watching television, reading a book, or petting a cat or dog. You suddenly feel an urgency to go to sleep. I'm not saying that all naps like this are walk-ins, but that's just an example. Perhaps you might feel an energy. There's any number of things.

Typically the soul personality that has been in residence in the body will exit completely, just as in a standard death, leaving no residue of the soul having been in the body, meaning it takes the entirety of its own being. The only residue left — in a death or otherwise — in the case of a walk-in is the imprint that soul has made on the cellular tissue and, of course, the bones and so on, the physical structure of the body.

The physical structure is an imprint that is required so that the cellular tissue, the atomic structure, and the whole business of the physical body can be adapted to the specific needs of any given soul personality in residence at any time. Should that soul personality exit and the new personality arrive, the body will take some time to change over. Don't be attached to the scientific, or at least pseudoscientific, explanation of seven years for a complete cellular changeover. It takes about two-and-a-half to three years for the cellular and atomic structure to repattern itself completely. This is not to say that this is spread out over that time equally but rather that the initial imprint of the soul coming into the body within the first three days — the initial body energy — changes over 70 to 75 percent. And the rest of it comes along slowly over that next two-, two-and-a-half-, or three-year period. Now, that's the mechanical process.

There Is a Strong Need for Walk-Ins

As far as the why — why walk-ins occur — in your current times, this is perhaps not such a mystery. After all, you have problems in your current times that the conditioning of your cultures' beliefs, nonbeliefs, experiences, and so on, have not prepared the vast majority of citizens to solve. Whereas a soul personality, coming from some other place, might be able to arrive with solutions that can lead to inspiration and action (especially since most walk-ins take place in adults so that the body would have a chance to react) or with a means and adaptability to grow, change, assimilate, acquire, and apply solutions in a more easily adapted manner than the former tenant, if I can say that, of the physical form.

So you know that many of the children being born today come in with these skills, abilities, and so on, but it will take them years to be able to apply doing what they can do to improve the world, to say nothing of many more years after that, to be accepted to do that. After all, you wouldn't expect a seven- or eight-year-old to be accepted into the business community as an equal worker. The business community might say to a precocious child, "Well, that's a great idea, kid, thanks a lot," but it wouldn't treat the youngster as an equal.

You need to have souls, soul personalities, that can immediately stimulate, apply, create, and adapt solutions to problems that everyone else has largely been conditioned to believe are unsolvable. That is why walk-ins are increasing at this time and are likely to continue to increase for about three to four more years.

The recent past equals, let's say, the past seventy-five years. Now, in the recent past, walk-ins have been half of 1 percent of people. This is actually quite a bit more frequent than people realize. But now let's say this is current.

Current as in 2002.

Right. Current as of today. Now you have something like 20 to 22 percent. (In 2016, 17 percent of the population consists of walk-ins.) This is because you need to have beings, souls, come in to create solutions where solutions seem to be impossible all over the world in all cultures and all ages. Think about it: As adults, you might see the world's problems, to say nothing of your own family's problems, in some places as too complex to solve quickly. Yet given different ages of people, such as in old age, there are problems. When you are very young, there are also problems. Generally speaking, the different ages of people do not always honor the problems of other ages.

Adults do not often remember what it's like to experience the problems of a teenager, or they tend to think of the problems of a teenager to be vastly less than their own or, perhaps even worse, vastly less important than their own. It is also that as an adult, one does not often think of the problems of senior citizens, in this case, let's say sixty-five and up, to have such problems, because in your society the idea has been acculturated that this is around retirement years when things ought to be getting easier. [Chuckles.] In fact, given your physical body's difficulties and so on, things often get harder. Given the challenges of economies and so on, things not only get harder but often become more complicated because you can't retire. So it is not so obviously simple. Therefore, the need for the walk-in is becoming startlingly strong.

Remember what I said before about this process on other planets, say higher dimensions, where you have a lightbody and so on. And remember that with these bodies being basically immortal, the so-called walk-in process is the normal birth process. In this sense, we are talking about a completely pain-free birth.

What if a physical body existed on Earth that did not experience so much as a personality? The person did not experience much pain, discomfort, sadness, or disappointment — all of the things that come about as a result of unhappy experiences on Earth. What if that were the norm? If that were the norm, you would find the physical bodies of most people would exist much longer and not change much over the course of life. By simply removing those aspects of stress and unhappiness from your life, your physical bodies have the capacities to live for at least 150 to 175 years, if you take away the misery, essentially.

One of the easiest ways to do this is to begin to embrace the walk-in process. Now, I'm not saying that it is meant for everyone. As you can see, it does not exceed 20 to 22 percent at its greatest amount. The important thing to note here is that the walk-in process is not one way. Many of you feel that you have done all you can do, that you just want to get on with your reincarnation cycle. You're ready to talk to God, and you'd like to get your life over. This is why an increasing percentage of suicides have been alarming public officials (and those who care about such things) for quite a few years. It does not appear to matter, for those who keep track of such things, to the quality of life you have or the privileges that you seem to enjoy. Generally, not specifically, for most cultures there is an increase in the suicide rate. I'm not saying this is good. I'm just saying that it is a fact.

How do you improve that? People have soul personalities; that's what people are. They are not physical beings; they are soul personalities within physical beings, all right? Consider the body in that sense as a vehicle. If people understood that, they would not necessarily have to live an entire life in a physical body. They could be born, experience some of the happiness of childhood, and maybe not have to struggle as much in childhood in your times. There's really not much to excuse the levels that children struggle, the pressures they have to put up with.

In some societies, there's plenty of explanation, but in the society in which you live in the United States, a lot of the struggling simply comes about because of a lack of caring — not from the parents, in most cases (some, yes) — by societies in general, which put priorities somewhere else. I don't want to go on about that too much, but at this time, suppose you knew, as a soul personality, that you could exit after, say, thirty years, twenty-five years, thirty-eight years, forty-five years — not that you must, but that you simply could, that you had permission, and you wouldn't have to go through a trauma to do it. You wouldn't have to get sick, and you wouldn't have to suffer. You simply have permission to exit painlessly, comfortably, and easily through the veils. You could talk to God, your angels, and your guides, and you could go through the usual process you go through after death, but in an entirely pain-free way. Someone could be born into your body without having to go through childhood and all of that in a painful way.

I'm putting it to you like this not as a salesperson but I want you to know that it is not only possible but, in many cases, desirable. If you know that as a society, I feel that the suicide rate will go down. Did you know — taking the suicide rate as a whole thing — fully half of the people now who are committing suicide are destined for the walk-in process. If you know that, I want you to know something else: In five years, if nothing changes, I'd be able to say 75 percent of those committing suicide were intended for the walk-in process. So why not just wait and let that happen? Your pain-free, physical body would go on, somebody else can come in, and you're all happy.

I'm not trying to sell it; what I'm trying to do is give you permission. Those of you who feel like you want to end it all, I want to give you permission to know that you do not have to suffer to move on.

It's going to become more common. Twenty to twenty-two percent of people on this Earth — think about that — within the next few years are going to experience the walk-in process. That's a huge amount. Even though that's the peak, it will settle down to somewhere around 17 to 18 percent, perhaps as low as 16 percent for the foreseeable future, well out into the future, hundreds of years, so that the walk-in process will become part of life.

Walk-Ins Help Eliminate Suffering

What is experienced? For one thing, they will not know they are going to exit. When it happens, there isn't much warning. Know that when you do come in as the new person, your attitudes might change. Perhaps before, for instance, you might have been in a marriage that was unhappy for both of you. Maybe one or the both of you wanted to stay in the marriage; it was a struggle. After you come in, it suddenly seems easy. You can both go your separate ways; it doesn't have to be traumatic. You can be friends; you don't have to be. Things get simpler.

Perhaps other things take place. There might be other things that could change. Perhaps there was a career decision that needed to be made. Perhaps there was something else. Think of all the decisions that seem to be stuck: You can't do "this" because "that" will happen. You can't do "that" because "this" will happen. Then you move on, and somebody else comes in. That being has its own life agenda. Everything is different.

Be aware if you're living with someone like that. The person has a sudden change, "sudden" meaning over two or three days, and you notice that the person is not interested in some things that he or she used to be interested in or that the person reacts to certain people in different ways. Perhaps the person is fonder of you, perhaps he or she wants to do specific things with you, or perhaps the person's life changes for the better in some way. If there is a couple situation, walk-ins only happen in a way that will improve the life for both parties. It doesn't happen simply to create an escape for one so that when the new one comes in, the trauma is left to be experienced by the other person who didn't experience the walk-in. That is not allowed because it generates suffering.

The whole purpose of a walk-in is to eliminate suffering, to create happiness, and to improve the quality of life for the being who's experiencing it. The same is true in the case of a loved-one situation, those beings as well. So don't worry that a walk-in's going to take away your loved one; more likely it will take away the aspects that you don't like, can't get along with, or find stultifying or limiting. That's important to know. But you will notice some change in that person.

The person experiencing the walk-in will have somewhat of a sense of continuity. You won't feel as if you're having a schizophrenic reaction. You won't feel as if two of you are in the body at the same time. There will definitely be a sense of change. There will be similarities in the personality, so you won't notice a radical change. There's always enough similarity because, well, think about it. It makes complete sense. The tissues of the body, right down to the subatomic structure, have all been adapted to fit a specific soul personality.

If you bring in somebody who has a radically different soul personality, he or she could not comfortably live in that body. What would happen would be — almost instantaneously — catastrophic illness and death. That is not the purpose of the process. That is why those of you experiencing walk-ins will feel a sense of continuity. Your personality will be sufficiently similar so that the body is not overwhelmed by your presence. Doesn't that make sense?

Therefore, the experience of adaptation by the soul personality to the body and by the physical body to the soul personality is greatly eased. There is no trauma. It is actually a more benevolent welcoming. It's the next most benevolent thing to the growth inside mother, the growth/birth process. In that sense, it is benevolent to the child growing within the mother, not necessarily for the birthing as it happens for the mother and baby as it exists today. But that's not the subject now.

Understand that the whole thing is intended to set up sufficient similarities so that there is no — to use a medical term — rejection of the soul personality to the body, the body to the soul personality, or both. If they're not compatible, it's not going to happen in any event. So there'll be that sense of continuity and familiarity and understanding and appreciation from the physical body to the soul personality and the soul personality to the physical body, and there won't be a sense of foreign-ness by either.

There will be, for the initial walk-in, a sense of difference. Yes, you're occupying the physical body. It looks a certain way, and certain likes and dislikes are inherent, but you — being in residence now, if I can speak to the one who's arriving — will feel as if many things are different. You might wish to do different things. You might wish to meet different people, go different places, or eat different foods, all of that. Those around you will likely notice this.

As we've said, in a relationship, nothing's going to happen to traumatize the other person. Generally speaking, the other person in the relationship or even a close friendship, or say, a child, you know, children, or even sometimes a very close animal friend, but generally this is only the case of compatibility from one human to another in a relationship of some sort.

You will always notice an improvement. But for the people going through the walk-in process, becoming new personalities, expressing through this already fixed-in-place body, you will be doing things differently. Many things will be easier for you. You will find within the body that the body itself has, as a result of the conditioning of its previous tenant with the physical body, skills, and abilities that you might not have brought in yourself. But those skills and abilities are there. You will be able to use them because they are present. You will bring in skills and abilities because of the nature of your personality and what you wish to do on Earth.

The specific result of the walk-in process is that the people in residence will be happy because they can exit in a pain-free way, go on with their reincarnation cycle, and simply experience the afterlife in the most benevolent way possible. The person coming in will be more. You will have what is left over to utilize, that feels good to you to utilize. What was left over that doesn't feel good will simply not be used anymore. Perhaps there will be anger or disappointment or cynical attitudes and so on. You will not have any of that coming in; you simply will not use it or express it. It won't be present. Things like that will be immediately noticed by your mates or by your loved ones — to their happiness, I'm sure.

You will also feel good about it because you will not need to use those things. They will be present if you ever need to use them, but you will probably not feel the least bit attached to them, because you will not personally identify with them. So you will bring in skills, and you will find yourself in a physical body that has skills; in short, things will be improved.

Soul Compatibility

What is the relationship between the soul who leaves and the incoming personality? Are they from the same immortal personality or from the same soul group?

Never. You would find that in a soul braid, but in the case of a walk-in, there is no connection at all, and I'll tell you why. If they were from the same soul group, the body would form an attachment to the soul that's leaving. If you're leaving, you need to feel completely unbound from the physical body. There cannot be any sense of familiarity that holds you, keeps you in the body. There needs to be complete release because the walk-in process at this level of existence on Earth, as it exists now with a physical body, is very different from the death process as you know it. The death process is a complete closing of the door. You can't go back to the physical body because the physical body is decomposing. It is returning to Earth. You must go forward, you understand.

With this walk-in process, however, the only way you can be pulled forward, attracted to moving through the veils, is if the door behind you is completely shut; therefore you cannot be of the same soul group. There must be a complete lack of identification with the physical body. If someone comes in from even the same soul group, which might be a wide variety, there will be sufficient identification so that you will not be able to complete the process; thus the process will not begin. It will not happen. So, no, there is no connection there.

Then how is there enough similarity between the old and new souls so that they can fit into a relationship and into the body?

The tissues of the body right now exist in a certain way that are adapted to your soul personality specifically. While this may not be readily apparent, microbiologically speaking, under the microscope, it is crystal clear when the tissue is actually living in your body. If you could use a microscope to examine living tissue within the body — which I believe has been invented but is not largely in circulation — it is possible to perceive how cellular structure differs from person to person. But the moment that tissue is removed from the body, it is removed from the energy field of the soul personality and takes on a fixed appearance. That is why right now it is not obvious, scientifically, that there is a difference, but there is a measurable difference, all right? Do you understand?

Yes, you're saying that the physical tissue conforms to the new tenant.

Yes, but it has been conformed to the old tenant. And the new tenant, you understand, must have similar personality characteristics. But as you've noticed when meeting people — you've met people, many, many people — from time to time, there are similar personality characteristics in this person or that person, and you know for a fact they don't know each other. You say, "Gosh," to yourself, or you say to the person, "You remind me of somebody else." But that does not mean that these people are connected by a soul group. It just means that their personality characteristics are similar.

Many personality characteristics — as counselors, psychologists, and psychiatrists study these things — can be listed, to a degree, at least in general groupings. So you could have similar personality characteristics while not being part of the same soul group.

So who oversees the process? How does the choice ... ?

Is there a supervisor?

Yes, how does this work?

No, it is nothing like that. You understand that these things of hierarchical explanation — hierarchical explanation in general is all a story told to human beings because your cultures on Earth, right now, all of them, are laid out in a hierarchical format, which allows you to experience stages of life in a way you can mentally understand. So recognize that all things that are said — "I do 'this,' and I do 'that'" — are all parables. But the actual process, I can give you a parable of who does what. But they're all parables, as might be told to children, in order to help them, to give them a helping hand, to understand, at some future time when they're ready to understand how the process actually works. Would you prefer the parable or the actual explanation?

Well, the actual explanation, of course. I'm trying to find out the process, the dynamics — how does it work?

This is the explanation. Those who are temporarily living in a hierarchical society are conditioned to believe that things are hierarchical by nature. But in fact, the whole hierarchical theory, or application to life, actually creates limits for you — as a race of beings — that are not helpful to you anymore. So I'm offering this shortcut explanation of how things really work so that you will recognize that natural attraction, not just the nose to the flower because it smells good, but the natural attraction that brings about benefit for both parties. "Gee, that smells good. Let's cut the flower and bring it into my office so that I can smell it." That's not very good for the flower, is it? But the better example is the bee to the flower. The bee gets the nectar and pollinates the flowers for the sake of the plants. Isn't that wonderful? That is part of the natural creation process. That's how it works. That's how everything works.

So this tells you to apply that to how it works in a walk-in situation. The natural attraction for the soul personality within the body is to be elsewhere. But in order to get to that elsewhere, there needs to be a process of leaving the physical body on a permanent basis, having no responsibility for that physical body whatsoever.

When you sleep at night, you go into the deep levels of sleep. You are always corded to your physical body in some way, regardless of where you go and what you do as a soul personality. A soul personality does not have to sleep, but the physical body does. You are still responsible to interact with the physical body; the physical body needs your presence. No matter where you are or what you are doing, you must immediately return to the physical body and wake up. All right?

This is different. This is something in which you need to be elsewhere as your soul personality. The attraction to that being elsewhere requires a total exit, such as the one you would have if the physical body died. Equally, in that same exact moment, somebody else, a soul personality somewhere else, off planet we can say (somewhere other than your planet), needs to be on your planet, needs to be in a physical body that is compatible with the soul personality coming in. That compatibility would create enough of a bed of welcome so that the soul personality coming in would feel safe and complete, sufficiently complete — to put it simplistically, happy to be here — and that has to happen in precisely the same moment, just as when the bee's legs touch down in the flower. It has to be an instantaneous thing. It has to happen in exactly the same moment. Everything has to line up for that moment to take place, and then it does.

Are these beings coming in part of what we have talked about as the Explorer Race?

Of course they are part of that because in order to be on Earth now, they have to be engaged in that process, or they have to welcome that process. So they are already a portion of the Explorer Race, or they are prepared to take it on as a portion of their responsibility.

Are they new souls? Is it a whole spectrum? Have they been on Earth before? Have they never been on Earth before?

Oh, it's, as you say, a whole spectrum. Generally speaking, most of them have not been on Earth in these times. "These times" I will quantify as the past 4,000 years. Most of them have never been here during these times. An infinitesimally small percentage of them would have been here, but only at a time when Earth was very benevolent — no conflict, no violence — including Earth herself, all right. It was very benevolent, meaning in the distant past or in the distant future. That's the only possibility of having had an Earth life before. So we're talking about beings who have not, in terms of your current appreciation of historical Earth life, been here before.

They're not part of the 94, 95 percent part somewhere?

They might be part of that, but the vast majority of those beings have not been on Earth before, either.

The Soul's Intention

Do the beings come in with an agenda in the sense of, "I see a problem. I see how I can make a difference. I see how I can help"?

No, that's mental. Agendas aren't like that. Soul agendas — soul personality agendas — are entirely based on capacities, so agendas don't really work. They arrived with capacities, things they can do. A bias toward capabilities, you understand? This comes easier, this child can draw easier. This child can do sports easier, like that. Capabilities, capacities, that's what they arrive with. And because certain capacities and capabilities are more needed on Earth at this time, they are welcome, in general by your society, culture, and physical tissues themselves (and your physical tissues being made up of earth and Earth knowing what is needed). All of these things are connected. Nothing is separate. Then the welcoming committee, the welcome mat, if you like, from Earth herself, is going to be laid out for those who have capabilities and capacities that can serve those needs.

All right, let's not use the word "agenda," then. Is there a bias to service and a feeling or desire to accomplish something on Earth because they can see what difficulties need to be resolved?

No soul comes in with that. Souls come in — remember, we're talking about mastery here. It's easy to get off track. Stay focused. We're talking about mastery. Mastery always means — whatever kind of mastery we're talking about — you are in the present moment. Mastery takes place always and only in the present moment, though it may leave in its wake other things, and other things might be getting prepared or aligned in the future. The actual mastery takes place in the immediate moment. So don't be concerned if I am adjusting your words to the present tense. All right?

So you ask, "Do souls come in with a specific intention?" In the past, karma — the desire of the soul to resolve what has been unresolved (that's my definition) — was the case, yes, all of that. Now that karma is no longer the case, all those things have been resolved, if not by one individual resolving all of those things completely, then by somebody. Karma is over. The soul comes in now without that, rather strictly with capacities, capabilities, but not with objectives. That is why so many of the children being born now are coming in without any specific lessons, because lessons are an intent by the soul to focus in a specific area, if not focus, then at least to have a tendency to follow these situations or have situations come to you that will allow you to learn about that. But then most of the children being born now aren't like that, and equally, that's one birth process, yes, the physical birth process. This walk-in process is equally a birth process.

Souls coming in during the walk-in process do not have that as a factor — no lessons. Without lessons, you do not have a purpose, meaning, "I want to go here to do a certain thing, and I can only do it on Earth." Those days are over. No, they come in with capacities and capabilities, and the only thing that might be defined as a purpose but is not the soul's purpose is an overall umbrella that might fit the situation, and that is service. But that umbrella fits all life everywhere.

What's actually happening is the inclusion of Earth now in all life everywhere, as far as the natural processes go; in short, what's happening is rapidly things are falling away that have been separating Earth and life on Earth from what is natural everywhere else. Or to put it in a — how would you say? — not trite, but perhaps simplistic way, Earth society is becoming more like an extraterrestrial society moment by moment. All citizens born everywhere else on other planets in other dimensions come in with capacities and capabilities structured not only for the soul personality itself but also to serve the needs of all others, according to those needs as they come up — not slavishly in service, but something that is available that you can do that somebody else can't do, and you can easily do it when asked or sometimes simply do it because it is something you are doing for your own pleasure.

You walk down the street singing a happy tune, and it cheers other people who needed cheering up. You're not doing it to cheer them up. You're singing a happy tune to yourself, and simultaneously, it cheers up those who need to hear it. That's service.

Okay. The capabilities and capacities of those beings coming in then, during the walk-in process, they're not being subject to the lessons of the previous inhabitants of the planet. It follows that they will more easily help solve the problems facing us on Earth.

Yes.

The Exiting Soul

These decisions to leave are not necessarily conscious, are they?

They are not conscious in a mental sense, no. But very often, you have had times in your life, just like everybody else has, when you've felt like, "Ugh, I can't go on. Do I have to do this?" That's the mental interpretation of the physical feelings in your body, but what's actually happening in your physical body is that, at this time, if your mind could interpret it in that moment — correctly — those physical feelings are telling you, "I can't go on the way I've been going on. I need to do it differently." But your mind says, "I can't go on like this anymore. I just want to get out of here," because you haven't understood the message completely. But you understand that, the real fact.

There is a sense of these loved ones leaving, and there is a sense that in this process, they don't get to honor the life of the beings who left — a funeral or a celebration or a wake. It's as if the parting souls are leaving without a celebration of their lives.

It's not important. It's not important for them. They're happy to go. The purpose of funerals is — now remember this — to comfort the bereaved. It's not really for honoring. The honoring is part of the comforting process to reassure the person, and it is not the bereaved. In fact, the bereaved aren't reassured by being told how great the people were who have passed. They are only reassured by being nurtured, supported, and loved so that they can go through the grieving process on their own in their own way. Nevertheless, such ceremonies are actually meant for the living. So I would have to say that given the great advantage of a pain-free transition, wouldn't you think that it would be better to have the pain-free transition? Or is it better to have only death as you've known it? Now, it's true that there isn't a funeral process or celebration of that person's life, but I do not consider that to be very important.

I would have liked to say goodbye.

Say it now, and mean it. Say goodbye to anyone who has that process, all right, including yourself, should you have it. Say goodbye in a heartfelt way when you are alone and can speak to your memory of that person. But if you experience the walk-in yourself, wait at least three to five days before you do that, or you might pull in that personality, and if you know about another person having had a walk-in, wait at least five days. Again, you might pull in that personality and make it difficult for that personality to leave. That's a whole other subject, especially when talking about pulling in a person, trying to keep a soul nearby, when someone has died. Some other day we'll talk about that.

The New Soul

What is the best thing that the people around the arriving walk-in, once it's obvious that that's what it is, can do in the beginning?

Don't be attached to the person being who and what he or she was, period. It doesn't mean that you have to be off-kilter. It just means don't be attached to that person being what he or she was. Don't be upset if the person isn't what he or she was. That's all.

If you feel yourself becoming upset, put some physical distance between yourself and the walk-in personality. That's all. How much physical distance? Twenty, thirty feet. And try not to look at that person. Turn around, and look in another direction. There are always lots of excuses for that. If you feel yourself getting upset, go into the bathroom, walk down the hall, or go for a walk, something, so that you can process it physically. If it's moving in some other way, experience what you need to experience. Go out, laugh, cry, or whatever you need to do. Most likely, you'll need laughter or amusement. Most of the time, that's perfectly all right to do in front of the person who is the walk-in. Sometimes it isn't. If you feel it's not appropriate, you know, stifle it for a moment, and run into another room and laugh.

The walk-in might suddenly be doing things that the other soul personality in residence would never in a million years have done, such as eating different foods or being interested in particular behaviors. Perhaps the person never wanted to go surfing and suddenly goes, or maybe the person suddenly wants to go tobogganing and had previously been afraid of the cold. There are radical changes that make you laugh in a loving, amused sort of way, not in a crazy sort of way. The person will not appear crazy. The walk-in will suddenly appear to be more adventurous. That's how they'll appear, but that's because your previous understanding of their personality was in a fixed frame of reference. Suddenly they overlapped that frame of reference in unexpected ways.

For the person near the walk-in, it is almost always an amusing and fun experience. It's going to make you smile more than anything. Smile. Laugh. Enjoy it. However, if it upsets you, put a little temporary space between you and the other person so that the person is not (how can we say?) distracted by that.

In physical mastery, we're looking to clear the cells of trauma from childhood and of all the actions that have happened to the personality in the body. So now this looks like the ultimate clearing, because the cells are going to change ...

They will change without restriction. There will not be something you will have to try to do. It happens naturally.

The new being will not have the birth trauma, will not have the childhood trauma, and will not have the guilt, shame, anger, rage, and fear.

Exactly right.

So this is pretty awesome.

It's wonderful!

We're talking about free beings.

That's right!

It's Natural for the Physical Body to Heal Itself

Might it be possible for a given physical body to have more than one walk-in? In the years past, occasionally and rarely that has been the case. But that will also increase. Perhaps a personality will come in for only a fixed amount of time. Instead of being born in a physical birth and, say, having a trauma and dying at the age of nine years old, you can come in as a walk-in, stay for maybe nine years, and then off you go and in comes somebody else. But again, remember, there will always be that compatibility if you are married to or in a relationship with somebody who's going through the walk-in process. It will always include and take into account your needs so that whoever comes in will improve the quality of your life as well. Walk-ins do not take place if they're going to make another person involved in the situation miserable, or they do not take place at that time.

It also sounds as if bodies are going to live longer, because with the new occupant healing the body, they should be able to live longer and more comfortably, right?

Maybe. What it will do is take stress off the body rather than putting healing into the body. So instead of being in a constant state of stress and anxiety and misery and unhappiness and all of that, that will simply stop. The natural process of your physical body is always to be healing itself. The physical body is the greatest healing factor in it's own existence. It's actually like a healing factory. White blood cells — think of all these things. It's amazing!

The vast majority of medicine right now is entirely structured as a complement to the way the physical body actually works. So if you simply remove that anxiety, stress, and unhappiness — yes? — the physical body's natural process is to heal itself. It will have more opportunity to heal itself, and it will be less burdened with the unhappiness of the previous tenants, who are no longer unhappily living their lives on Earth. They are happily moving through the veils, talking to God, the angels, and the guides and teachers, getting on with their lives elsewhere.

So all in all, it is, as people say, a win-win process that supports everyone. Most importantly, it is not an anomaly. At other levels of existence, it is the only way birth takes place. So it is a tried and true factor of living in many other places. If you all know that, it will not seem so foreign and strange.

This is very comprehensive; it's very clear. I wonder if Isis or Zoosh, or anybody else who wants to speak has anything to add to this. I'd like it as comprehensive as possible.

Certainly. We will take a brief intermission. [Pause.]

✳ ✳ ✳

Walk-Ins Improve the Quality of Life
Isis

Isis. Greetings.

Greetings. Do you have an overview or anything to add here? Speaks of Many Truths did a wonderful job, but is there anything else, from your point of view, that you'd like to add about this process?

This engagement of what is being called the walk-in process, I would rather call it the benevolent birth process. It is benevolent because there is no discomfort for anyone.

I'd also like to say that in other societies, funerals are different. The funeral does not require comfort for the bereaved because there is no bereaved. The personality that has departed is needed elsewhere or wants to be elsewhere. The personality that arrives is needed "here," wherever that may be, or is needed "here," wherever that might be. So the friends or family of the previous tenant are happy for that soul to be wherever he or she is. And it's all right to celebrate his or her life.

I think that the time of celebrating a life is still perfectly acceptable, so I wanted to make that comment. But short of that, I do not feel the need to correct, or say anything else about it unless you have a specific question.

Well, I don't know enough about it to actually ask specific questions.

It's definitely going to change society, though. You're going to have people who are workers, managers, executives, politicians — across the board — who are suddenly going to change and be more creative, more capable, more happy. That's one of the most important factors, because people are unhappy for a wide variety of reasons, but one of the main reasons is that they don't have what they want. They might not be able to get it. It might be literally impossible, or there might be so many blocks in the way that it's seemingly impossible. In these circumstances, the new personality will have different wants. Maybe the wants they have will be easily acquired, or maybe they will simply not feel any sense of urgency. That can change things too. There's a variety of possibilities.

The biggest change that everyone will notice immediately is that this person is obviously happier. "What happened to Tom? He seems to be perfectly happy." "What happened to Sally? She's not grumpy anymore." "Isn't it wonderful? It's a pleasure coming to the office now, 'cause I don't have that old sourpuss next to me." It's a joy to have this person around now. "I went to lunch with her the other day, and it was great. I've never been to lunch with her before. I always shuddered going into the same room with her." That kind of thing. Those kinds of comments will become increasingly typical.

Yes, and that will radiate out over the whole Earth.

It's very nice, because there's so much improvement in the quality of life without you having to climb Mount Everest to accomplish it. Suddenly life gets easier and better, and you really haven't had to do anything to bring it about. It is a natural process, which is typical to life elsewhere.

You understand what's really being said here is that the burdens of the required subjects in the school you are in on Earth are being removed from you. This is one of the burdens. The burden has been a long process of learning, growing, changing, suffering, adapting, and struggling. All of this is being gradually lifted from you — not immediately. For some people, it'll be an immediate exit. But even for those of you who remain, having people around you who aren't miserable will improve the quality of your life simply because their lives have improved. In short, life changes, and the load of books you've been carting around (because school here is so tough) — well, school's going to get easier.

This tells you something important. It tells you that, yes, you've been in school. Yes, it's an advanced PhD program. But what happens to people in PhD programs? Eventually they graduate, and then they begin their professions. They learn how to apply what they've learned, some of which they need and some of which they can discard. In short, once they are practicing their professions, their lives get more interesting, and often, compared to their college days, a lot easier. That's what's happening. Your life is going to get a lot easier. I'm not saying you've graduated, but you are no longer in school in the same way. School's getting easier, and that will be a continuing trend.

Earth School Is Getting Easier

Say more about school being easier. We're still in training to become creators?

Yes, but all of that training doesn't have to happen here. There's only so much that can happen here. Just like with any school you go to. You go to a teacher, and that teacher provides you with all he or she knows about a given subject, including not only knowledge but also experience and their means of teaching. The teacher provides you with everything he or she has to offer and every way he or she knows how to offer it to you as a member of a given class. Then you go on to another class and another teacher and another subject perhaps or another nuance of the subject you're interested in.

The main thing is that school is always changing, and as you acquire more knowledge, you are able to assimilate more or be more specific in where you put your interest. So school is changing because the requirements of the program — you go to college and you have certain subjects that you have to take, yes? — are being reduced because you can only learn so much. In any school, the teachers can only teach you what they have to teach.

This is a different school; you don't necessarily have teachers per se. You teach each other; life teaches you. But you can only learn so much here as life is.

You're going to stay here. You're not suddenly going to evacuate the planet and go somewhere else. What's going to happen, then? What's going to happen? Life here is going to change. You are going to stay here, you as the Explorer Race. You, as human beings in general, are going to stay here on Earth — not you individually. You come, and you go, but as a race of beings, human beings, you will stay here, and things will get easier. It's as if school came here for a while, all right, and you came to be here in school for a while. But school is moving on. As you move on in your natural cycle, as a portion of the Explorer Race, you will go on to the next place where school is taking place.

Where's that?

Wherever it may be, to learn the next level of your creator training. You will know that when you need to know it; you don't need to know it now. If you knew it now, it would only distract you from what you are doing here, and what would happen?

We wouldn't get "here" done.

Exactly right. You wouldn't get "here" done.

So the walk-ins are going to become happier, and is that going to ripple over into the other 80 percent who in a few years will not be walk-ins?

It appears to be 80 percent, or even 78 percent, all right. But remember that this goes on into the future, on a year-in/year-out basis. So life just gets better in general. Nice, huh?

The Natural Process of Life

Now granted, I'm not saying this is your deliverance. There are still lessons. But the big change is that the terribleness and the struggle as this process goes on ... the cumulative impact change will be that things will feel more possible, that the impossible — to achieve a desirable goal — will seem more possible, and it will be easier to bring about. In short, struggle will decrease.

Yes, and you've heard in the past, many times, that there are all these people, figuratively speaking, all these souls, who want to come to Earth to do all these things, and the line is much longer than Earth has the capacity for.

So this is how it's going to be here?

It isn't exclusively for that, as you've heard. It also serves to shorten up that line. Everything compatibly serves everything else in the natural process of life. So the natural process of life is being restored to Earth incrementally as it feels comfortable to those living here. It can't happen like that [snaps fingers]. You wouldn't learn anything from that, plus it would be too sudden. It has to happen gradually.

Well, this is dramatic!

It's wonderful, isn't it?

Yes, yes, this is.

The so-called walk-in process, which is a form of natural birth, is really something that is a gift for you all. If you can look at it as a gift from Creator, from all those who love you just for being yourselves, you don't have to be anything different. If you look at it as a gift, it will feel wonderful in every way. And the wonderful thing is that even if you look at it fearfully, your fears will be soothed, and you will be able to experience the process in the most benevolent, nurturing way. So know that even if you're frightened of the process, you will gradually find your fear reduces, and you will welcome it.

Remember, life goes on. This isn't all there is. You and your immortal personality go on — live on in some other form, in some other place, with wonderful beings you're happy to be with and who are happy to have you there. So know that we're not talking about loss in any way. We're talking only about gain in a happy way for all beings. It's a little better finish, wouldn't you say?

There is another element that you didn't address. It seems as if who I am is becoming irrelevant.

No, no, who you are shifts from being something future oriented to being a completion process. Remember, you imprint the tissues of your body so that when people come into you, they will receive the gift of all you have accomplished as well as all you came in with, in your natural gifts. So you will leave, by the very nature of its process, a legacy for that person who arrives who has similar characteristics and traits personality-wise. You will leave a gift, and you will not exit until you desire to go and are needed elsewhere.

So don't feel as if you've been given notice. You didn't get the pink slip. It will happen when the time's right.

No, but the identity situation: the new being comes in and is going to have to say "I" to talk about what he or she did ten years ago because otherwise it's going to get complex, right?

Yes, and it will feel completely natural after a time. During the first thirty or so days, you'll feel awkward. You'll want to say "somebody else" or "the other one" or something like that, but initially, you'll realize that socially you'll have to say "I," but inside you'll be able to separate that. You'll know that isn't you. There won't be any sense of attachment to what went on in this body by the other soul. You'll have to say "I" in social situations as to what happened in the past, but in time as the walk-in process becomes more known, understood, appreciated, and assimilated, other language — "lingo," as you say — will develop. But for right now, it's perfectly all right to say "I" and not worry. Don't worry about becoming confused about that. By saying "I," you will not form a personal attachment to what was done by the other soul in the body in which you now reside. That will not be present, because when you say "I," you know you'll be saying it for social reasons. You'll be saying "I," but you won't really mean yourself. All right? So you'll say it just to put others at ease — a little diplomacy training for everyone.

CHAPTER SEVEN

How the Walk-In Adjusts

Zoosh

November 2, 2002

When I talk about the walk-in phenomenon to different people, they get very defensive and angry to think that it could happen to them. Why is that?

Sometimes when people have this reaction (obviously you are referring to a couple of friends), it is usually caused by various things. One, they might have a religious discomfort with it, and we have to honor that. In other cases, it might simply be that they are already feeling rushed enough in their lives, and the last thing in the world they want to hear is that they might, even as a possibility, have less time than they thought they had. So you can see why that would be something that might bring out a pugnacious quality in people.

Of course, there is the possibility that they have been informed by their teachers and guides that such a thing might occur for them sooner rather than later, as this is going to become a more frequent occurrence over the next few years. Such a discussion with various souls on Earth is taking place increasingly often.

Now some people might legitimately feel that such a thing is not proper and not reasonable and therefore, on the basis of what they believe for whatever reason, might simply say so. That reaction is the core problem between different religions and philosophies. Religions and philosophies in their own right do not create wars or arguments, but in people's dogmatic desire to create truth, they do. The whole problem with religions and philosophies in general, including specific beliefs about any topic, is that the word "truth" gets mixed up in there. Generally speaking, religions and philosophies were never intended to be about truth; they were intended to be about inspiration. As you know, inspiration might vary widely from one person to the next. The artist is inspired one way, the business person is inspired another way, and so on, and the inspiration they each receive might be compatible were they to change hats, so to speak.

Given the nature of your culture's attachment to truth as being the ultimate pursuit of all mental aspiration, it is this actual reasonable goal that creates so many differences and has literally created one war after another. My suggestion is when it comes to your religion or your philosophy or even your beliefs about any given subject, don't be so attached to truth; rather, just let it be your inspiration. Be open to other possibilities, or at the very least, allow others to have their inspiration as it functions and lives for them.

If I were to do a survey of thousands of people, is this defensive attitude an attitude I would find in a large percentage of them?

If you were going to do it across the board and explain what a walk-in is, putting it in sympathetic terms — that it is a possibility that people will be able to shed their burdens and move on in a gentle way as compared to the usual way death takes place, like that — I think you would still, even with that explanation, get a great deal of resistance. Understand that this book is not only meant to be a manual for those who are associated with the experience, either experiencing it or being around it, but also intended to be somewhat controversial. So you can say very easily, even within New Age circles and broadening that out to the metaphysical and broadening that out to holistic circles, it will be (at the very least) controversial. It's not about the truth.

All of the material I've ever given to anyone has always been about inspiring them, encouraging their imaginations to sing, be inspired to do more, broaden their horizons. It has never been about "this is the truth." Spirit's job is not to give the truth; it is to encourage you to open up your vision or your potentials or your beliefs or your capabilities. This information is not about giving you the truth so that you can live it and force it on others who already have their own truths, at least in the moment.

Walk-In Abilities

You've said that one of the advantages for the planet would be that the souls coming in would have skill sets and abilities beyond those who are walking out.

This doesn't mean beyond the capabilities of human beings in general but beyond the individual's focus. You might have a limitation that's entirely reasonable as an individual, meaning you as an individual are a good driver, and you can conduct a business fairly well, yet you are not a pilot or do not have any particular interest in ever becoming a pilot, either in the air or at sea. So taking that into consideration, one might say that's a limit, but it isn't only a limit. It's also a direction, a focus, an interest, and even to some degree a demeanor, part of the personality. So those who come in might have different personality traits — a different demeanor. It won't be radically different as has been discussed before, but it will, in some cases, be significantly different or, at the very least, noticeably different.

The skills, abilities, and inclinations that they have are likely to be different; therefore those loved ones who live with or even work with a person who is a walk-in will probably notice unexpected changes. Perhaps the person was afraid of sushi and made jokes like, "Is it still alive?" and all this kind of stuff. But out of the blue, he or she says, "Let's go have sushi." While this is a minor change, it would be unexpected to those who know the person.

That implies that they've led lives — I think you said "not on Earth." Is that true? The walk-ins have not had lives on Earth before?

Oh, no. That is not true at all. They might very well have had lives on Earth. Why would you even want to have beings who walk-in — remember, what are these beings' jobs in general?

To make everything more benevolent.

Yes, to make everything more benevolent. But you know as a hard worker running a small business that to make everything more benevolent, you have to slog through the pits sometimes to get things in order, wouldn't you say? Especially when they've been well disordered, either for "this" or "that" reason, so you are in the process as an individual making things more benevolent. But it doesn't always feel benevolent in the process, you understand. So for them, we want — and we encourage, yes — people to come who have the capacity to make things more benevolent but also have the skills and abilities, the patience, and (perhaps more to the point) the endurance to do what it takes to bring about that benevolence for themselves, their families, their communities, and ultimately the world.

Then compare that to what you said that bothered me a little bit about the innocent soul who has always had its teachers. It was told that it could go to Earth and live inside its teacher [chapter 4]. It sounded so innocent and so unskilled and so inexperienced that ...

But you understand the wide range — think about it. We're talking about a walk-in as a phenomenon, not as an unusual characteristic, not the occasional walk-in. It will become a more frequent occurrence. So while there will be situations like that with souls who have that opportunity described that way, it is not exclusively the situation. What was going on was an example, so we talk about an example, but the example is not intended to be, what? It is not intended to be the truth. It is intended to be a way.

Let's say that there are several beings on Earth who are in the middle of something important for Earth but perhaps they started late and their bodies are worn out, or they just don't have bodies anymore. Would they go through a process of review and possibly come back as walk-ins without going through the process of birth again?

That is very unlikely. If you have lived a life here, the chances of you coming right back and having another life, regardless of what you are doing, is very unlikely because you would need, and desire, to have some experience in learning about that. Even though time is not a rigid thing in other places, and you could, theoretically, come right back to that (now we're talking visual, so understand we're talking about someone going out, experiencing, and coming back in relatively the same timeline), it is very unlikely, but it is not impossible.

No matter how important something is, very often as you've noted in the past, teachers and other beings who seem to be vitally needed are sometimes lost for one reason or another, and the people wander around for a bit saying, "What will we do?" But life goes on, and other teachers are available. Perhaps they don't resonate with you the same way as the previous one did, and that forces you to apply what you had learned, put it into your life where it fits, and go on. After all, the best teaching gives you things to apply. Inspiration is fine, but you have to decide how practical it is by doing it. If it becomes practical for you by doing it, then wonderful.

The Soul Braid Experience versus the Walk-In

What is the difference between a soul braid and a walk-in? Is it important to know whether it's a soul braid or a walk-in, and how do you tell the difference?

Generally speaking, with a soul braid, it is a much more subtle change. When a person is experiencing the soul braid, he or she will notice a much milder degree of motivational change. It will be something that does not feel sudden or abrupt; rather, there will be a sense of continuity. Your personality is still present, but you suddenly have new interests, and things that were difficult for you once before are now easier — not easy, but easier. That would be an example of a soul-braid experience.

With a walk-in, you would feel radically different. You would even very commonly feel frustrated and uncomfortable. This is not always the case, but with people who have not had walk-ins before [see chapter 12] or who find the whole walk-in experience entirely foreign — meaning no exposure to New Age, metaphysical, or even philosophical understanding — it could create rage and discomfort and frustration and anger, especially if their lives are very demanding. So what would occur, then, would be a radical change. If you have a walk-in experience and you're the parting soul, then the walk-in will be radically different. If your life is not very demanding and overwhelming, you will not likely experience frustration and anger. There will only likely be frustration and anger when there has been resistance for a time, meaning that the soul walking out is past its point.

Say, you were walking down a hallway with lots of open doors, and the first open door looks inviting, but you're so busy and you have so much to do, you walk right past it even though it looked wonderful. You keep on going until you're actually a little past the last open door and then, almost as an afterthought, you rush back. You fight your way back, and you get your fingers around the doorframe and just barely pull yourself through. That would be a situation in which the exiting soul, because it was so distracted by the life that person was living, not only almost missed the opportunity but, more to the point, almost missed a benevolent experience. Thus, no soul that's going to exit a body that goes on living and becomes a vessel for another soul is ever forced out.

You might ask, "What if they miss that last door? What happens? What if they insist on staying on?" Then they will stay on, but all the challenges, all the things that were going to happen that would have felt like opportunities for the new soul coming in, that the new soul would have loved and really enjoyed, would feel very likely — not absolutely, but about a 70 to 72 percent chance — like challenges and discomforts, outrageous, you know, like "What's going on?" kind of reactions in the soul hanging on. But no soul is kicked out for a walk-in.

It is always and only a free choice based on the soul's desire to walk in or exit. It is always based on the soul's desire, just as in a natural death, meaning that the soul walks out and the body dies. The soul chooses to leave. Creator doesn't come and say, "Well, your time is over," and grab you as a soul by the scruff of your neck, wrench you out of your body, and say, "Let's go." You choose to leave. It's the same thing exactly in a walk-in experience.

For the walk-in, the change would essentially (but not necessarily) be rough. It would be a significant change. You would feel a sense of vagueness. There would be almost a sense of lack of personality for a while because as the new personality experiences the physical body in which it finds itself, it sort of explores the physical body for a day or two — experiencing sleep, experiencing the waking state. During these few days, the person might feel vague, and people around him or her might notice that you seem to be vague. Don't assume the person has any disease; it might just mean that he or she is experiencing this phenomenon. So if you have had that type of experience, consider the possibility that you've had a walk-in, and that is not a terrible thing. It could prove to be a great benefit.

Since your destiny (and this is key) as the walk-in soul is entirely different from the destiny of the previous soul in occupation, there is no reason whatsoever to assume that the outcome of your life will have anything to do with the outcome, or even the feared outcome, of the previous soul's life. That is important because destiny is not cut in stone but often there is a tendency toward a certain destiny, and that can sometimes be changed based on what you do in your life. In this case, it is also a change that happens. That's important to understand because sometimes people (souls), when they come into the body as walk-ins, almost feel a sense of obligation to live on the way the previous soul was living, and it doesn't feel comfortable.

Say the previous soul was an angry person, creating problems, even an alcoholic. The new soul coming in, that's what it knows. That's what the body does, and that's what the body knows. Yet when you go down to the bar to try to drink with your old cronies, it just doesn't feel right, and it gradually becomes something that you don't really want to do anymore. Before you know it, you find yourself at Alcoholics Anonymous, and you have a whole group of friends. It's not easy letting go because your body craves it, yet you just don't identify with that lifestyle anymore. If it happens out of the blue, that could very easily be a walk-in.

When the soul who walks out leaves, how does that work? Do the teachers talk to it and assure it that it doesn't have to worry; it's not abandoning anything?

There's a lot of conversation that happens in the deep dream state, usually for months and months before the exit takes place so that the moment is very gentle and completely relaxed. Walk-ins/exiting souls do not usually happen in traumatic situations. I will say that on the basis of walk-ins up to this point in time on Earth, about 3 percent have happened in traumatic situations. By that, I mean car accidents, such as when after a person wakes up (and might be injured) and feels radically different. The person doesn't feel anything like he or she did before. This can happen that way, but don't ever expect it to — as I say, 3 percent in that way. Generally speaking, it happens gently and easily. You flow right out of the body, not unlike you do in a natural death. It just seems completely natural; you just step out of the body and go on with your life. You go with your teachers and your guides, and life goes on for you but elsewhere.

The Walk-In Usually Adapts Well to the Family

You've discussed this a little bit, but maybe you can expand on it. The walk-in comes in, and as you've said, if it's a husband or wife or there are children or a job, he or she immediately goes about the life that's there, taking responsibility for it until perhaps it can sort of wind it up and settle it and then go do what it wants to do.

No, that's not necessarily true. Think of it this way: Think of marriages as you've known them or even as you've heard about them. Marriages are not always wonderful; husbands and wives do not always love each other as much as might be ideal. Husbands and wives do not always make the best parents, even though that would be ideal. Let's look at it another way. Let's say that the marriage has been struggling and that it hasn't been much fun for anybody, but the people are doing the best they can. The walk-in comes in, finds the spouse to be very appealing, literally finding his or her good qualities, and does not even particularly feel attached to old fights, arguments, or disagreements. Perhaps the mate brings something up that would previously have caused a big battle or, as you say, the battle royal, all over again, and the walk-in says, "Yes, you're probably right about that," and on he or she goes. To the mate, it's like, "What?" The mate is a little shocked and happy and doesn't say anything but is happy about it. This could be a walk-in.

Maybe the walk-in comes in and sees the good in his or her children, not just the things to criticize. The walk-in doesn't just think about the children as they were when they were little babies or toddlers, when they were cute and lovable no matter what even though they were dependent and required a lot of care. They are cute and lovable like that. That's for sure, no matter what. As they get older and develop their own personalities, they're not always as cute and lovable as they were when they were babies, and sometimes parents miss that. So that's just universal in terms of Earth, but recognize this: When the walk-in comes in, the walk-in is not at all attached to how the children were when they were babies unless they are babies now, you understand? Walk-ins are not attached to that; they find the children to be appealing and enjoyable. They like the children.

It doesn't have to be something where the walk-in comes in and doesn't feel at all attracted — is disenchanted — by the experience of the family, and as you say, winds it up and goes on. It's not that at all. Normally the case would be that things just get better all around. Remember that the walk-in situation (the exit and then the walk in, yes?) happens to improve the quality of life — period. It creates in some way, 92 percent of the time, an improved situation for everybody in the immediate unit. By the "immediate unit," I mean family, and in some cases where people are not married and don't have children, close relatives, or close friends, the immediate unit would be work or some other thing where you relate to people. Generally, it will improve things for everyone. That is a given in the walk-in situation. It is very important to keep that in mind. You hear about people who have a walk-in and go out to explore, take six months off from the marriage, and say, "I have to find myself," whatever. It's not always a midlife crisis; sometimes it's other things.

As you said before, if the marriage isn't going to work out, there will be someone better for both of them.

That is the case, but normally the case is that things simply get better. It could be that there are people waiting for the others — for someone to leave. Then you find the people who are waiting, and you love them so much better, but that is the exception. Generally speaking, the walk-ins come in and often like what they find. You have to recognize that the wife or the husband, depending on the sex of the walk-in, is experiencing demonstrated physical Earth life from those closest to him or her. If you fall into a situation where there's a marriage and children and close relatives, these people actually demonstrate human physical life to you. So even if they may not be, over a period of time or for the next fifty years, say, your all-time favorite in those moments when you first come in — for those first few months and years — they are going to become some of your favorite people. You will feel very much like their teacher, even though you can't talk to them that way. You will tend to emulate them.

This brings out an important point. When walk-ins come in, are they more likely to be imitative? That's another way you can tell whether someone's a walk-in. Say someone has always demonstrated a certain personality, a certain way of being, and then suddenly, you don't get the feeling that the person is quite the same anymore. Maybe you actually liked the way the person used to be better, maybe not, but the person appears to demonstrate qualities that are more imitative. Perhaps the person is likely to be more easily influenced by things that people say and do or is likely to be influenced by the television, as it's constantly on. In short, the person is going to do the same thing young children do when exposed to other children — be imitative, which is exactly what you would expect in the case of a birth and a growth. So be alert to that. If your husband or wife, brother or sister, or whatever, suddenly becomes a little different and very imitative, it doesn't mean that person is a walk-in, but it could. We're talking about something that is still relatively rare.

The Exiting-Soul Agreement

There's a lot of talk in the metaphysical world about contracts and agreements before we come into the body. We make agreements with certain people to do certain things. Now, what happens with that when the exiting soul maybe hasn't lived long enough to fulfill all of the agreements or hasn't met that person for whom he or she was going to do something? What is the obligation? Is that ended when the soul walks out? Or is there some responsibility on the walk-in to fulfill some of those agreements?

For starters, regardless of what anybody has said, I must say that I do not agree that contracts even exist. A contract would be at the very least a promise: "I will do this for you when we meet" or "We will do this together when we meet in some way." It has to be vague. Potentials change radically. People die naturally, and their bodies return to the earth. They will have learned their lessons they came in to learn. They will have had the opportunity to fulfill what they came in to do, at least on the primary levels. If they feel, after they've stepped out, that they want to do more because they might have had discussions, generally, loosely, nothing heavy — no heavy contracts, no blood promises — and they feel a desire to help another soul, even after they've walked out and the life is over, they can (if they choose) do something with that soul in some other lifetime as they go on in their reincarnational cycle. Everyone easily sheds these things. No responsibility exists to do that. I know people say karma is real, but my whole point (as I've said before) is that karma is over because you've done all these things.

Now, lifetimes are not carved in stone. As you know, rivers meander over time; it's just the same for a lifetime. Souls meander in terms of their potentials and possibilities, especially during times like this when change is all about you. There are no rigid contracts anymore. If you exit, well, you exit. Let's face it. If you hadn't walked out and allowed someone else to walk-in — you understand, if you had said no — well, then you just would have died. A walk-in/walk-out situation is not a threat. It just says, "Well, you can get away without suffering," to put it in it's most mundane terms.

Because the person is done? Is that what you're saying? And the body is still usable?

You did what you needed to do, and you can leave. You have the opportunity to leave like that. You decide, because of discussions with your teachers, that it is all right with you if your body goes on and becomes a vessel for another soul, especially if that soul has some familiarity or similarity to you so that your body, because you have an affection for your body, does not feel as if a foreign invader has landed. As a rule, you usually will not make that a requirement but a strong preference, and it is honored.

You brought up something interesting. You said if you exit, then the body's usable; otherwise it returns to the earth. That stimulates something in me that the way that the experience of a human gets into the general fund is that the particles that have that experience return to the earth as the body decomposes, right? But here, with a walk-in, 40 percent of that person goes out to be transformed in some way, and it doesn't go into the earth. That means the earth has enough experience; it doesn't need any more. Is that right? It has enough of those particles that are contributing to the ... ?

I think you're making a simple thing unnecessarily complicated. It's very simple. The body is what it is, regardless of what soul is in it at any time. It is always earth, and whenever it returns to the earth, it becomes as it always has been. It is earth. It does not bring qualities from the souls of the beings who inhabited it while walking Earth. It's not bringing those qualities to the earth because Earth needed it; it's just the opposite. Earth gives you opportunities to explore qualities in yourself that you might not have been able to explore otherwise because of Earth's great spiritual advancement. But you do not give Earth qualities, no. The body is simply like a library book. She says, "Okay, time to return to the earth," and she has no particular attachment to your qualities. That's why the body breaks down the way it does. You are not passing out favors to Earth; you are not favoring Earth with your qualities.

I thought the experience each soul gained, then, was available to the next group of souls because of the experience of the particles.

It is this: We know from previous discussions (do we not?) how advanced Earth is.

Yes, quantum mastery.

All of these things, the particles that make her up, fully engage when they are involved in a body for a human being (or any other being but especially human beings in this case) in your personality while not abandoning their Earth qualities and capabilities and their own immortal personalities as particles. But when the soul leaves, the particles rapidly release the qualities associated with the soul as it demonstrates them. In the case of a physical death that is released very quickly, the particles are their earth substance in a different form as the body gradually becomes earth again. The particles, in whatever form they wind up, are of earth and of their own personality. It is as if an actor lets go of a role he or she has been playing. The particles, however, always remember who they are (in the body or beyond), just like the actors remember who they are — that there's a performance, even though they might get very involved in the role. They know that they are different and can be different when they're offstage. It is more like that, if that helps.

I do not rule out that a given soul might come in and exhibit some characteristics and qualities that are so unique that its energy might add certain personality characteristics. But it will add it during the life; it will add it simply by sprinkling your personality around as you do, being yourself in life — the way a cheerful person can cheer up someone who is feeling a bit down. So it tends to be demonstrated as part of a physical life rather than something that Earth did not have.

CHAPTER EIGHT

Your Walk-In Experience Is Supported by Your Physical Body

Reveals the Mysteries

September 23, 2002

All right, this is Reveals the Mysteries. First, a comment for you for your support and enlightenment. There's a reason you are not recalling details from your past. As you know, when souls come to incarnate on this planet, if they remember all that, they are in such an evolved state (as all souls who come here must be), they would most assuredly do things, act, communicate, and be the sum total of what they had been up to that point.

Of course, this planet would be very enlightened with a beautiful society and warm population — nurturing, loving, wonderful — as it is in other dimensions and as it will be in the future, as everyone is striving for now. But it is not that now. It is in the striving that people will re-create it, expand it, and make it more. This you know, and the walk-in phenomenon is a similar situation. Like a drop in an ocean, so the walk-in phenomenon functions the same way.

The walk-in soul must also let go of all that it is to enter this dimension on Earth. It can, on a feeling level — that's most important to understand in your depths of being — access the feelings that it had accumulated in previous existences. This is often experienced when you have such experiences as a sudden feeling of confidence or a sudden feeling of peace or even safety. In short, it's a sudden feeling not prompted by anything in your surroundings. This is almost always a circumstance of that depth of connection on a soul line having to do with your previous experiences, incarnations, and talks with teachers — who and what you were, really were, as you came in — before you dropped your awareness on a conscious level of who you are.

It's another reason we encourage people to go into their feelings to cleanse the connection, which isn't always pleasant, but it passes. It's so that they can feel their feelings and experience the full depth of their beings in the present, as they are, and as needed to be reassured by the feelings of your total being who, even in a moment-to-moment experience of your physical life here, will be assured and supported by teachers, guides, and others. In short, your soul being, as it expresses itself in a physical self, is truly nurtured and supported, but the only way you can really experience this is through physical feelings.

These same physical feelings can transform your experience of life. When such a feeling comes through, it is often during moments in which, as you look around at your life, you did not receive any mental stimulation that things are getting better or that they might get better and you'll get through this. Nor do you, even in that moment, experience any sense, meaning using your senses of understanding — sight, sound, touch, smell, and so on. You receive nothing stimulating a conscious change, no. You feel suddenly, unexpectedly, self-assured or loving or sometimes even joyous, even breaking out with a laugh, which, as people might experience it around you, seems incongruous, to say the least. Yet when prompted by that, it often makes the path easier as you move through the events of the day, and things become much easier because you are able to move from one form of life to another.

What form of life might that be in the situation that you find yourself in as a representative of the walk-in experience? Of course, as you are finding yourself (as is so typical of walk-ins) in someone else's life, instead of being born as a baby and being in your own life, it is difficult and even seemingly, on the face of it, well, why would you do it any other way, yes? It's necessary to perform much the same way as the previous soul performed in order to bring about the desired results, be it personal, career-oriented, or even in a career such as yours [publishing] that affects the lives of many.

When you try to do things that way, even though you know it doesn't work for you, you almost immediately experience a sense of blanking out, memory gaps. I have to tell you that this is intended, because as you proceed further and further into the immersion of your soul into the physical body, you inherit it as a welcoming vehicle to embrace you and allow you to live life to the fullest degree you can on Earth as it is now. As this happens and as time goes on, your physical body becomes increasingly aware that to utilize the methods and means of the previous incarnation in that body is unhealthful for your soul and your personality.

Of all the physical beings you will ever meet who are likely to support and nurture the real you in your physical body, the real walk-in you, the real person in heart and soul — the being who will do this the most effectively, not just with the best of intentions, but the most effectively — is your own physical body. It's not just because, as has been discussed before, your physical body is made up of Mother Earth's body, but also because your physical body had knowledge and experience of the previous incarnation, whoever that might be for a walk-in.

That knowledge and awareness is on such an intimate level that it goes beyond what any other being in your physical surroundings (and very often even any other being whatsoever) could know to the degree of intimacy that your physical body knows. Therefore your physical body is the quintessential teacher and supporter of the true you, the walk-in you, in your body. With full approval of your teachers, guides, angels, spiritual instructors, and all beings who supported and welcomed you so that you might have the walk-in experience at all, it will proceed with its understanding and in cooperation of material mastery and teaching mastery — which as you know are portions of Mother Earth's capabilities. The application of that will turn out to be the various things that often seem like symptoms, meaning you will be prompted to do something. How can you be prompted? You will not receive instructions. Your physical body will not try to control others to bring you your demands, none of that. Rather, you will experience a certain need or desire to do something. That happens. It happens other ways too.

The Physical Body Blocks the Walk-In's Memories

There is another way that something happens that really commands your attention and reminds you that you are a walk-in. You might know this sometimes, and at other times, it might seem simply frustrating. Your physical body will block — literally block — memories from the past. It does this not because it is capricious or trying to annoy you (like other circumstances and people and happenings might annoy you) but rather because if you remember the behaviors, the frustrations, the angers, and the general demeanor the previous individual in you would have demonstrated (not just with that decision or what happened or what resulted from what happened in that time, but the full-bodied experience), everything that was felt then and all of its consequences — that's the key to understanding this — would be felt if the memory was allowed to come through. Those consequences contributed to the original being walking out of the body, because it just felt boxed in and couldn't go on with life the way it was. There's no way your physical body will allow those conditions to repeat themselves, so what occurs is something very similar to when a soul is born in what we're calling a natural birth, and that is the baby will try to do the same thing.

That's one of the big reasons a baby cries when there is no apparent physical cause, because a baby knows, especially when it is quite young, within the first few months as a being, how to do something, how to resolve something — how to have the knowledge, wisdom, and experience to create a resolution, even without the physical capacity to bring it about — to make something better in life. Yet the baby is being forced, just the same way your physical body literally creates a sense of force that does not allow the awareness, no matter how conscious, that such wisdom is available. It does not allow that wisdom to be present because that wisdom is associated with not only the total being whose conscious awareness must be dropped to come to Earth but also the physical body, even at that early stage of being an immature physical human, as a baby. The physical body is aware, even at that stage, that were you to remember, apply, and experience the solution, that solution would be inappropriate and perhaps even (in some cases) catastrophic for you to apply as a human being baby in a society and culture in which you live.

Therefore, the physical body does the same thing that the walk-in experiences. It will support, request, or ask for — otherwise known as stimulate — something external to happen to distract you as a being. Much more often, meaning about 98 percent of the time, perhaps *almost* 98 percent (97-something percent), it will create what feels like forgetfulness, and it is that forgetfulness for baby that will prompt it, out of frustration, to cry out. That is why when parents are walking a child, it will sometimes feel there is something wrong with it, its perception, because it can feel that, especially if they are close and loving baby, which is typical for parents or even siblings sometimes. The parents will feel that rage, anger, and frustration, and they will feel they are making some mistake, they have overlooked something, which is why they will do everything, sometimes repeatedly, yet baby still cries with that same feeling emanating.

I say this for not only walk-ins to help you to understand, to nurture you, to remind you, to support your wisdom to live, but also for parents who have had that experience and know that the physical body blocks that knowledge because its full impact would cause some detrimental effects, as one experiences this maddening frustration as a walk-in or as a baby. Of course, as a walk-in, there is a greater degree of maturity (in that sense) — conscious maturity, mental maturity — and life experience to a degree that can be called on that allow and make it possible. The adult walk-in could perhaps demonstrate characteristics other than crying out in rage, but feeling that frustration can be maddening and unsettling.

I bring this point up because it is a practical reality of experiencing a walk-in. It is not because one is getting older and [chuckles] is no longer as sharp mentally; it is very specifically intended to protect the walk-in soul from the devastating impacts that could cause one of many conditions. One I've suggested is that the full-bodied recollection with all of its attendant experiences (not just recollection of the piece of knowledge that's needed, but recollection of how that knowledge was acquired) and what went on around you at the time (along with all the frustrations, angers, fears, motivations, and so on) caused the physical body to be profoundly affected by that. Not just that, which is significant to a great degree in itself, but also other things that the physical body, in its wisdom, is attempting to prevent. Regardless of the full range of experience of your feelings and circumstances of the time in which that piece of knowledge is attempting to be remembered by the present soul in the body, there were other things that happened.

Sometimes it was a result of that full-bodied experience of everything, meaning a path was chosen that, although it seemed appropriate and reasonable at the time, was long and circuitous. This caused the soul as well as the practical day-to-day life to wander about in an area where there was no hope of truly bringing about happiness or even accomplishment that would lead to benefit others — in short, off the path, wandering around. The physical body has this full knowledge. Is it not fascinating to realize that the physical body in an instantaneous moment has full command of this awareness because it physically experienced it?

Regardless of what people say, with the cellular structure changing over, and all of this business, there are parts of the physical body that remain a constant throughout your physical life. These parts function as a physical memory process leading and supporting the material mastery applications of the physical body in these moments of critical choice. So the physical body feels-knows that the best choice is to simply not remember to protect. Think about it, walk-in individual. Think about what you sketchily recall —

speaking to all walk-ins here, of course — from the past. Sometimes such recollections will simply not be available, but they are perhaps burdensomely recalled, even in an external sense, meaning you don't remember it. You can't remember it as an experience — no sights, sounds, and smells. However, they are sometimes burdensome when suddenly recalled, because people might say, "Oh! I remember how you used to be," and then tell you a story that will perhaps even make you shudder on the basis of how "you" were.

This will sometimes happen to remind you in a somewhat humorous way, because of your disconnection from that past experience, that it is better to be who you are in your body, and your physical body brings this about because of its Mother Earth capabilities. Sometimes spiritual mastery is understandable the way it is applied by the mind. Sometimes even material mastery is understandable when given these markers (as physicians say), or landmarks, having to do with the physical self.

You Are a Creator in Training

Teaching mastery is not always understood because teaching mastery is usually understood after the fact. This means something you realize now and has a great impact on your life or makes sense to you regardless of how it came about was often prompted by, say, receptivity, openness, awareness, or simply the capacity to generate, support, or create ideal circumstances for you. It means your physical body will feel, but more to the point, your physical body has helped to create or literally created on its own — with Creator's approval, of course. That is something that has prompted a profound change, not only in your understanding of your reality but also how you proceed with life after that. You are truly experiencing many levels there: spiritual mastery, material mastery, yes. But after the fact, you sometimes realize this has been a full-bodied teaching mastery experience.

What about the other levels of mastery, such as dimensional mastery? Dimensional mastery is rarely if ever understood until *after* one's life is over, when one can see how the circumstances of the life one chose to live in those times and in that body (in the full experience of life as you knew it in that body) to understand in greater depth your own personality, which is the main reason personalities emerge into any form of individuality to pursue life and experience from its point of origin. That is, of course, to understand more about yourself as an individual with the initial goal of returning and sharing that from your place of emergence and in fact ultimately leading to a blossoming and a creation of a place yourself, from which other beings will emerge. This is clearly demonstrated by the way women give birth and how men contribute to that — to remind you gently and always physically of how creation works.

There is also the simple drive. It is not a drive as you understand physical drives: the need for sexual contact, the need for food, the need for shelter, and so on — not that kind of drive. It is a drive that literally supports all life that you experience: the drive to know more about yourself rather than the pleasure of feeling sure of who you are when you were in that being — wherever it was, wherever it started — before you emerged as an individual personality to experience life.

Now, such drives are the underpinnings of the reason you go on with life — walk-ins, whoever you are, or even souls as you come into the body — very often when circumstances are frustrating or difficult or seemingly impossible not because of the knowledge mentally that things could get better, which is true, but because of that drive to know more about yourself. Is it not fascinating that such simple things are easily overlooked, and these simple things have to do with dimensional mastery, even though they might be applied to spiritual mastery, material mastery, and of course teaching mastery?

Of course you do not really think about such things, and with quantum mastery, which has to do with the mastery of consequences (the full range of circumstances moment to moment, every single experience you have: smelling a flower, noticing a bee flying about, or being hit by a spitball in class and being annoyed as a youngster), be it pleasant or unpleasant, is being coordinated by the master of physical experience. This has to do with all consequences that affect all actions, forever in the past, in total in the present, and in all future possibilities, for all beings living on Earth's surface. Clearly a definition (wouldn't you say?) of something that sounds very much like a creator.

The capacity that Mother Earth has to support and create life on her physical body for all beings is in effect. You would not benefit by knowing this and living a life without having that wisdom affect your life. Not only do you not need to know it, but the occasional reminder of it gives you the sense of awe and wonder helpful to appreciate how you (as an individual walk-in or simply a soul born into a body in the usual, natural way) and your life and day-to-day activities are supported by such amazing creative powers — that of creators in training, such as Mother Earth, who has proceeded further along the lines of learning how to be a creator than you have.

As a creator in training, you want to be around other creators in training who have gone further than you have — just as in any school situation in which it is very desirable for students to be around other students who've gone past what they are doing so that they might receive the benefit of the advanced students' experience — here in the most intimate way on Earth, whether as a soul in a natural birth as a baby or as a walk-in. You experience literally such amazing creation in your day-to-day, moment-to-moment life from Mother Earth and Creator, who trains her. You as the student are coming along and making progress around and within the physical being on the most intimate level, in your physical body, using Mother Earth's capabilities. You're a senior student, so to speak, here. You find yourself in an experience on a daily basis that can be maddening and frustrating, simply being, "I don't remember, and I wish I did."

Here is this explanation, the reason why: You are literally being protected. How many times do people hear that, whether they are religious or spiritual or whether they are simply hearing that from their parents? "I'm protecting you from this." [Laughs.] You've said that to others, and it has been said to you. Yet it is a real thing. Your physical body is your first and foremost intimate connection with your capacity to live on Earth in this amazing creator school in its full levels of mastery as a physical being — granted, separate from your soul. With the total awareness, complete understanding, and physical memory of what was in you before, as a walk-in, your physical body literally shuts off your capacity to recall something, even if it seems to be absolutely vital to recall it. I could tell you stories. There have been times when people who were walk-ins have been in circumstances in which they might question the physical body's blocking them from remembering something.

A Walk-In Story

I will tell you a short story. There's an individual who was not as spiritually involved or interested as most of the readers, but still had some practical understanding that there had been a shift within her. This individual was driving down a road, and always as a driver, conducted herself in such a way that she was consciously, and sometimes unconsciously, performing the duties she had always learned and known as a driver. She thought of herself as a reasonably good driver, but others did not always share that opinion, as you note while you drive your vehicle in traffic. How often it is that you have momentary experiences with others who think that they are wonderful drivers and your personal experience does not always agree with that? Very often you do the same things yourself when you notice after several miles that you don't really remember the previous territory, although you're sure, in your recollection, that you were consciously present but perhaps not as consciously present as at other times.

You find that as you are barreling along the road, you experience these moments of gaps. Here for this particular driver, she was driving along, and if she had continued to drive as a person who used the driving habits and capabilities of her previous incarnation within her body, would have reacted in certain ways and would have brought about, unintentionally, her own death. Her reactive systems that she learned from before, in her previous soul's inhabitance in that body, would have caused her, when prompted by a stimulation (as psychologists like to say) like something in the road, to react incorrectly, because she was not as physically present as she might normally be, let's say, as a good driver.

Because she was in that slightly altered state when she saw this unexpected thing, she would have suddenly done what drivers often do when they see something unexpected, and she would have turned the wheel to avoid hitting that thing. But that thing she saw in that time and that method of driving that she was falling back on, which had to do with how driving was learned by the previous incarnation, would have been a catastrophe for not only her but also the others who would have become unintentionally involved.

You understand this all happened in a split second, as car crashes or near misses often do. Understand this happened within — I'll give you a range for the sake of your enjoyment of the story — about one-quarter of a second. She saw something suddenly, unexpectedly. She gripped the wheel, and in the next split second, she would have turned the wheel in the way the previous driver did. But she suddenly had a complete blank-out experience. It was almost as if she shifted from being a driver to a passenger, simply gripping the dashboard in front of her, and even though in total terror, she had no capacity to turn the wheel to the left or the right. She simply went through the phantom experience; in that moment, she saw something that had to do with another existence.

When you come in as a walk-in, for even the first few years of that experience (but more often in the first few moments or first few months or weeks), you will sometimes see things dimensionally that are different. You might see a landscape, for instance, that is not the one you are in physically, especially if you are on, as drivers often say, "automatic," driving along, not really remembering or noticing where you are and in a few miles suddenly notice that that is the case.

When you are on automatic like that, things happen. So even though she was in abject terror, she simply didn't remember how to function as she — meaning the previous incarnation within her as a walk-in — would have functioned, seeing any object in the road. There was literally another road crossing the road she was driving on with cars and people and so on. Instead of immediately slamming on the brakes (which would have been serious business for the cars behind her) or jerking the wheel to the left or the right (which might have had similar results for others), with this abject terror and with her hands literally gripping the wheel (which might cause her knuckles to turn white in that moment with such an extreme grip), she could not remember what to do. It was as if she suddenly forgot she was driving and couldn't remember how to drive and "poof!" (all this happening, you understand, within a split second) she went right through that moment of seeing the overlay from another place, another time, and suddenly was fully and totally aware of the road once again.

Now, this is almost, what you call — as youngsters might say, not to be too colloquial — a wet-your-pants experience. Not quite, but almost. Often what people do after such an experience is the first chance they get, they pull over and shake a little bit or ask themselves, "What on Earth was on my mind!" Or they get out of the vehicle and walk around. But the woman continued on down the road and experienced something that is not unusual for walk-ins: She could suddenly see the physical surroundings, even as a driver whizzing past them, in a way that the surroundings, including within her car (objects in her car, the land, the people, the cars, the plants, the animals, the mountains, everything) were pulsing, scintillating with life, as if there was a living, breathing energy interacting from all forms of life to all other forms of life. Granted, it didn't last forever, but it was right there for a moment, and she could feel this incredible, uplifting experience. Of course, she wanted it to go on forever, as anyone might. It didn't go on forever, but it was there.

She took it as a reminder that Creator and her angels, teachers, and guides were looking over her, which of course is always true. But what was going on in that exact moment was her physical body dropping a veil and allowing her to see with her physical eyes the interaction of all life with all other life in this beautiful matrix as one looks at it almost like looking through water but not quite. That motion happens at the edges of things, be it a tree, mountain, or car. The edges of things are not firm and solid or clearly defined as separate from each other. The edges soften, and there is clearly a breathing and an experience of shared energies from one thing to another, that that experience was present for her for a few seconds. It was the kind of recollection that caused her to change and embrace life.

After that, she drove down the road and remembered, with a smile on her face, that amazing life-affirming experience and embraced her life more. She went on and tried new wonderful, healthful things that she'd been shy to try before. She experienced people in different ways, having been a very shy person previously. She went on, accepted invitations by other women that she worked with, "Oh come out with us. Let's go to this talk or this discussion. Let's go out after work and have coffee and talk. Let's go out and do 'this' or 'that' or come home and have dinner with me and my husband and children." She went on to experience life completely differently, embracing it rather than holding back or feeling shy.

She engaged life as walk-ins often do, regardless of the wisdom that is in existence in the depths of their beings, which is not easily mentally translatable, at least not at first. But the feelings were present, and the feelings within her expanded, and she became more social and experienced with people and what they do. She had been holding back because of the conditioning of the previous soul in her body because of very clearly understandable circumstances — which I'm going to pass over for the moment in the story — that prompted her to hold back from life. But she suddenly saw and felt how life literally breathes in and out and between all other forms of life, even if those forms of life are in transit, meaning that the car is not really a car. But what made it up?

There's an interchange with all other life, seeing that and feeling that moment and fully experiencing in those few seconds the full capacity that she could physically experience and, even to a degree, mentally remember, which sometimes prompts the feelings that were present in those moments of experience so that she could use that experience to carry on with life, to be herself in *her* body and live.

So we have a story that supports the experience of the walk-in, which is challenging and has parallels to the experience of the soul being born in the natural way as a baby. Walk-ins do not always remember, even though they might feel it is essential to remember, what they "need" to remember because if they remembered it, more than the recollection of that piece of knowledge would be experienced. Your spiritual master, material master, teaching master, dimensional master, and quantum master physical body loves you too much to allow that to happen.

CHAPTER NINE

The Personality Allows the Soul to Reveal Itself

Reveals the Mysteries

November 15, 2002

What would you like to talk about?

Zoosh said that a walk-in does not feel the same type of emotional intensity as someone born in the conventional way. Can you discuss that?

That is true, but only for a given time. Depending on the individual, that period of time could last from, say, three days to a month or more, but I do not think that it would hold indefinitely. As a matter of fact, it is possible that, should the new souls become not only acclimated but blend in with the life, the ongoing life of the body, they might even become more sensitized than the average person because it is clear when you think about it. The physical body might be older or adult, but the soul in terms of Earth experience is young and tender.

At first, there is a period of time when the body makes certain preparations. Some of this has to do with the soul that departs. The body extends — extends it into an overlap — that chemical preparation, not a numbing situation, to that which comes in. This allows the new soul to ease in to the intensity that the soul might not have felt in a while or ever. What happens is that, after a time, it is possible for the walk-in to go many different ways.

One way might be that the walk-ins get overwhelmed by a stimulation or distraction or constant demands for attention by this, that, or the other thing in your modern society, and they might tend to remain in a state of confusion during which they would be uncertain of their feelings. Another possibility is that they might become sensitive, as children might be, though there is not that much expected of children. Say you're in the body for six or

123

seven months as a new soul. A six- or seven-month-old would not have much in the way of responsibility, if any, but a six- or seven-month-old walk-in in an adult body might have a great amount of responsibility. The biggest hurdle that walk-ins have to face is probably the attempt to confront and work out an application of their souls' desires with the given circumstances of the body and life they find themselves in.

If they become too sensitive, they might become reclusive. This can be noted. I'm not saying it should be considered a problem, but it might be necessary to entice such beings out into the mainstream to meet people, and the more they meet people and feel better about them, the sooner it will pass. But if you're asking whether they have the same emotional bodies, meaning feeling bodies, no. The feeling body is there. They do not bring in an emotional body per se. It is there. It is only that it takes a while for the soul to adapt to the demands of a world that is about material mastery. As a result of those demands and that material mastery school, it can take a while to adapt.

I understood it very differently. It was on a tape in the archive series (people sometimes sent in tapes of their personal readings because they felt the information they received was important to others). Zoosh was talking to someone and said that this was the person's first life actually being born through a human and not a walk-in situation, so the emotional intensity was more pronounced than had been experienced as a walk-in previously.

You'd have to talk to Zoosh about that. You cannot expect the beings that talk through any channel to agree on everything. As a matter of fact, as you've noted over time, very often they do not agree at all. That is actually acceptable since different points of view might relate better to this reader or that reader. Regardless, it is not something that is calculated but rather based on the personality, perception, and experience of the being speaking.

I have read that many times Earth is almost an overpowering experience for new souls because of the emotional intensity. You can get lost in it.

You have to keep in mind that if you are looking for a formulaic answer, it is not there because we're dealing with people individually. Individual personalities will react differently even if in an identical mechanism, and physical bodies are not what I call identical mechanisms.

I was thinking that this is a way to experience Earth but not to get lost in it.

Getting "lost in Earth" is the intention. It is not considered — and this is an interesting point — that a person or a soul has lived an Earth life unless he or she becomes fully engaged in it. If a person remains outside of the boundaries or is reluctant to participate in social events (because many people are like this) and refuses as a soul to engage with the physical body, then he or she will come again.

I see. So rather than being concerned about a soul — that's a whole new way of looking at it — getting into the deep melodrama and losing his or her focus, that's the point.

The point is not the so-called melodrama because "melodrama" is just a word of judgment in this case. Rather, it is that the drama of life is intended to bring out what you came here to do as a soul and to show you your skills and adaptability, as well as to show you the skills, adaptability, knowledge, and wisdom of others. In short, on Earth, even if you have a serious problem, you cannot expect to have others show up to resolve it. You have to ask for help. Granted, sometimes people show up to resolve it, but that is the exception. On other planets, if there is a serious problem, beings show up to help immediately or at least when the time is right for that personality.

When a soul has not had much experience on Earth or on a planet where there is a lack of communication, as on Earth, then it can be difficult, and sometimes the soul refuses to engage in the so-called dramas of life. If the soul refuses to engage and withdraws sometimes in an obvious way, as in what is called mental disease, or sometimes in a less obvious way, as being an isolated person (there are many possibilities there; a person might be unreachable in a relationship or choose to live as a hermit, going out and living somewhere far from other human beings), then most likely, unless that was the soul's purpose, which is not likely, the soul would have an opportunity (as the Mother of All Beings calls it), which essentially amounts in my eyes to a requirement to come and live again.

Then the next time the soul engages actively?

That's right. Probably then you will talk to your teachers after that life, and say, "What could I set up differently that would encourage me to engage more in life?" Your teachers would give advice, and among you, you would decide what to do. You wouldn't just repeat it in an identical situation.

So what about those who sit off and watch and evaluate people who think they are mentally superior? They're sort of withdrawn, and they comment more on the action rather than actually engage in it.

There is no absolute. If you're looking for the formula that says "this" means "this" and "that" means "that," you're looking in the wrong place, because it depends what the soul came here to do. So there is no formula. You can't say that if this person is living out in the country all alone with no one else around, just the dogs and cats and horses, then he or she must be "this." That is not true. You can't point a finger and say to another person that such is the case of what I've been speaking. That can only be done after life when it is decided by the soul itself in communication with the soul's teachers and guides that it has not fulfilled the purpose of the life. In which case, the soul will come back to do it over not because it's being punished but rather because it has that privilege or that right to do so.

The soul might choose not to. If it chooses not to, it can't go back, meaning it cannot go back and relive the life it lived. The soul also can't choose to not go forward with that choice of education, learning, or experience. If the soul chooses not to come back to Earth, which occasionally happens, then it will have the opportunity to live out that lesson more slowly on other planets. It might take ten, twelve, fifteen, or twenty lives on other planets to come to the same conclusions or expectations or ultimate purpose that a single life on Earth might accomplish. Some might find that Earth life attractive, and others might say, "Well, I don't care if it takes fifty lives on other planets. That's the way I'm going to do it."

I can see if they got into a particularly tumultuous emotional situation ...

Not just an emotional situation but also if they got into a situation that was physically terrible or frightening. Emotions are not the enemy; they are the cure. They are always the cure because they will drive you toward or away from something that you need to be near or far from. They — emotions, also known as feelings —are the only means you have to solve anything. They are not the problem.

That's an interesting statement.

Well, think about it. As Zoosh has said, if something is annoying you, you might be inclined to do something about it, but if you do not have annoyance available to you, why would you ever do anything about it? So the feeling body, and what the mind calls emotions, is not only the friend but the necessary foundation to material mastery. Without the feeling body, material mastery is not possible. For that matter, material functionality at all is not possible. Think about it; the foundation of all life is love. That is a feeling!

You Always Serve Each Other

You said something interesting earlier. I had assumed that each soul generates or creates its own feeling body, but you said that it stays with the physical body after the existing soul leaves.

To a degree, yes. When the soul departs, you take your feelings — that whole part of you — with you up to a point, but as you know, many feelings cannot be resolved as you move through the veils, as they're called. Those feelings are shed, but where do they go? Do they just go in some dustbin? No. They will return gradually to the physical body from which they came. Otherwise, the physical body has bits of itself floating about out there that are lost. Anything that's shed by the departing soul will return to the physical body. Even in the case of a natural death, the same thing happens. The bits that cannot go along, for whatever reason, will return to the physical body, or in the case of a natural death, usually they just stay in the physical body.

But there might be some bits that have to return in a walk-in situation. What I mean by that is the feeling self, the mechanisms of the feeling self, all remain in the physical body. But that which has motivated you as a soul to depart or to allow your departure (those are two different things: to depart or to allow your departure) goes with you for a ways in order to support that decision so that you continue to move out. If it didn't go with you for a ways, you might just step out of the body and become instantaneously lost.

Now, there needs to be a reason to leave and go on. It is not a mental reason; it is a feeling. You get up and go, so to speak, and your guide is there to help you to go where you're going, but your guide does not take you. Your guide performs the function — the reason it's a guide — to guide you to get to the right place, but it does not pull you along nor does it push you. That which causes you to move at all are your own feelings. They motivate you to move on, and some of those feelings can go with you as a soul, soul feelings, all right. Some involve conflict, for instance, "So-and-so loves me, and I don't want to go on because he or she loves me and will miss me," which is typical. That can go only to a point, and it cannot go where you're going as a soul to move on through the veils of recycling life. So eventually that falls away, and it returns on pretty much the same path that you have taken with your guide (in front of you, next to you, or with you). Your guide takes a physical trail. The bits that fall off and need to be elsewhere because they can't go with you return on the same path right back to your physical body, and it is up to the next soul who comes in to find resolution there. Resolution may not be necessary, of course, because you are there, and those bits, in the case of the example, had to do with, "So-and-so loves me and will miss me." But you might find yourself in that relationship, so that will be resolved simply by your being there. It doesn't have a motivating factor on you.

How fast do they come back — a minute, a day, a year?

I don't think that's really very important, but it would be very fast.

What if the impetus to leave was more painful? What if there were feelings of rejection or depression? Just imagine what might cause someone to leave.

No one ever leaves his or her physical body because of a feeling of rejection — ever. You leave because of pain, physical pain. Pain's ultimate function is to escort your soul out of the body and help you move on. In the case of a walk-in, you see, it's different, but in the case of a natural death, it is pain that causes you to move on. You can feel a tremendous amount of rejection, but that's not going to cause you to move out of your physical body and stimulate a physical death. However, when we're talking about a walk-in, you could just be unhappy. Then you might have rejection plus all kinds of other things. Even then, no matter how those feelings are, you will not leave your physical body. That cannot cause a walk-out/walk-in situation. It cannot. You can only exit from your physical body if you have some place to "walk" *to*, meaning there is another life waiting for you, there is something you can go on and do, or there is possibly, and this happens more often than not, something that you're *needed* to do. You are needed elsewhere.

Just remember that the walk-in situation, especially in the past, has been the rare situation in which someone walked out because he or she was needed elsewhere and instead of having a physical death, left the physical body behind to be actively used by another soul who walks in. But nowadays it's becoming more common. Nevertheless, you cannot exit as a soul if you are not actually needed elsewhere.

What an interesting concept. Give me some other instances of being needed elsewhere.

It could be any number of things. For instance, possibly as the result of your personal experience throughout all your lives, plus the Earth life you have just been living, you have a particularly unique perspective that could be helpful to explain to certain people to whom you could be a teacher to help them to understand, apply, or prepare any number of things in some other life. There might simply be people you need to join — anything, any reason to live — but it cannot be abstract. It cannot be like there are three or four souls on the other side of the universe who might be happier if you were to join them as a soul. That's not enough of a reason. You actually have to be needed. It's not just that you would be welcome, and they would be happy to see you. That's not enough. You have to be needed. Others cannot proceed with whatever they are doing without you there. So they wait (sometimes they do; this is typical) for you to get there, or if they can't wait (perhaps whatever they're going to do is needed by others, and there is no waiting that is acceptable), then out you go.

For example, you had a friend recently who was in that situation. She had been needed for a while. The other beings were waiting. They waited in terms of Earth time for a few years; in terms of their time, it wasn't as long. They waited as long as they could, and then it was like, "Right now! Now!" It would be like someone banging his or her hand on the table and saying, "Now, now, now." But it isn't that kind of demand. They were banging because they were needed elsewhere, and because they were needed elsewhere, off she went. Another being stepped into her body to allow her to have a benevolent death and resolve her situation with her family, which she could not do.

Can you say what sort of thing was needed? Can you just expand on that a little bit?

This had to do with a teacher, and the teacher was desperately needed on another planet to resolve (and I have to be vague here) problems of functionality, basically how things work, so that others who needed to do something could make things work that needed to work for others. It's always for others — for others, for others — and it goes on like that because we all serve each other all the time. The teacher was needed and the situation was urgent, so she left.

"The teacher was needed," so she was going to be the teacher, or she combined with these other beings who … ?

Combined with these other beings. They had been waiting and couldn't wait any longer.

That's one of the most profound things I've heard you say: We serve each other all the time.

That is true; that is a given. Others have said this.

That's very interesting, and that goes all the way up to the point where Ssjoooo responded to the need in this cosmic day [see Totality and Beyond, Explorer Race book #20.].

The important way for you to think so that you will understand how life works is that it goes all the way up, all the way down, from side to side, and from here to there and everywhere else. In short, there is no "up" and there is no "down," but those directions have been given before to give you some sense of pathway to follow so that you could make headway. If there is no direction and you find yourself in space able to go in any direction, you might conceivably, given all the directions possible, remain stuck for a time.

The Heart Is the Center of Your Being

Back to the feeling — so the physical body is holding these feelings when the soul walks in, and if those feelings are strong, it's going to impel that soul to work the situation out, to resolve it before it can do what it needs to for its own purposes.

That's true, but it's desensitized for a while so that it can ease into it. It doesn't just crash into the situation. That's why, even if the soul walks into a body for which there are tremendous demands and so much going on for a while, the soul might just muddle through for a while with things not being done very efficiently and people saying, "What's wrong with her?" That's because the soul is literally muddling through, probably working at the full range of the capacity that it has to offer (which is not very much), just as a child wouldn't have much of a capacity to offer immediately. It does not take as long as a child's maturation. We're not talking fifteen to twenty years to become established, but it takes a while, especially if that body is engaged in a life that is overwhelming in the first place, in which the body's doing much more than is intended for any given life in any event. As we know in this particular case, that body was doing at least three times more, given the circumstances of the pathway of that particular individual.

I don't know how you see. Do you see through my mind or through my eyes, or do I somehow present a picture?

We always see through your heart.

So if I don't feel it, you don't see it?

It's difficult for you because you tend to compartmentalize your functions. You assume that thought happens in the mind, but there is nothing the mind knows that the heart does not know; however, there is much the heart knows that the mind does not. The heart is ultimately the best reservoir for knowing you — who you are, who you could be, who you might be, where you've been, where you're going, where you're from, why you're here, and so on.

Just know that the center of your being is the heart — not only physiologically, but also if you were to put a sphere in the body or around the body, the center of that sphere would be the heart, and all the lines would radiate out from there. That's why the heart, which stimulates, supports, and nurtures feelings, is always the first to know and the first to give the message to other parts of the body — what's coming, where you're going, where you have been, why you are here, and so on. The best thing people can do if they want to understand their lives in those terms (not only what's going on now, but what has been going on and what might be coming) is to get to know their hearts and their feelings.

If you get to know your heart and your feelings as they feel in your physical body and can interpret what those physical feelings mean, you will not only be able to understand yourself very well, know what is good for you or what is not good for you, and know how to be in given situations — literally how to be — but you will also know what's coming around the corner. Maybe you turn left, not right, and so on. To sharpen your instincts, get to know your heart and your feelings.

On other planets, of course, that's one of the very first things youngsters are trained to do. On this planet in more ancient cultures, that was also one of the first things youngsters were trained to do. In your time with the enamoring of the mind, not only is that not one of the first things the children are trained to do, often they are not trained to do it at all. Therefore, they do the best they can, which is also known as muddling through.

Can you say the soul is most connected to the heart?

I wouldn't say that it is *most* connected to the heart, but I would say that the easiest way to get in touch with your soul is through your heart; however, your soul is not exclusive. If you want to find your soul, communicate with your soul and have loving engagement with your soul. The heart is the easiest path because the soul will feel, as any being would when warmth and love is radiated, at ease and safe. Of course, you're going to be more open when you feel at ease and safe, to say nothing of loved or liked.

The Body Needs Time to Adapt to the New Personality

So any soul that comes into the body is the personality, and there is a sense of an "I-ness" in the body that is different from the soul? Does it feel separate from the soul?

Yes. That's why that time to prepare needs to take place. It's like a marriage because the original body formed up around the soul in mother, but this situation is different. The soul leaves and the body becomes a vessel for a different soul. So the body was prepared for a soul that is no longer present, and the body is a little uncomfortable, but it has had time to prepare. Like with any relationship, there needs to be a time of getting acquainted. That's why it's all right for the new soul to express itself differently in the body and to be itself, even though it might be different from the previous soul's expressions, because that's how the body learns to adapt to the new soul. It is really very much like a relationship, getting to know each other and feeling at ease with each other more and more over time and then feeling perfectly comfortable with each other, as if you've always known each other and have been old friends forever — like any other relationship.

Of course, certain things immediately function quickly and easily out of necessity because of the fact that life must go on, so there's that. But in terms of the full embracing, "Happy to have you here," the body hugs your soul, and your soul hugs your body saying, "Oh, it's so wonderful to be with you." That kind of thing takes time as in any relationship, and you need to give yourself that time.

In short, as the soul coming in, don't expect everything to work perfectly immediately. It will take the body a while to adapt to your personality, and it will take your personality a while to adapt to not only what's going on in the body but the residual things left over in that body from all of the life that has been lived before your arrival. So you're going to have to deal with that, but then you were trained, meaning you were told that you're arriving in something that is already a fait accompli; something's already been established. You're arriving in an establishment.

It is your job, first and foremost, to create equilibrium in that establishment, which will be your foundation upon which you can go forward and build your life from there. It is during that time of establishing equilibrium that you, as the soul, get to know your physical body, and your physical body gets to know your soul, so it works very well.

Granted, those around you might be a little bit at a loss to understand what's going on, but there will not be radical differences between your soul's personality and the previous soul's personality. There needs to be enough similarity so that the lives around you — whatever situation you find yourself in, even if you're not in a relationship — can at least feel as if you're different but there is continuity. There clearly might be a difference, but generally it's "you" from their perception. You're different, and they can adapt to that.

I read something Speaks of Many Truths said about the body being prepared for the purposes of the soul that incarnates in it, and it gave me such a good feeling that there's such possibility. There are unlimited possibilities. It's like a plastic thing you can mold anyway you want.

That's a wonderful way to put it. It's very much like the sculptor who looks at the block of clay. There it is, sitting in front of you, and for the amateur sculptor, you might look at it and think, "Now, how can I shape this clay to look like something?" It is that attitude that might happen in the first few days or weeks from the soul's point of view, but as you get more comfortable with the physical body, then what happens over time is more of the attitude of the professional sculptor. That person looks at the clay and sees either what he or she wants to show in the clay or sees even the way the clay seems to express itself — that's the artistic point of view — and simply removes parts of the clay to reveal what he or she sees in it.

I've heard that said about marble.

That's right, and this is really the progression that the soul takes. We are here, you, me, and others, contributing to this book to encourage the soul to move from being an amateur sculptor to being a bit more of an artist who reveals by involvement. You have to put your fingers into the clay. You can't just think about it. By being involved, you reveal all of the potentials and capacities that will be more than what was here before and, in some cases, less. Maybe the previous person had the fabulous ability to produce beautiful handwriting, for instance, and you are not motivated to produce beautiful handwriting and don't seem to have quite the same capabilities. If you work at it, you can do it because the body has been trained to do it, but it is a struggle. If you don't do it for a living or if the demand is not placed on you, then you don't really have to.

The point is that it is our job here with this book to help the soul engage in the physical body, not just to mold the physical body, but to become receptive to the physical body's capabilities and capacities. Thus, together the soul and the physical body begin to perform a dance — the sort of dance where someone is not attempting to always lead. Imagine dancing with a partner and your partner's always leading. There might be times when you want to lead because maybe you know the dance step and your partner doesn't, so the lead has to change feet, so to speak.

I feel another way of expressing that. Since a walk-in has to leave it's memories at the veil, there is the exciting possibility of working with the body to see what the soul wants. And the walk-in allows the soul to reveal itself because, to the walk-in, it doesn't remember, so there's this possibility of seeing who one is in the physical by that process.

But the body does not inhibit the soul from revealing itself. What happens to cause that inhibition is usually the soul feels overwhelmed by what's going on in the body's life, which is why that's when they will start to engage equilibrium, slowing the life down, slowing it down, and slowing it down until they get to the point where they can establish equilibrium and build up from there. So it's not usually the body that inhibits that.

I have the exciting sense that a walk-in doesn't know who it is, and there's a chance of revealing oneself to oneself on Earth.

Yes, you're right. Here's a way to know whether you might be a walk-in. Say you wake up one morning and, no matter what your life was, you suddenly feel that you could be anything, you could do anything, and you could go anywhere, even though you know for a fact that you have to go to the office. You have to do your work and do your job and take care of the kids. You have to help everybody get dressed and ready for school, regardless of the routine you have to do. You still feel suddenly — out of nowhere — that you can be anything and you can do anything, all of this. This might be a sign that you've had the walk-in experience, provided the other signs are there as well. It could also be a sign that your teachers had a good talking with you and helped you to remove a block. Things can have different meanings.

In this life, regardless of whether you're a walk-in or simply a soul doing the best you can to live your life, try to give yourself more latitude. The people around you might not always encourage you to try new things, but give yourself a little homework. Here's what I recommend: If you go for walks, walk down a different block one day. If you read magazines, try to look at a magazine that you haven't looked at before just to see it, not to be trained in someone else's interest but rather to be stimulated by the pictures. If you talk to people, talk to someone new or talk about something different. In short, try something different in your life in the next month or two just to see how you feel.

If you feel a tremendous sense of vigorousness almost as if a flower wants to bloom within you, you will know you are proceeding on the right path. Maybe you need to do more of the new thing you are doing. Maybe you simply need to do more new things. The main thing to take note of is that in your age of specialization, even people who are not specialized in careers (like physicians and so on) have come to feel as if you have been stuffed into a notch or forced to be a sprocket or gear. Expand the teeth in that sprocket or gear: Try something new or do something different to see whether you can enjoy life more.

CHAPTER TEN

How to Live as a Walk-In

Reveals the Mysteries

November 22, 2002

What would you like to discuss today?

I would like your understanding of how it works in natural birth when a soul comes in, in relation to contracts and agreements we make with people to be our wives, mothers, brothers, fathers, sisters, husbands, or bosses, and so on. It seems we make arrangements; we create scenarios for our lives. It's as if it's laid out loosely before birth. Would you tell me how it really works? This is for the birth soul now, not the walk-in.

In your linear world, it is typical to think of things in worded fashion, so that's why the word "contracts" comes up. For people interested in this subject generally, it is typical to think of things that way. In fact, before a given life is ensouled, what happens with that soul personality (and any other soul personality that is likely to come in contact with that being, let's say, during his or her life) is as follows: Picture it with no words at all. It is a picture. It is as if there is a radiance of color, and the radiance that goes out to the beings that you are likely to contact is a color that might be a bit more distinct.

In this case, I see the color as something like a light blue with a tiny bit of lilac mixed in. The beings who you come in contact with are a little bit beyond that color, and that is more of a gold and white light mix. So it is all done. The color represents and is equal to (one and the same) the energy, so it is an actual contact. Now, this contact takes place, whether the beings that you will interact with as a soul are on Earth yet or not, so it's very likely that some of the beings are on Earth. If they were able to do it, though, it would be a distraction for them, okay. So they're not usually able, but if they are able to do it, though, theoretically, they would feel a slight vibration, warmth, or tingling, something very slight.

On the other hand, if the beings are not on Earth yet, not born yet, then they would still feel it, but it would be more distinct, more clear, because not being on Earth yet, there would be the clarity of more consciousness, not necessarily totally. It depends on what they are doing and where they are, but there would be an awareness. Imagine it this way: You would get a feeling, and it would make you smile. You would have a warm feeling. You would know, "I'm going to be with so-and-so again" or "I'm going to see so-and-so again."

Remember, beyond Earth, beyond the drama here, everyone is a friend, and it's a good feeling. So it is like that. It is all done, then, with feeling, and representative of that feeling is the color here for the sake of a linear, physical delineation so that it isn't just energy. Energy can be felt in many ways, and it can be confusing to try to describe something that does not have any apparent physical characteristics other than being slight. So the color is added for the sake of accentuating what goes on. It is not ever anything that is worded or contractual.

I realize that your question did not mean to suggest that, but I think it is important to underline that because in the cultures and worlds in which you now find yourself (if you understand my meaning), the past has been very clearly anchored in and developed toward more and more words for the same thing. The intention being that you can make your point clearly with different shadings of a word that might mean generally the same thing. But what it has done unintentionally is create confusion because many people will use all these different synonyms for one thing. While they might mean entirely different things in the dictionary or to people in general, they will mean that one thing used on an individual personality's basis for that definition. In short, all these extra words have not helped and have often made things more complicated. So the simple and clearest means of communication is always through feeling, which is sometimes seen as color.

Is this color radiating from the soul about to incarnate who is going to be interacting with these beings?

Let's not go into that because that becomes unnecessarily complicated. Let's just say yes; it radiates from that soul. But when I say the source, we're talking about the source of energy and color in general, and I think it is not good for the purpose of this book to get too complicated, as we are doing now. This book is intended to be practical, not just theoretical.

All right, so the way it plays out, then, there is — based on these broadcast feelings, let's say — a loose scenario set up that you will interact with this or that person and that soul and this being in that way through the light, right?

Yes, but there is nothing like what you would call fate in which what you say, what you do, the circumstances, the moment, the time, and the actions are set up. It's more like a feeling for the people, the souls, whom you will interact with. It's a feeling, but it's an intended feeling. It's not a contract as one would sign or shake on. It's an intention that is fulfilled not by some external authority but rather because both souls in the case of two intend to do it, feel good about it, and plan on it, and it happens like that but not in that order. I'm trying to be clear without being excessively complicated.

So the life goes on, and these souls show up in college, in school, in business, at home, at the office, and at the gym. You end up interacting with these beings in some fashion?

Yes, that's right, and sometimes they might encourage you to do something. Sometimes they might encourage you to not do something and lots of other possibilities.

The Walk-In Follows a Path Similar to the Exiting Soul's

Now, the soul walks out. Are all those (let's call them) agreements null and void, then?

I understand your application of that term. They aren't null and void. They all remain in effect, because the body built up around that soul is (since we're using legal terminology) nonbinding, meaning that the body built up around that soul was going to see certain beings, yes? If any of those remain in effect — meaning beings you were definitely going to see — then because the body built up around that soul, those things would be there as potentials. So everything shifts to potential and that which was a potential before — souls that you might interact with — also remains but only slightly less. Everything clicks to being slightly less potential.

Then when the walk-in comes in, it's the same for him or her. What was described before for the birth soul is exactly the same set up for the walk-in with the difference that the physical body still has within it the potentials of meeting these other people. If those other people do not have any purpose in the walk-in soul's life, then they do not meet at all. Only if there is some purpose or meaning do they meet. In that sense, you might say the walk-in soul has a wider variety to choose from.

There might be, say, one or two people they would not have planned on meeting but, when coming into the body, have the awareness on the soul or spiritual level that these people will potentially meet. If it might be advantageous for one or two of them to meet or interact in some way, the soul might then add them to the list of potential beings that it is planning to interact with. In that sense, the walk-in soul has the advantage there. That is the only inclusion that I see.

So the walk-in soul has the same kind of potential meetings with different beings as the birth soul?

Absolutely. That's how you learn, grow, and ultimately contribute on Earth and, of course beyond, once you go on.

There are new beings coming in who haven't been on Earth before. I can see how the birth soul, having had many lives, has all this variety to choose from: things that it wants to do that it didn't get a chance to and people it wants to interact with in a different way. I can see all that. But what if you have someone coming from beyond the system who doesn't have any prior relationships with anyone?

Be aware — perhaps I'm not making myself clear. This birth method of the beings you will interact with, this is the system universally. That might alter your question. If it does alter your question, consider it, and restate it. If it doesn't, then continue.

You mean everywhere, everywhen, everyhow? It all works like that? Anyone who incarnates, that's the system? Whether it's on the other side of the totality or in this galaxy or anywhere?

That's how it works as far as everything I have been guided, taught, and inspired. I have never seen it any other way.

So the walk-in soul has that same "preview of coming attractions" kind of feeling in which there are adventures and special beings to interact with. Is it based on need? What is it based on?

It's based entirely on, not unlike the birth soul, what the being wants to do here and what it might wish to learn here. As a bonus from the being's teachers, it could also be based on what the teachers might include as a potential possibility, not a demand, that the soul could learn here if it chose to either connect the dots, as you say (notice the shape of things, the flow) or go through it as a potential lesson. Doing that could be valuable for the soul to grow and appreciate the total life on a broader level. It's not a requirement but available, not for everyone but often. Am I making any sense at all?

That's really interesting. I just thought that was an Earth thing because of the karma and the Explorer Race requirements for growth. I didn't realize it was system-wide. I had a whole other idea. I thought the walk-in came in without any support. You've pretty much explained what I wanted to know.

The important thing to remember is that the walk-in has similarities to the previous soul, and if you could get them both in the same room at the same time as physical human beings, they could not help but notice their similarities. In a brief conversation, you would agree on many points. At the same time, ultimately — no matter how similar it is when the walk-in arrives and the other soul departs — the similarity tends to decrease as time goes on as the walk-in soul begins to express his or her own personality and traits and so on. The similarity is not ongoing except in a slighter and slighter and slighter way as time goes on.

This is important to note because sometimes there are changes in direction, such as the new soul has other things to do — not necessarily with other people, but might have other things to do in life, perhaps a career change or working in a different way. As a result, the attitudes of the beings you meet or even already know toward the new walk-in soul (the body that formed up around the previous soul; yes, you arrive in that life and there are beings one already knows) might suddenly shift as the walk-in soul shifts within that body. People see it, or they don't.

In the beginning, they generally don't see it. They might notice something subtle, but your attitude also changes, and ultimately their attitudes change. Whereas things might have been going one way very clearly in the previous life in that body, with the walk-in's life in that body, things might go in a completely different direction because the walk-in's life might not have that much to do, say, on a career level, with the body that one has walked into, the inherited temple, so to speak.

The change will not usually be sudden and crisis oriented, but it will have duration. Perhaps a different direction is needed. There will be a direction that will come about on a slightly dramatic level, perhaps intense. If you don't understand something, then it is intensified so that you understand what's going on. This might not be something sudden and extreme and horrible. It might be an accumulation of repetitious experiences that would continue to let you know, one way or another, that you need to change directions, even try something entirely new if you are going to be able to carry on or gradually close out that part of your life so that you can move on and do what you came here to do.

Most of the time, not all the time, the new soul will not make radical shifts. It is the exception for walk-ins to arrive in a marriage and leave the marriage to go off and do other things. That is the exception. It is not typical. What usually happens in the marriage is that the new soul arrives, sees a whole other level of personality characteristics in the loved one and in the children or grandchildren and so on, if there are those. Usually, there is a greater closeness, not the other way. It's just that one hears about the other way because it seems so dramatic.

In the case of changing your employment or the way you do your work, if you work for someone else, you might conceivably change jobs. But if you have landed in a businessperson's body, for example, and you find yourself working, say, in a manufacturing business or in a service-oriented business, you will increasingly — almost always — be pressured by those around you, whether they were in the life of the previous soul or not, to change the way you do things in ways that cause you to feel as if you (the new soul) are coming more to the surface. In the beginning, it will be very intimidating not to do that because you will feel the body as the body of the previous soul, and you will feel somewhat intimidated.

Some people will feel more or less intimidated, and it isn't actually intimidation, but it is somewhat overwhelming. You will feel overwhelmed to do things the way that body has been set up to do things by the previous soul. However, as time goes on and the body gets used to you and you get used to the body, you'll begin to try to do things a new way on your own. If you don't know quite how to do that, externally you will be prompted by those around you to do things in a new way because the old way will simply not be accepted. I think you have heard of such things.

Exercise Your Personality

It is important for all walk-ins to understand that exercising your own personality is important. You don't necessarily have to make dramatic changes, but you might have to shift in the way you do things. You might find yourself in the body of an athlete. Maybe the athlete has in the past gotten up at six in the morning and gone for a run. Well, maybe you're different. Maybe you'll get up at five and go for the morning run, or maybe you don't even go for the morning run. In short, maybe you do things differently, but you're not going to stop being an athlete right away unless you have something major that you need to do. You might continue to be the athlete and add other things to your life.

Here's the key: Understand that it is difficult in the beginning to define your own personality in the body because there is no immediate support for that. But after a while, there is not only support for that in the body but a desire by your physical body that you begin to express your personality. The body will be waiting for you to express it, and the body will no longer give support for doing things the old way because the body, by that time, is clear that the old way has to do with the previous soul. The body is physically clear that the previous soul is no longer present. There is no support to do things the old way from that soul; therefore, the body has by this time, as I say, adapted to the new soul's manner of doing things, even though the new soul might not be conscious of its ways of doing things.

The interesting thing we have, and this is typical on Earth as you know, is that you are not very conscious of these subtler things, but your physical body is the first part of you, in the case of the walk-in, that becomes crystal clear as to who you are as a personality and everything that makes you up. It's very clear on that point, and that's why it does not support the previous soul's manner and methods of doing things. Therefore, if you try to do things that way, in the beginning you will be able, but after a while, it will get more and more muddled until you are just confusion incarnate if you keep trying to do it that way. Say you want to do things in your new way, but mentally you feel muddled. You don't know what to do. Then what you need to do is to get to know your body, and I'm going to tell you how to do that right now — all you walk-ins out there.

Thank heavens you have a vehicle that you can fall back on that knows you and everything about you in terms of what you can do: "So this is what to do." Pick a situation in your life, any situation that's happening that is complex or difficult or that you feel confused about or that you simply cannot make up your mind about. For example, one day you feel "this" way, and the next day or later on the same day, you feel the "other" way, so you feel muddled. Then you can either write these things down or, I recommend, say them out loud.

Step aside from people for a while. If you have to go to the bathroom and lock the door, do it, because you need to say something out loud. This is a physical thing that you're doing, and it has to do with physical mastery, so it's good. You're working on your spiritual side anyway. What you do is you state the situation, whatever it is, even if it's something simple. You just say, "This is happening." Then you say, "Would it be best for me to _____," and then you say one choice. Then become aware of your physical body, especially in the general area below your neck and above your genitals — in other words, the trunk of your body. You just go in there and feel that part of your body, and notice how your physical body feels.

If you feel warmth or relaxation or physical comfort for that, then you know that would be a good thing. You can even make a note if you want to or remember it if your mind is clear. Then wait until those feelings pass, and get relaxed in your body. It might be a minute, or it might be a couple of minutes, but we're not talking about seconds. Wait until you are relaxed. Then say, "Or would it be best to _____," and state another possibility.

Again, notice how your physical body feels. If any part of the trunk of your physical body feels uncomfortable or you feel an uncomfortable feeling in another part of your body — we're talking about feeling warm — then make a little note or remember mixed feelings. Say to yourself, "Maybe this is part of the answer." And go on through, stating out loud, waiting a few minutes between each one that you say, "What is the best way to do it?" Keep going on until you finish all of the ways that seem viable. If you get a strong warmth on any one of those ways, then it is good. If you get one or two mixed reactions, some warmth in your body or some discomfort, then take note to try to remember what you said. You can play around with that, meaning there might be factors in that way of doing things that are good and other factors that aren't. Try to rephrase the statement until your body feels physically warm.

It's time-consuming, but only in the beginning while you get used to doing it this way. There has to be no distractions so that you can completely step aside and feel your own physical feelings. Remember, now, your physical body knows you completely. It is not confused in any way that you are the previous soul, and it stands to be your best possible teacher once you understand your feelings.

From everything I've heard, this process is going to have such a powerful, benevolent effect on Earth that at first it doesn't really matter whether people know that they are different souls or whether they're operating differently, feeling differently, acting differently.

Exactly.

So how will knowing this help the walk-in?

Because of our recent material, talking here. Whether you know you're a walk-in or you figure you might be a walk-in, you can use that technique (although you could use it anyway even without being a walk-in) to state out loud what might be the solution to something, as we discussed before. In the past, not being a walk-in but the original birth soul, you might have been crystal clear about how you solve things when a problem comes up. But all of a sudden, out of the blue, the same problem comes up that you've solved in the same way all the time. You've always solved it that way and "bang!" suddenly your usual solution doesn't work. That might be a clue you might be a walk-in. Therefore, it might be good to try that exercise we've given to see whether it helps. So that's one of the big ways this can help.

Use This Book to Simplify Your Life

Now, as a walk-in, you know you have a mission, but it's critically important that you know you don't have to find it. We've already discussed that. You have a mission that you will probably fulfill here on Earth. The exception is that you might be here to learn something, as stated before, that you will apply in another life some place else, so you will fulfill it there. Don't go hunting "here" and hunting "there" and picking up "this" rock and moving "that" bush to find your mission; rather, use this book as a solution to solve your difficulties. You will find methods and manners and applications that work for you and help you to become more fulfilled and complete as a person. Use it as a resource to know and understand yourself and to know and understand about walk-ins.

The book is actually intended to simplify your life. So if there are bits of it that get too complicated for you, just skip right over that and find the parts that will help you to simplify your life. Ultimately, that is happening for everyone on Earth anyway.

When there are problems and solutions are presented to take care of those problems, then they are no longer problems. That simplifies life for the person who has the problem and ultimately for everyone so that the problem doesn't turn into a big thorny knot, which is what you have many of these days. Time will allow these thorny knots to disappear and for problems to be mere ripples for you to resolve in your own benevolent ways.

CHAPTER ELEVEN

The Walk-In Support System

Isis

December 11, 2002

When souls say they review their lives or discuss their lives with their teachers during the exit process, they do not actually have memory of their lives. When you get to the stage of life review, a settling takes place in which you sort of pause before you move on. The ability to access your life does not actually come from the soul that left but comes from teachers and, what I call, a membrane. If you were to look at it, it would be like a flow.

There is not a direct connection anymore to the soul because the soul, at that point, due to its vulnerability, can only take in so much. It cannot function as an Earth person to remember discomforting things that happened because, and you can identify with this, by that time, the soul has come to the point that it is of the same energy that, say, ETs are. They cannot handle the discomfort level you have on Earth; therefore they cannot have, what you would call, recollections.

The exiting souls do not have any linear memory function at all. So the only way they can go through a review and understand things when they review some parts of their Earth lives (which is only an "if," not everyone does) is either from a teacher or from this flow. It's hard to describe it, but it's there. It would be as if you were to stick a finger in, and only that which is compatible with you in that moment would be available to you. So the linear functions of memory of the exiting soul are left to the walk-in souls to resolve or discard according to their personalities.

That is why certain memories are prominent. They are not prominent on the basis of their importance to the previous life. They are prominent only on the basis of compatibility with the walk-in souls. It is no different. Imagine the souls who leave can only sample, let's say, certain energies of the entity that they are compatible with. So the souls who walk into the body, while they can have the full range of recollection of memory, will only taste (if we can use a word describing another body function, but taste doesn't come into it, you understand; that's an analogy) certain memories, and those memories will linger. Therefore, the ones that linger are not necessarily the ones that were important to previous souls.

There are several reasons for this. One, the new soul coming in has slightly different personality characteristics because at the point of coming in, the soul has to be very much in tune with the soul going out. But as time goes on, that soul who has come in can express more and more of itself as it lets go of the memory motivation; memories motivate a person or sometimes cause someone to withdraw. In short, the soul has an effect on your personality.

As the incoming soul begins to exercise its own personal motivations as any soul does, it will have less access to the memories of the previous soul. The other possibility is that the soul will pull certain memories up and make them more prominent based on personal motivations. In short, the new soul will use certain memories to support — by that point, within the way its mind is functioning in this world, to justify or motivate — its actions based on personal expression of its personality. So it is like a selective recollection.

Of things that could aid the person, right?

Yes.

The Flow of Memories

The soul that exited touched into this flow in the life review. Was that flow pertinent to it or the history of the galaxy or the universe or what?

It is not associated with such things because it's not associated with the physical world. Remember, the soul that leaves is no longer a part of the physical world that you know. The thought that you have right now of the galaxy, the orb, whatever, all this has to do with the physical world. There is no connection to anything associated with the physical world. The best way to describe it is otherworldly. It has no context in descriptive terminology associated with your world at all. It is strictly (how can I put it?) a spiritual function. It is hard to describe. It is other than what you say.

Yeah, but I'm just having a really powerful, some sort of energy flush here. So everything we've talked about in all these books, no matter what dimension, is part of what you call the physical world? Where there are worlds and galaxies ... ?

Everything we've talked about is described in terms that can be understood in your physical world. That's why from time to time the beings say, "This doesn't relate directly to your physical world" or "I'll explain it in terms that you can understand." In short, it is as if you were talking to someone who had a framework of understanding. In order to communicate the best possible flavor again (we'll use that term) of the worlds you are describing, you have to frame it in terms that he or she could make sense of, in your case, and also pass on your interests to others who are interested in a similar fashion. You understand?

You are asking us to put things into terms that involve feelings. How difficult is it to put feelings into words that involve something that is similar to visuals but without sight and has the impact of visuals but has other senses that simply are not experienced on Earth? In short, we can only give you (how can we say?) a flavor of those other things. So everything that has been described is true within the context of the terminology that you can use on your planet as it is now, as you are now. I might add that anything that any spirit describes or any inspiration you get will come in those terms out of necessity, because what good does it do you to get a description ...

Of something you can't fathom.

... of something that you cannot fathom at all, as you say? It would only cause confusion and possible serious consequences, meaning how could it possibly help your mind to begin thinking in terms that are not compatible with your world?

They are not compatible with thinking at all, right?

They are not compatible with thinking as you know it. In short, it could have a serious impact, as Zoosh once described, I believe — a person going to another dimension and staying there and coming back afraid. You could come back the wrong way. It's a similar situation. We want to help you understand the answers to the questions in which you are interested. We don't want to damage you in the process.

No, I understand.

From Autopilot to Pilot

The soul is this gentle, vulnerable thing that can't take the toxicity of negativity, but at what point does it merge into the immortal personality, which is much stronger?

Well, let's take it the other way first. At what point is this gentle being able to come into the body? At what point is it able? Why isn't the soul crushed when it comes into the body as a walk-in?

Oh, why? Good question.

It isn't crushed because it uses the previous personality sheathed within the body. The body forms up around the personality. So the walk-in soul uses the previous personality as a suit of armor until it can adapt. That's why there's almost no recognition for many walk-ins at first because it is using — the soul is using — the personality as a suit of armor so that it can gradually adapt. What's on the inside, so to speak, is that area where the two souls are exactly alike. There are traits that are identical, which allow the exchange to take place. That's what's on the inside, and that's what contacts the soul that comes in.

What's on the outside of the so-called sheath are all the traits, all the mechanisms, and all the adaptations that have occurred within that physical body, allowing it to adapt to the previous personality and also allowing it to function in the world in which you live. That is why over time, as the walk-in soul is learning to adapt, there is a gradual alteration in personality. The new soul's personality emerges over time. In some cases, it might be over a few days. In other cases, it takes longer. In some rare cases, it is almost instantaneous, but that is practically unheard of. So it happens when you come in, and I think it's more important to know that because it has to do with the walk-in's practical day-to-day living.

Does this sheath gradually fall away?

Not unless you are ready to have it fall away. The only way you as the new soul are ready to have it fall away is that you become accustomed to the world you find yourself in at a higher rate of speed, because the person's body is an adult, and there is experience already built up. There is the experience built up of having been a baby and gradually becoming accustomed to the time it takes the baby to evolve into the child and then to the young adult and so on.

Having that available, you as the soul who comes in can adapt more quickly, but it still takes a while for you to adapt to the world using the experience in the physical body associated with the previous personality. Then your soul, in that sense, gets accustomed, adapted, and attuned to functioning in this world, and as that happens, you take over functions that would have been running, as it would feel, on automatic. And the automatic has to do with all the previous experience that happened before you got there. When you feel more in tune with the world in which you are functioning, you take over those functions, and those automatic functions are submerged. They don't actually drop away. I'll tell you why.

They don't drop away for quite awhile if at all. That's the reason there are times when you are very tired, physically tired, or there are times when you are distracted, meaning there are many things going on at once. Or if the distraction level is so great that it is more than you as the new soul can handle — or other possibilities, things that are overwhelming for one reason or another to that new soul — then what happens is that you go back on automatic, and the previous soul's pattern identified and stored in the body, stored literally at the atomic level in the body or the particle level, emerges to act almost as a soldier to say, "I'll be your personality for a while. You can be quiet and retreat for a time." There isn't that communication, but it is like that, all right? And the new soul is quiet. It retreats and tries to adapt or apply itself to its overwhelming situation at that moment, going through one thing after another until it sorts it out while the previous traits — not all the traits, but many of the previous traits of the previous personality — are observable if, of course, the person is awake.

There's even a subtler thing. Suppose this happens during a time when the person is asleep. Then what happens is that you might actually experience similar dreams that you remember — you understand, not the deep ones, but the ones that you'll remember after waking — that the previous personality might have had because that's how that personality relates to its almost conscious self. Those are the dreams that you remember, the ones in which you are almost conscious and not quite awake yet.

The reason I bring all of that up is that there will be times when the walk-ins feel confused. That means that they will not be sure even after they have come in and are well settled in the body. There will be moments when the previous personality's traits will emerge suddenly. This doesn't mean you are having a conflict within your body or there is a war to dominate the expressed personality, none of that. It means, rather, there is something going on with your personality, your soul, that you are struggling with or in conflict with, and it's too much because your soul does not yet have the capacity to deal with internal conflict, all right? Therefore, you will not shut down, but you will retreat a bit, and the warrior aspects of the previous personality will emerge.

I use the term "warrior" advisedly because very often what lasts from the previous personality will be the survivor techniques, the survivability. So these are all grouped under warrior, whether it is "warrior" who goes to war (meaning the fight to survive) or "warrior" who prevents war (meaning techniques for getting along and solving problems before it goes to war). You understand, these are what I call basic material mastery functions that come under the heading of survival, and in that, I classify them as the warrior.

Well, that's wonderful. I mean the whole situation is set up so that this innocent soul coming in, even though it has to take on its responsibilities right away and live a life that it doesn't understand, it has that whole support system of what was there before then.

Yes. You have to understand that in a normal birth the soul comes in and is protected by the adults. The soul is a baby and appears as a baby to be absolutely dependent, and it is. Therefore adults around that soul in the form of the baby protect you and take care of you. But when you come in as a walk-in, most people have no idea that there is a new, vulnerable soul there. You do not look like a baby, and no one rushes up to cradle you and nurse you and take care of you, so something has to.

Yet you are, in a way, as vulnerable as that baby.

That's right. You are that for some time. Therefore, there needs to be something that can protect you and take care of you, and that is the sheath of your former personality.

It's fascinating how it works.

Earth Mastery

In your interest in the practical, you might not want to answer this next question, and if you don't, that's okay. I think it was the Mother of All Beings who said, "I guarantee that there will be a place for any soul who doesn't finish its training on Earth to complete its clearing or learning or training or whatever." Where are the souls who are leaving Earth going?

They will essentially choose, and it can't be some vague choice; it's like a between-life choice. You choose to be incarnated or, as you might say, reincarnated. It would have to be a choice, all right? If it's at the level of a conscious choice, "Okay, I've decided," like that, then what will happen more likely than not is the soul will be incarnated again in a past time on Earth. Just go into the past.

You go into Earth's past, during the human time here, which will not be erased; it will simply be available to those who need it. It will not be largely populated, meaning that it will be at a time when the population of Earth will be, you know, perhaps a few million.

It might also be an alternate version of Earth, if you need Earth, all right? The only way you will need Earth — it doesn't mean that you've been bad, [chuckles]. Let's get over that. It means that the functionality of Earth at all the levels of mastery available — the complexity of Earth, the schooling capacities of Earth. This is what you want. It might be interesting for you to understand this because it is going to put things in an entirely new light for you. Those who need Earth and want to go on will receive advanced creator training. That's who will want to stay on Earth, not beings who have been "bad," but beings who want or, because of what they will be doing in other lives, *need* advanced creator training beyond that of the civilization or culture in which they were living on Earth and beyond what they had the opportunity to experience.

When they are in a version of Earth in the past and there's, say, just a few million people on Earth, it will not be a version that is about struggle and all of this business. It will be a version in which advanced creator applications can take place. You know all the levels of mastery that Earth has have been discussed before, but this book stands on its own. So I reiterate that Earth herself is a spiritual master, a material master, a teaching master, a dimensional master, and a quantum master, which is the master of consequences. Therefore the souls who stay on will not function much at the level of spiritual mastery and material mastery. They will, rather, function primarily at the levels of teaching mastery, dimensional mastery, and quantum mastery. Those levels, while available to you now to learn various lessons on Earth, are not the areas that most people or souls function in, somewhat but not that much. The ones who stay on will function more in those areas because of what they will or might do in lives to come. Those are the beings who will stay on because they are not done here.

Can you give me an example of a time or a place or a situation in which they might go?

Instead of joining the Explorer Race and becoming a creator, they might go directly from that advanced training to another planet, where they would need to be advisors and have abilities that are, to the population, sometimes considered the sort of things that creators can do. They might have the capacity to influence the natural world in some way, or they might have the capacity to interact with beings on a daily basis who influence the natural world to the benefit of the population.

They might be able to make connections to the population in such a way as to teach them how to do these things. In short, they would have advanced skills and abilities available to them that the population where they are going would need to learn. Their personal magnetism or their personalities or their appearances or something about them, that quintessential something when you meet someone that is so special, is not always special to everyone. It's special to people in a certain capacity — not necessarily leadership, but perhaps as a beloved teacher or a special friend who would be able to pass on these abilities to others. That's an example.

Another possibility, since you are interested in more difficult or challenging worlds, is that they might go to a world and appear to be as a visitation of someone in recent times on your world. For example, you are experiencing on your world visitations by various beings from creator levels who represent themselves — its not a lie; they're using that energy and it is provided by Creator — as various beloved beings who are remembered, at least in your beloved stories, for example, as Mother Mary or Mary of the Magdalene or others from Christian or other religious influences. They are being seen in one form or another and sometimes leave patterns in physical objects that last for a while.

These things are done to remind people that the spiritual world is real even though you do not always have reminders of it in your day-to-day world from other human beings you recognize as reminders. So sometimes you need reminders of the world that you have been conditioned to believe is the spiritual world, which almost always has to do with the cultural conditioning in your world now with your religion, even if you're not practicing your religion anymore, or a religion. It might not even be a religion, but it might be the popular religion or the authoritative religion or the national religion. You could see someone that is a figure from that even if you're not that religion.

In short, the cultural conditioning is important because what we were talking about before is a factor of life here. The language that you speak must be understood by those who are being spoken to. Sometimes the language is of words. Sometimes it is of sight. Sometimes it is a feeling or a combination thereof. Those are examples, not exclusively the only applications.

Okay, so a lot of the reported instances of people seeing angels or Mother Mary or spirits or healing energies or whatever, these are individual beings who are doing this?

No. Some of it is. The majority of it is exactly what they're seeing. But some of it, for some people or some groups are these types of beings. That is a good thing because these types of beings usually, as a result of the Earth experience (Earth-like living experience), are able to know exactly what will uplift and inspire Earth people as a result of having been one. Therefore, when given, or let's say granted, the availability of Creator's love and energy or the love and energy from these other beings and so on are able to portray it as an artist might, in a way that most lovingly inspires and communicates to Earth people on the basis of their awareness of what works.

Sometimes, you understand the spirits of angels and so on are not always the most practical in their application. Here's an example. Let's use angels. (This happens a lot.) The angels allow themselves to be seen by those who happen to look up. They see angel forms in the clouds. Many spirits are seen in the clouds for various reasons. Sometimes they are influencing or contacting various beings on Earth. Sometimes it might be the animals, the fishes, and so on. But sometimes they are angels that have come to be seen by human beings. And while it is very nice to be seen in the clouds, very few people will actually look up at the clouds at that time. So it might not be the most practical way for an uplifting mass sighting.

Those who come who have had the Earth experience might instead create something that is actually seen by people and might leave a mark on something physical. I believe there was something awhile back in which a mark was left on a water tower, that kind of thing. Because people recognize that inspiration has to be (people who have lived on Earth and are using these energies) blessed by the Creator to use them, you understand, they recognize that inspiration has to be more than fleeting. What appears in a cloud — as the cloud is like paint in that it moves; it allows itself to be moved to take up the form fleetingly — is just as relevant, just as valuable, but it is not lasting.

Whereas a mark that is observable even in an evolving pattern on an old metal object will last for a while, people can look at it and say, "That really looks like so-and-so," and the feeling associated with that. See, that's it. It's not just that it looks like, "Oh isn't that interesting. It looks like _____." It's not a mental experience when they look at it. It's that when they look at it, they get this tremendous feeling, and they identify it as the shape or form. The feeling comes first because it's real, because it's the purpose of that object in that moment, to impart the feeling, and it's lasting. Then someone might describe to you, "Well, see, there's 'this' shape and 'that' shape," but you get the feeling first. Most people get it; some people get it after.

Can you give me an example of times and places on Earth where exiting souls who want extended creator training to do some of the things you just discussed would go? When and where would they go?

They would go to the times that have existed in the past that interacted with other times on Earth. There are, in the distant past on Earth, civilizations that could interact with other times, meaning they had windows or doors available to them.

The civilizations were advanced-benign. When the civilizations were advanced-benign, they could have windows available to them. They would not necessarily want them, but they could have them, or some segments of society might. Those windows would be available to access other times on Earth, usually, rather than other places, other planets, because you are on Earth, so there's a reason you access other times on Earth. That's the kind of civilization.

You wouldn't necessarily know anything about those civilizations because if you were to see them now, they would appear to be that which is almost extraterrestrial. There would be aspects of the civilization that would remind you of contemporary styles of appearance, not necessarily what the citizens in your culture might wear, so to speak, but what citizens in other cultures wear or how they might behave.

CHAPTER TWELVE

Mother Earth Welcomes Every Soul

Isis with Reveals the Mysteries and Speaks of Many Truths

May 14, 2003

Isis. Now, I'm here and there's also, to my left, Reveals the Mysteries and, to my right, Speaks of Many Truths. So in the future, you will notice, as you occasionally have in the past, a sense of melded personality. Let's go ahead. What would you like to talk about?

Thank you for telling me who is here. Robert faxed me a short piece you gave him that said a walk-in's physical body's astrological attunement will always be to the time, place, and date of birth of the original soul, and he said I should use it to ask for additional information.

Yes, the reason we do not elaborate too extensively to Robby is that we are counting on your ability to focus questions that would extract not only information of value but also help to make the information practical, as you are (how can I say?) touring in a physical body on Earth yourself. Therefore, your questions often support the practical reader, so take a moment to see what you can come up with to focus the tide of information available.

So the soul chooses a time of birth to set up certain, you're calling them, life-trend tendency patterns. Basically, this is saying that the walk-in in the physical body is still attuned to the original birth date of the original soul, not to the date the walk-in entered.

Not to the original soul but to the original date of birth of the physical self on its own. Granted, the original soul would be in agreement, and that's the key to understanding this. The original soul is in agreement to what is offered in the way of the physical vehicle on Earth. It is not that the soul directs the body.

One must remember that the body, after all, is representative of Mother Earth, who is much wiser and more experienced than the soul, regardless of where the soul has been and what it has done. We know the soul has not been a creator nor has the soul fostered, nurtured, or even supported life to the extent that a planet can do, to say nothing of what Mother Earth can do, as she has shown.

Therefore it is like an offering, you understand, that Mother Earth makes, and the soul acquiesces and says, "This will do quite nicely, thank you very much." Given this offering, the original soul comes into the body and, you might say, enjoys the ride to the best of his or her ability for as long as the Earth body is available.

In the walk-in situation, when the walk-in takes place and of course the original soul departs nonviolently, then (in most cases) what you have is that the same vehicle in its touring capacity — loaned physically from Mother Earth and supported throughout its physical journey by Mother Earth and Creator, of course, and others — remains attuned to the original soul though that soul has departed. The new soul that steps in, or the walk-in soul as we're calling it, is able to readily adapt to the condition the body is in and the life of that body due to the similarities between personality constructs, meaning the basic personality of each soul has sufficient similarity so that they can adapt to each other's creations.

That walk-in soul is able to anchor in the physical body during the duration of its engagement with that physical body. Now, by "anchor," I do not mean that it readily adapts, as you know very well. But it will have enough of an anchor so that regardless of how bumpy the road gets, it is not going to fall out, even though it might be baffled, or confused, for a time. That is ultimately the reason for this book: to support those walk-ins and, for that matter, those people who live with them or know them so that the best means can be found to get along in life regardless of which turn life takes you on or which turn your body reacts to in the way your body has been conditioned.

One must understand not only the conditioning that the body has experienced in the life with the original soul but also Mother Earth's part in all of this. Granted, she offers her being to make up the physical matter of the body, and she does so freely without attachment or desire for personal gain because it is not in her nature to live life as a human being. For her, it is also like a voyage of exploration.

Mother Earth and the souls of any planet that are creative ... oh, you have sent some of your space probes to test planets that are in a dormant stage — not particularly creative maintenance, you might say. Such a personality, a soul of a planet, has many capabilities and possibilities.

Mother Earth, however, is freely expressing a great many of them, much of which has been discussed in other books. But the important thing to understand is that Mother Earth herself is experiencing something entirely new — which is to create in her own way, working with Creator and other beings of course, to offer her body, the bits of her body, to make up the Earth's physical human body.

You Are of Earth

Now, I'm going to give you, especially because of the phrasing of your question, some of the mechanics of that. Beginning, of course (as scientists have understood well), with the birthing process. But let's talk about the spirit, the heart, and the soul of it. The baby's body begins to form in the mother, and in the beginning, it is (for the most part) very quiet. It doesn't move around too much. Then eventually the mother begins to feel something moving inside her, quite a magical feeling many times. At this time, the soul is not really in residence. We're talking about the first three months. It is possible that the soul might stop by to get some acquaintanceship with the physical body and mother as well, but it would be a brief visit.

For the most part, what is occurring is that Mother Earth literally loans some of her own soul to that baby, and the baby is naturally part of Creator, yes. But Mother Earth's soul or her personality is in that baby's body literally up to the time of physical birth, in greater or lesser quantities, because by the time of physical birth, the soul is in and out rapidly, almost like an alternating current.

In that first three months, the mechanism of discovery, options for each and every baby, Mother Earth literally feels and experiences the human representation of her own personality, needless to say a small facet of it, so that there is not an overwhelming feeling from the mother, the physical mother. Yet what you find is that Mother Earth literally feels life from that individual state of being.

Understand a key concept here: Planets and souls that ensoul planets most of the time (with only one exception that I'm aware of) have not known and will never know what it is like to be an individual because their component personality and soul makeup is entirely unified not only with Creator and all the beings who support Creator but also with all planets everywhere. This is how planets know, as the soul, the basic creation process, to keep itself together and to function according to its own needs as a planet, as opposed to functioning and adapting to the needs of those who might visit your person and take up residence, as in various populations and so on.

This all comes about through a mutual sharing not unlike instinct, as you understand it, in animals and also in human beings but much broader, deeper, and more varied than that. So it is instant wisdom — vertical wisdom as Zoosh calls it — on a timeless level, and it is a unified experience. I'll talk more about that at some point, but I want to give you that much so that you can understand the similarities and contrasts with Mother Earth's soul and your own.

Here we find Mother Earth literally having an experience for the moments that she is paying attention to each individual baby whose soul must be present. Do you understand what I mean by that? That for the baby to be inside Mother Earth, to feel safe even at that, as science might call it, chemical stage (the cells, and so on, dividing). Even so, for that to take place, there need to be feelings of welcome, love, safety, and nurturing, and to be able to assimilate those feelings, there needs to be a personality present to welcome these feelings in the baby.

That personality, that welcoming personality, is a portion of Mother Earth. You can see how all of this is very loving and sacred and spiritual and important, I feel, for you all to understand at this time. So for the first three months, then, as primarily those feelings are going on, there is the welcoming and nurturing of the baby, and perhaps in some cases a little stirring that the physical mother might feel from time to time. Sometimes she's not sure, but I can assure you there is some stirring going on.

Now, as time goes on and baby begins to develop from about three months to six months, it is not at all unusual to find the birth soul beginning to move in and out of the baby's body to experience some sense of what physical life is like. This is especially important for souls who have not lived in the dimensionality, as you refer to your place of being, and also critically important for souls who have not experienced a human body before. So it is a time of familiarity and, to a degree, orientation.

Yet that soul is in and out a lot, talking to teachers and other beings who advise the soul, and every moment the soul exits, Mother Earth's soul presence is loaned to welcome the tissue growth, welcome the structural changes, and just imbue the physical body with the joy and expectation that it requires in order to want to live on its own as an individual (as you experience individuality). Otherwise, baby would never want to leave mother, and every doctor (and some mothers) have stories about the babies who seem to be reluctant to leave. So what you have here, then, is a welcoming and orientation all the while with Mother Earth experiencing these moments of individuality, something unique in her perspective. I mention these things to give you a sense of how unusual this is.

The Status of Mother Earth

Now I will speak about an aside here before I move on to the next trimester, so to speak. For the planets to function and welcome various populations — plant, animal, human, and so on — is not a typical process. Remember, it is unusual, to say the least, for planets to experience individuality. They must have a great degree of homogeneous wisdom to call on. Therefore, this experience of Mother Earth is not only providing her with the unique opportunity to experience individuality, but (because of her connection with all other planets everywhere) through her, other planets (according to their desire to participate) can also experience this.

You have heard from various ETs over the years that Earth has been a magnet to various ET civilizations, meaning they come and observe and so on, to see how life is on Earth and observe it from a distance, for the most part. I can assure you that this is but a small portion of the magnetic attraction when compared to the observation going on by the other planets. They are fascinated, and they are interested. None of you has begun to do this, however, because you have to understand that you need the status of Mother Earth to do this.

Zoosh and others have explained how many levels of mastery of Mother Earth have been attained in order to be as flexible and available to the Explorer Race for all that you are attempting to be and to become. All of these things she must be — many levels of mastery, so to speak, on the spiritual and material level and other levels — in order to accommodate herself to your needs, and as I'm explaining now, to accommodate you to her personality.

The Transfer from One Soul to the Other

Now we move on to the last trimester, so to speak, the six-month to nine-month period in motherhood. Now we find the soul, birth soul, much more in the body. It is in and out quite a bit, that experience of, say, four or five minutes at a time. One might find that "in and out of the body" very much the case. There will also be times when the soul will be in the body completely, meaning there is full engagement of the soul that will be in the body at birth. During these times, one often finds that the physical body of the baby is entirely inactive. Of course the physical functions, the blood circulation and tissue evolution and all of this, are going on.

When the soul — remember how sensitive souls are; tremendously sensitive — comes into the physical body of the baby, there is a tremendous awareness of all that is happening inside the physical body of baby and to a lesser degree what is happening within the physical body of mother herself. To experience the maximum amount of awareness, the baby's body becomes as still as possible. In these moments, mother will not feel much motion from baby.

This tells you something important. When baby is kicking and moving around and flexing its muscles and so on, this is also something that Mother Earth is doing, largely in her personality in the physical body, in her personality to imbue the physical body of the baby with a joy for living and a joy for being physical, so that when the physical body of the baby emerges from the mother, there is already a desire to be as physical as possible. There is the desire to move, to flex, and to experience from the inside out the joy of physical expression, something that is entirely new for some souls. It is like no other experience that can be imagined.

However, as an adult (and for those of you who can remember childhood), if you can remember moments of exaltation when you just wanted to jump up and down, and when you did jump up and down or waved your arms about in happiness, it is this exaltation you feel that relates directly back to the way Mother Earth prepares your body so that you can experience the joy of physical life. Of course there is much more, but I mention this so that you have some marker or landmark, so to speak, to realize why one sees this. It is typical to see this in a baby and in small children and how they attempt [to express that joy].

Now, what parents have not seen, when they've held their babies hands, how their children want to jump up and down even though their bodies are not fully capable or fully aware of their capacities? What parents have not enjoyed seeing their children lying on their backs and kicking their legs and looking absolutely joyful about it? Simple pleasures of youth, you know. So all of these preparations are lovingly provided by Mother Earth. Yet for herself, she enjoys the experience, albeit temporary, for each baby, the experience of being an individual.

The reason I bring up this elaborate description is not only as a gift so that people can enjoy it but also to explain the mechanism. One might ask, "What about the mechanism of transferring one soul to the other during the walk-in?" What occurs is that there is a moment, you understand, when the body does not experience the birth soul within it and the new soul has not arrived or has not engaged yet. Sometimes souls will move toward the physical body and pause for a moment, perhaps receiving last instructions from their guides or teachers, but more often it is a case of being shy to enter. This is what is experienced whether the person is asleep or awake. At that time, there is a momentary feeling, a physical feeling — not of dizziness, but an actual physical feeling — of what I call spirit. It's a gentle feeling, almost like a touch but not quite.

For some people, this will cause them to relax completely and perhaps even go to sleep; that's not uncommon. Others — who are perhaps spiritually aware, who are involved in various spiritual practices or shamanic practices (which require a great deal of physical awareness) — might notice a tingling or a sense of experience similar to what they have been training to do or even what they have been doing. They might say, "Well how is this possible if the soul exits?"

It is possible to observe it before the soul exits because there's an overlap in time. Picture, as a drawing, a point, yes, the point representing the physical body, or if you like for the artist to draw the physical body in repose. There is the birth soul preparing to exit and the walk-in soul preparing to enter, but neither has actually taken place. There is an overlap. One might draw an arc, for instance, over the physical body in repose in that way.

During this time, Mother Earth again allows her personality to enter the physical body of the physical being. Her personal being and the soul that is exiting, the birth soul in this example, that's what it feels. It feels the tingling. As the walk-in soul is coming in, it will also feel that tingling. You understand each has personality similarities and compatibilities. Effectively, the walk-in soul is conjoined briefly with the soul that is exiting. That's why there would be a memory, you see. You could draw a dotted line between the two souls, one that is exiting and one that is entering. Also a dotted line from the passage, one might say, of the walk-in soul into the physical body and of course a dotted line from the physical body to the soul that is leaving to embark on its journey.

Then there is a moment of encapsulation provided by Mother Earth. The physical body will of course completely be comfortable with this personality of Mother Earth, whom the body remembers and feels at all times, really as a foundation, regardless of what soul is in the physical body itself. This foundation is what supports life for the personal soul in the physical body at any time. It is also ultimately what will create the longing for the physical body to return to Mother Earth and to be a portion of that being, exclusively. When that longing becomes strong enough, death occurs (as you understand it) in the physical, though all souls are immortal in their essential personality, and the souls go on. Be reassured of that.

The Preparation of the Physical Body

The bridge personality, you might say, is Mother Earth's personality at the moment of the walk-in when the soul that is in presence, the birth soul, exits. There is often a moment of acknowledgment. The exiting soul is joyful to be going on with its personal life, to be shedding some of the difficulties of Earth life and supporting the soul's growth so that it can adapt and offer more in future incarnations. There is a sense of joy there, yes. There is also a sense of joy of experiencing this moment for the walk-in soul, this highly spiritually charged moment of joy that is not a birth but rather that moment of exaltation I referred to before that you have all experienced.

I think most of you can remember a moment of being joyfully happy. The walk-in soul that is coming in experiences the exaltation, the joy of coming into this physical body, which is already prepared for it and is able to provide the experience of Earth human individual personality that a walk-in soul is enthusiastic about participating with. So there is that moment.

Some souls, and I mention this to you on purpose as the participant, will take longer to adapt to the physical bodies they enter, perhaps because the body wasn't prepared in the best possible way for them to come in. A personal note here: Your body, Melody, could not be prepared in the best possible way simply because of the three-souled combination. It was not possible for those souls to prepare your physical body for a one souled experience. They did the best they could. That's all they could do. This is why in your case such a long duration of adaptation was necessary.

During the times when it was difficult to feel who and what you were in that body, the physical body was flooded with Mother Earth personality. This was done (1) to support and nurture the physical body during this exceptionally long engagement transition and (2) because the physical body had been adapted to having more than one soul within it. Mother Earth's soul and your soul allowed the body to feel the combination of souls present that would make the physical body feel at ease so that the single-souled experience would not be foreign to that tri-souled physical body as it had been conditioned. So naturally this took longer.

I will say to the reader that it is not completely unknown for people on Earth to have more than one soul occupying a physical body at one time, especially in the past thirty or forty years when there has been some desire by souls to experience greater and greater quantities and capacities of life forms. But while one might experience one soul in the physical body and at other times two souls (not for you, Melody, but for the reader here) in the physical body, it is highly unusual to experience three souls at once. So this, for you, Melody, has been a challenge.

During this time of adaptation up to the point of your being informed that you were a walk-in, because it was at that moment that you were prepared (having tried everything else) to do whatever it took to be able to engage with physical life or say, "That's enough." It was necessary because your mind in the previous soul, which was (for the most part) fully enthusiastic about the mental process on Earth, was less enthusiastic about the physical process. Your soul coming in, Melody, is just the opposite. It's more enthusiastic about the physical process, the feeling process, and less enthusiastic about the mental process. You can see right there the challenge and contradictions. So what occurred for you, then, was a great deal of difficulty in adapting.

During that time of adaptation when you felt as if you were overwhelmed in your singular soul, you would go dormant at times. What you did was very much what a baby's soul experiences when that soul comes in during the final trimester, the six- to nine-month trimester. Your soul became very quiet in your physical body and simply became heightened in sensitivity, feeling everything that you could feel, including the blood coursing in your veins and the synaptic pulses in your brain, to try to understand the nature of physical life because of the inability (literal inability, ability up to a point, but inability) of your tri-soul to prepare your physical body for one soul.

The challenge was that your soul had to go deep within your physical body and observe your physical body's autonomic functioning to reacquaint itself — you, Melody, and your physical body — with the times in the past when your physical body had only one soul. That engagement allowed you to find a way in which you could become, as they say, grounded or connected to your physical body. This took time, and during that time, your physical body was flooded with the personality that it knew and loved and cherished, Mother Earth's personality.

Those who were around you during this time literally did not know who you were or what you were about. It was as if they were talking to a complete stranger — not an incapable person, but someone they did not recognize in your personality. Those of course were the times they were interacting literally with the personality of Mother Earth expressed through your physical body in the way she felt would be best. It had to be best for you first, Melody, meaning it had to be benign, acceptable, not entirely unlike the personality that people would know you as yet sufficiently receptive so that you could feel, see, observe — in short, experience through your senses — life and good things about life.

During this time, you were primarily observant of life and not capable of being observant about the daily details of business, finance, and other things around you because you were attempting to engage not only with physical life but also your own physical body. This engagement with your physical body took time. About the time you were at your wits' end (which is an appropriate statement because you were prepared to do whatever it took, even if it was beyond the mental), you were ready to engage not only in new spiritual practices but also new physical practices to become Melody in your physical body.

I have included this elaborate personal explanation here so that the reader can appreciate the difficulty and challenge of the walk-in experience. I might add for the walk-ins out there that your chances of experiencing such a difficult transition are highly unlikely. However, because there are some of you out there who will have the experience, at least for a time, of more than one soul's activity in your physical body, such confusion and difficulty and lengthy (not to the length of time that Melody experienced it, but several months) experience of soul transition and awareness in the physical body could take place.

I also say this to those who live with these people: If they experience an unusually bland personality opposed to something significant or expressive that was present before, they should not be alarmed. Certainly, they should not use this as an excuse to avoid any health matters that need to be attended to.

You Are Given the Gift of Ignorance

Be aware that because the walk-in phenomenon will continue in your future, it will allow many of you who've been struggling in your physical bodies to move on, for the most part, in completely peaceful and nonviolent ways. It will also allow these souls who will come into your bodies in benevolent ways to engage life in the most benevolent way for all beings on Earth as you transition not only through your Earth incorporation and economic world order process but also in preparation to experience the more spiritual awakening of all human beings on Earth. Those souls who choose to walk in will be more capable of doing that, and the souls who choose to exit will have the joy of transiting out of the physical body without pain, with ease.

Now, I do not expect you all to be comfortable with that, but I'm putting it to you in those terms so that you can adjust to it over time. There's no point in trying to fight it, for those of you who feel you want to. "I'm going to stay in my body no matter what." I can assure you, the soul's transfer from the body, as in the case of the natural death, is always a joyful experience, not just because in the case of a natural death there is discomfort present most of the time in the physical body, but also because of those who come to welcome you when you move on. It is exactly the same for a soul exiting the physical body in a walk-in experience as it is for a soul exiting the physical body in natural death. Granted, in the case of a natural death, there is greater time to experience the move out in, say, a gradual death in the way it usually occurs. I'm talking about a nonviolent experience or a sudden experience. There is time to move in and out when teachers and guides talk to you and so on. I'm talking about the actual transit from the soul, exiting from the physical body to move on with its life beyond that physical body. That process is exactly the same.

In the case of a sudden death as might occur to, say, a soldier or someone hit by a car, something like that, the process is also identical. The guide or, you might say, angel will come in a gold light (some of you might experience initially as a white light), welcoming and loving in an unconditional manner, and will prepare you to move through the veils and onward in your journey of soul discovery. This occurs for the soul that is exiting the body as well. I assure you it is welcome, it is a joyful experience.

The idea of Mother Earth, that part of her ensouls every baby, every infant, is so beautiful. How did that come about? Was it because the Explorer Race needed it? How did this start? Why did she do it?

Exactly as you surmised. For the Explorer Race, you find here a unique situation unlike on other planets. On other planets there is no strife, you understand. There is no struggle or discomfort to speak of, in most cases. Therefore, the soul did not feel the slightest resistance, the slightest reluctance, to being fully engaged in the process. Let's just say that the process would be the same on another planet. It's not usually the same, but let's just say that it is for the sake of comparison. The soul would be perfectly happy to be in the mother and in the forming baby body simply because there is no struggle, no discomfort whatsoever. There would be no need for a gradual conditioning process based on mother experiencing the slings and arrows of daily life.

Therefore, on Earth, because of the human experience of temporary ignorance (not remembering who you were, all that you are, and so on), you can experience discovery, or as Zoosh likes to say, "the gift of ignorance," the joy of discovery through your ignorance. This process must be gradual, must be gentle. Therefore Mother Earth, literally, can identify completely with the material matter of all your physical bodies — it being her material matter sparked by Creator. She would naturally extend or be a portion of that material matter at all times.

It is a gradual process that is required for the soul to adapt itself to what is an entirely unknown experience for the soul, meaning to ensoul a physical body when the physical body is experiencing not only a lack of awareness of who it has been, who it is, and so on, but also a soul experiencing a physical body on a place where there is discomfort on a moment-to-moment basis in a greater or lesser degree. This is why there is the gradual process of Earth.

It's not simply scientific fact that the human being requires nine months to experience the gestation and all of that. That is the scientific explanation of the fact, but it is not the reason why. The reason is that it takes the soul fully that long to adapt to the experiences of discomfort even insulated within the mother's body the way the soul is. That is why it is the way it is.

The Benevolent Sharing of Souls

The exciting thing that comes up for me is the bodies that we inhabit are infused with Mother Earth's Quantum Master energy. How do we build on and use that? What can we do with that?

You don't engage it. Remember, you would not expect a baby to produce such mastery as you might experience it in society. Rather, just be aware that it is present, and do not automatically assume that there are some things that are impossible for human beings to do. This does not mean that I recommend that you walk to the edge of the cliff, and say, "I can fly like a bird" and then jump off. You would definitely discover your similarity to a stone rather than a bird.

The law of gravity, yes.

Yes, however if you want to go on a hike and you are at the top of a hill, you can sit down and imagine yourself flying as a bird, and if a bird happens to fly by and you feel you want to, extend (not go out of your body but extend) from your body to the bird. If the bird is comfortable with your extension, it will allow you to come aboard, so to speak, and experience the motion of its wings. Even though you are in your own physical body sitting on the hill when the bird flies by — even though you are completely in your body (make sure you are not driving or doing anything like that but sitting down relaxing or standing and relaxing, if you like) — you might very well feel the bird's body as part of your own, perhaps even getting a glimpse of what it sees and experiencing it.

In the past, this has been something that has been a gradual training that mystical men and women and shamanic men and women have been trained to do for various reasons. Now even a person untrained in this can experience it in a benevolent way.

Just make sure there's a bird flying by because if the bird veers off when you expand or imagine yourself being in its body ... either way, extension is something that would require perhaps a little spiritual training. But you are quiet, you see, in those moments on your own in the physical body, relaxed without any demands on your physical body. You are heightened in your awareness of your own physical being, so your physical senses are heightened, and you look at the bird and you essentially extend. You stay in your body, but you extend your own heightened physical awareness to include the bird. So if the bird suddenly changes its path of flight and veers off one way or the other, immediately disengage with the bird. It is doing something else. The bird is not comfortable with your joining it at that moment. But if it continues on soaring past you or perhaps makes a gentle arc and flies around in your general area, regardless of what it is doing, then remain in that engagement.

Enjoy the experience, and then let it go. Return to your physical body, and simply say, "Good life" in the direction of the bird, thanking it for its participation while at the same time wishing it a good life and blessing it simply with that word. Say it with feeling. Don't just say it as if you were saying, "Chocolate with strawberries" or "paper." It is a salutation. It is a blessing. It is a greeting.

I say this to you not because I'm trying to convert you all to mystical men and women or shamanic men and women but rather because such experience allows the benevolent sharing of souls. In those moments, the bird also experiences your physical body as a unique understanding in that moment of human beings, who and what they are. It understands in that moment all the things that human beings (to the extent that it is safe for the personality of the bird) are really all about and why they are so complex and unpredictable. After that point, I can assure you, such a magical moment for you is equaled by the magical moment for the bird; it will pass the experience on to other birds, to its loved ones and to those with whom it communicates.

It is typical among birds, plants, animals, lions — everything — beetles, to behave in a general personality. They have unique personalities of course, but they also have their form of species personality. While you have this as an underlying experience (for human beings, as the Explorer Race), you are doing so much and expected to do so much while you have that ignorance of who and what you are that you do not fully engage in your species personality. Of course, having that ignorance, you cannot.

But the animals and plants, not being members of the Explorer Race and not having to forget who and what they are or what they've ever been throughout all times, do not have that experience. So the most difficult and challenging thing for the animals to understand about the human being is the unpredictability — the unpredictable nature of human beings.

Don't feel as if you're doing a disservice to the bird in that moment. Honor the bird if it suddenly darts off. Then you will know it is engaged in something else, and as much as it appreciates you, it is busy. So just wait. There will be another bird along before too long.

You Are Welcomed by Mother Earth

Is the body consulted as a member of the decision-making process in a walk-in situation? Is it asked whether it wants the new soul? Does it acquiesce or decline? Or is that not the way it works?

No, that is not really it. You have to understand that the personality of Mother Earth, as you can tell by the population of human beings on Earth, has already welcomed human beings as a population. So that is built in. When Mother Earth's personality floods into the body at any time or even simply because your physical bodies are made up of Mother Earth's body, that welcoming of the Earth human being (and any soul that might occupy that human being) has already been fully engaged down to the cellular and, for that matter, atomic levels.

So, no, the body is already in a welcoming state for any soul who comes in to be a soul in a human body, all right, only in the safest possible way. Don't worry about the spirits running into the human body or possession. None of that would ever happen due to the highly complex and protected nature of this process, very similar to the natural birth process. Then if this works out, the physical body is prepared to engage or to act as a vessel to carry the soul and to allow it to express life up to that point in time when the physical body desires to return to Earth. The physical body being, in that sense, entirely on loan as a human vessel. So let's say the welcoming mat is always out until that time of returning to Earth.

I might add as an aside that even though it is not a great affront to a personality, she would much prefer a simple sheet around her physical body, or if you want, a simple box without any great effort made to seal all the cracks and then a burial. But the old way of burial is best, meaning allowing the physical body to return to the earth and engaging in the earth without elaborate contraptions, if you don't mind, to slow the natural process of returning to the earth. That is up to you. Just come to that in your own time.

Right. This is off topic a little, but large animals who take a long time to gestate, they're coming to this place of negativity also, even though they're not in school. Is Mother Earth's soul also involved in welcoming the soul into an elephant or a dolphin or a horse or any animal?

Certainly. In the case of animal souls, most of them do not choose to come to Earth more than once during this time of the Explorer Race experience here simply because of the difficulty and discomforts involved, unless they are living in a highly isolated area away from all of the strife that takes place, perhaps sometimes in the sea or in the rain forest. Nowadays, human beings are pretty much everywhere, so they generally do not come for more than one incarnation on Earth. Of course, this time of gestation, regardless of how long it is, requires Mother Earth to be very welcoming. Their bodies are made up of Mother Earth too. And they are infused with a great deal of welcoming and support, and their souls enter gradually in a fashion similar to your souls simply because of dealing with the discomfort.

Of course, they are not engaged in the same way as your souls, meaning they do not arrive with ignorance. They are rather fully engaged in their own personalities — who they are, what they've always been. So they have a great deal of spiritual capacity to deal with the difficulties and the struggles and the challenges of discomforts of Earth, and they call on that freely. So the process with the soul's welcoming is easier in that sense because of the animal souls' or plant souls' remembering who and what they are and who and what they've been, having a full engagement with that during the birth process, which supports such challenges of Earth socialization.

She must be one incredible being. The humans come from everywhere, the plants and animals come from everywhere, and she gains a feeling of that experience from every one of them. She feels it. She gains the wisdom of it.

Like a mother who carries her baby, like an animal mother who carries the baby within herself, she feels the nurturing and the great love. Mother Earth feels this nurturing and great love for each and every soul who experiences life on Earth in a plant, a tree (even a portion of a tree, the leaf), a bear (or a portion of a bear, say a claw), or a human (or a portion of a human being, say, the heart). For each and every soul, there is that welcoming, mothering, nurturing, and support, saying literally, "Welcome to my life."

Yes, I understand for the first time why the term "Mother Earth" is used. It makes sense now.

Cycles of Life Experience

Let's take this line from the paper that Robert faxed of the preliminary material you gave him because it's fascinating. Here are the exact words, "The time of birth is intended to provide your physical body with the means to know how to focus a life-trend tendency pattern according to the attunement of personality expression." Now that's incredibly rich. How does that work?

Consider how Mother Earth engages in a cyclical experience that is in modern culture broken down into the simple expression of time. You know that Earth revolves on a general axis; thus, there is nighttime, there is daytime, and there are seasons. In short, cycles of experience are normal. This is built in to the physical human experience as well. There's childhood, and then you grow up. You're a little older, and you experience things differently throughout your life. In short, you are fully engaged in a cyclic experience throughout your entire physical experience of life on Earth, Mother Earth, in order to provide you all the uncountable millions and billions of individual personalities — not only human but of course animal.

Let's talk about the Explorer Race, about humans who have existed on Earth throughout existence as you know it, or at least the time of experience of the Explorer Race. Each and every one needs to have a unique personality of his or her own, even though you might reasonably say, "Well, people born in the summer have certain similar characteristics, and people born in the winter have certain similar characteristics. People born in the daytime have some characteristics that are similar. People born at nighttime have some characteristics that are similar." So people who are born during similar cycles, examples that I've just given, might have some characteristics in their personalities that are similar.

So what that describes, in the tapestry of words that were offered, is a sense of feeling of how rich and cultivated each unique personality must be. While the word "time" is used in that description (that is your modern cultural social expression), the actual derivative from that word, the actual precedent to that is cyclic. This is how Mother Earth engages your personality.

For the sake of being scientific, I will bow to scientists' needs for a moment. Figure simply on the basis of arcs of delineation or measurements in minutes — quantifiable portions of minutes, quantifiable portions of seconds, and so on — how each minute, second, and hour (accumulations beyond that and so on) is expressed through the motion of Mother Earth moving on her axis or rotation. Each moment of moving even in a portion of a second might be reasonably compared to showing a different side of her personality in that moment. So we will leave science there for a moment. I just wanted to acknowledge it simply for you to understand this without getting unnecessarily difficult.

If you consider all the beings that Mother Earth must support with the physical properties that make up your physical body and how each of those physical properties must welcome in its own way the unique soul as it would express its personality through that body, then Mother Earth will use every measurement of expression on a physical level to provide that personality. You might say she will also use her mass, meaning, oh, to make an equation of this, mass (M) times time (T) equals soul personality (SP): $MT = SP$. Not actually "equaling" soul personality but rather equaling the welcoming aspects of the physical body that allows soul personality to exist.

You have to consider each molecule, each atom, of Mother Earth's personality as she rotates, giving you not only your cyclic moment of engagement with the physical matter that makes up your body but also providing you with a portion of the structure of Mother Earth's body in that moment of cyclic passage that you literally are fed by. At all moments, your physical body is engaged in that cyclic presentation of Mother Earth's personality, whereby your physical body first came to being and, equally whereby, your physical body was first born.

You know there is a form of astrology that calculates your astrological emergence on the basis of your birthday, hour, and minute, if possible (as provided by physicians and nurses present), as well as goes back nine months and calculates your personality based on the astrologers best guess of your moment of conception.

I want to support that type of astrology to be done in the future. I feel it is of value. Granted, astrologers are working within their best guesses, but even general guesses, say, of five days "this way" or five days "that way" or ten days "this way" or ten days "that way" will give the ensouled person a great deal more information of their tendencies, their possibilities. For the individual who, regardless of what astrology (as is available for those of you who wish to go into the greater details of what is possible, and certainly astrologers do this) can offer them even in its greater detail, what has been the stone in the shoe (perhaps it's not appropriate to your times, since it's more to do with horses) or what has been, perhaps, the nail in the tire, that has been difficult for astrologers to explain is the apparent capricious actions that do not seem to relate to your sign whatsoever and what often causes people who do not believe in the value of astrology to deride its benefits.

That can mostly be explained and understood simply by making, for the astrologers, their best guesses in the conception moment and figuring the astrology based on that. That conception moment will give you some understanding of when that portion of Mother Earth's body engaged, meaning her mass, in that moment of cyclic experience that you call time with that moment of conception, to ultimately become what you know as yourselves. I want to support that form of astrology and those astrologers who care to do it, and I will make as much contribution toward that as they would care to ask about.

In terms of astrology, you see the difficulty there for when the walk-in soul comes in. It has some bearing on your astrological experience, but it will not have a physical bearing. It will, however, have a spiritual bearing, and spiritual astrology is possible, meaning that it will have a bearing on tendencies. It might influence physical motivations and so on. So in short, there is some reason to take note of it. But the challenge here is that most people will not even be aware the walk-in has taken place, so I don't want you to become overly concerned about noting the moment.

It's more important to pay attention to the full page rather than a single letter on the page, which is the foundation of understanding, appreciating, and working with the walk-in experience, whether it is you or someone you know and/or love. I'd rather you engage in that than attempt to become overly engaged (even as a professional astrologer) in the moment of a walk-in. That will be infinitely harder to calculate for most of you.

Some of you who are spiritually aware might have a feeling or might notice a change in your personality and so on. For those of you who have that or can even pinpoint a day when it took place, then do that, and at some point in time (wait a couple of years at least in order to be fully engaged in your new body), if you wish to give that date to an astrologer who is interested in such things or perhaps doing walk-in soul research, then by all means go ahead.

But I personally feel it is more important to pay attention to the Earth date and time and, to the best of your ability as an astrologer, the conception time. If you wish to triangulate, so to speak [chuckles], understand that the Earth date and time and the conception date and time are the most important to figure astrologically. The walk-in date and time is less important astrologically, but would come under the headings of what an astrologer might refer to as an influence.

Well, I think this is absolutely brilliant. How's Robert?

We can push on for a brief time.

The Walk-In Relates to the Body's Physical Memory

Okay. Do we have time to go into how the physical body actually has physical memories of feelings from the birth soul, which can then influence and create feelings in the body that could possibly confuse the walk-in soul?

You understand that this is what comes under the heading of what I call conditioning. The first soul, of course, has no feelings. Souls do not actually experience feelings in the way you understand feelings on Earth, meaning a feeling on Earth is something significant, something you notice, or something that is measurable or at least present. A soul's feelings are so subtle compared to that that even beyond here — beyond Earth, say for example — a soul would experience what you would now understand as a very subtle feeling. If you are in a quiet state, you will notice it. But generally speaking, most of you are not in that quiet state unless you are meditating or relaxing, perhaps just before sleep, perhaps just after waking up as long as no alarm clock is involved or any sudden waking method.

In a time of complete calm, you might notice the subtle feelings of the soul. But outside of the body, say, before here or when your soul continues on, subtle feeling is everything to the soul because there is no discomfort to deal with and there is no great complexity of life as takes place with the Explorer Race on Earth. Rather the soul's life is, by comparison, much simpler.

Granted, a soul might be able to experience arcs of experience from one planet to another, vast engagements with other life forms. But all of this takes place in a location, so to speak, or an experience of life, where there is no discomfort whatsoever. So the soul is wide open to the experience, and the slightest nuance is available to a soul. Therefore, you understand that the soul's natural way of being is to experience feeling on a subtle level. "Subtle," not meaning subtle for the soul when it is engaged in such experiences, but as you would feel the soul's feelings as the soul is in your physical body on Earth. You would have to be relaxed to experience that and be aware of the soul's feelings.

Now, other than that (I realize I'm taking your question by portion), the soul's feelings are not so much the case. Rather, what is occurring is that the soul, meaning the individual personality, reacts — yes, acts and reacts — with different things in life. Your body's being 100 percent receptive to your soul's personality with the underlying foundation and connection to Earth — all that she is, all that she knows, all that she experiences — happens in two ways. One occurs at the moment of birth and the other at the moment of conception, so that's the foundation.

Your body is essentially affected by the impact of your soul or your personality's action and reaction to various events based on who and what you are in your soul personality as expressed through the Explorer Race form of being, meaning not remembering where you are and so on. Your body becomes conditioned to your personality's actions and reactions to various events around it.

Now your question was, "What about when the walk-in experience takes place, and that soul exits the body? How does the walk-in soul deal with that physical conditioning in your body that the physical body will relate to cyclical experiences, also known as experiences in time that have caused the body to feel (physically) in certain ways?" The body, in that sense, reaches back and identifies certain experiences happening at certain cycles. Or to be social about this (to honor your terms), the body will reach back and explain, so to speak (not mentally but demonstrably) in a moment of instantaneous memory recollection — meaning the body is always aware about everything that has happened at any time, but the body is gentle with the walk-in soul and demonstrates a feeling — it will pop up an example or two of how that feeling came about in the past.

Even though there might be 100 reasons why the body has become conditioned that way, the body will pop up an example or two, and the walk-in soul then identifies why it's experiencing a certain feeling based on one or two incidents that the physical body gives as a memory. The physical body does not want to overwhelm you with 100 or so or maybe 200 or 300 experiences that caused it to be conditioned that way. It is gentle in that sense with you, being made up of Mother Earth, who has that capacity and that quality. Your question is, "How do you as the walk-in soul deal with that?" It is your job as the walk-in soul to begin to condition your physical body according to your temperament when you come in.

That's another reason for this book — so that you can be informed that it is your job to condition your physical body. If you feel an uncomfortable feeling, let's say for the sake of the example, you feel something come up where you have memory recollections, "Oh this is why I feel this way" or "This is what's going on for me," then it is your job. If you feel different, then it is your job as the walk-in personality to condition your physical body by attempting some version of that in the safest possible way you can. For example, you might feel different and experience in that moment confusion, perhaps feeling that you want to do something differently but simultaneously you get a physical feeling that doesn't want to do it, a conflict, all right? It might not be great, but it might be present.

You must understand that your physical body might very well be attempting to warn you that something is not safe, such as my humorous example before of walking up to the edge of a cliff and jumping off and pretending to be a bird, which I do not recommend. As I said, you might discover what it's like to be a stone. What I'm saying is first you must assume that your physical body is warning you of something that is perhaps not safe to do, as in my example. But after having read this book, I am hopeful that you will begin to show your physical body that your personality is different and therefore your personality could very well experience this in a different way. Let's pick out something that many people do but not everybody does, all right?

A typical example is swimming. Not everybody swims. Many people do. It is something that is actually natural to the human being, but if you have not experienced, say, a water birth (which I believe is done from time to time in various cultures, certainly in the past, and even being experimented with by some in the present), you might not, as a physical body, be aware of the fact that swimming is a natural thing. In the case of a water birth, the baby literally swims out of the mother to the surface or is supported to the surface by someone standing by. The baby naturally swims. It's not surprising, since of course the baby has been nurtured and cultured in life surrounded by water, an essentially water-like fluid, inside mother.

Say that you don't swim, that you don't go in the water; your experiences of going into the water in your life were not supportive or didn't work out. Swimming didn't work out for you, and you avoid water. In that case, when your personality comes in, perhaps you would have a desire to go down to the water and your body would give you the message, "It's not safe. Don't do it. Don't go on the boat," and so on. Therefore you avoid it.

Over time, your walk-in soul engages more with your physical body — your physical body begins to adapt to your walk-in soul and you, as the soul, the new soul, you as the walk-in soul — and as you become more expressive, then what occurs is that maybe you say, "Well, I'm not prepared to learn how to swim yet, but maybe what I'll do is I'll go out on a boat to see what that's like." Perhaps you look at a big boat, and you say, "Well, I don't know about that. It doesn't feel right. It's too overwhelming, and there are too many people on it. Perhaps I won't feel good, and I might have a bad experience." So then you think about it and look, in this case, at a small boat. If the boat is small enough, it's almost an extension of your body, a rowboat, for instance, or a canoe or something like that that you can paddle. Therefore, because of your physical engagement with it, you actually feel that the water is safe and a fun place to explore. It can even be a motorboat. But if it's a motorboat, it has to be one in which you operate the controls so that you are actually fully engaged in the physical process of being on the water in this small vehicle.

That would be an example of how to condition your physical body to your soul, your soul's expression, and to help your physical body to let go of the previous conditioning of the physical body that had, on the basis of the previous soul's presence, informed your physical body that the water was not safe for you, that you couldn't swim, and that you were uncomfortable in boats and so on. Therefore, you decide that, well, maybe in this small and not overwhelming way, in this small boat, it's all right to go out on the water.

In short, in the case of my example here, you simply condition your physical body to who you are in your physical body, and your physical body adapts to you. Before you know it, maybe you don't go swimming but you find yourself going out to the water, the lake, the river, or the ocean (wherever you live) and looking forward to getting in your motorboat (or your friend's motorboat or even a rented motorboat). You whiz around on the water feeling as if it is a joyful experience and so on.

Hmm. But what about the situation where you've trained yourself to use the body as an indicator of what to do, and something comes up with loving, physical warmth to guide you in a decision that might not be appropriate for the walk-in soul but is a physical memory from the previous soul?

Now, that would mean that is something good for you to engage in, and if you're uncertain that it would be, then it's good to proceed slowly and take it step by step. Make a step toward that direction if you feel that warmth, but generally speaking, if the warmth is present, it is a good thing to do, because your physical warmth, as you have been taught, is something that shows you that something is good to do. So take it in steps.

Let's say, for instance, you see an old love, yes, or an old friend, and the warmth comes up. You feel nothing but friendship toward that person. But with your current soul in the body, yes, your interactions with that person might not feel quite as wonderful as the previous soul's. Then you simply slow down your engagement with the person. Perhaps you make an attempt to communicate with the person and get to know them a little bit better.

Or perhaps you acknowledge that physically you have great warmth for this person. But perhaps, with your soul in this body, your relationship to that person is meant to be something different.

Maybe your relationship is not meant to be as a lover (if it was in the previous relationship) or a business associate (as it was in the previous relationship) or any other relationship for which there might be warmth. You might be meant to still engage with this person but in a different way. That's why one slows down the process a bit, perhaps writes letters (or in your current time, computer letters, whatever they're called), and there is some way of establishing the relationship, to feel good about it. You talk on the phone when you are ready and explore other ways of being with each other. Perhaps it was a business association that had worked wonderfully well to a great advantage and perhaps to your mutual advantage in the past, but now perhaps it's more important to get to know each other on a friendly level, perhaps by going fishing or skiing together or camping or simply playing chess. In short, if you are uncertain, slow it down, and go one step at a time.

Very good. Okay, how are we doing?

I think perhaps it would be good to stop for now. It was a long session, eh?

I want to say that this combination is incredible. There's a great warmth and wisdom and knowledge of you with the added physicality of the other two. It feels really good.

I'm glad you like it.

Yes, it's great.

You're welcome. Good life and good night.

CHAPTER THIRTEEN

The Transition of Your Native Personality

Isis

January 9, 2004

As you grow and change and become more of your actual personality — which as a walk-in has to have similarities to the previous personality or it's not compatible to be welcomed into the body — and as you become more attuned to yourself as you differentiate from the previous occupant, you need to begin to express more of yourself in ways that are identified with you. Obviously you are very flexible.

Now, as a walk-in, your capacity to perceive others is going to be significantly greater, but you have to understand that, as you grow and change and become more of yourself, so does your capacity to perceive externally. Everything that is external grows and becomes clearer. So right now your perception is still somewhat attached to the previous tenant's capacity. Now, you have to give up some things to establish who you are, but you still maintain enough of the former soul's capabilities so that you can function when you come in as a walk-in.

The issue to keep in mind is that you are learning. You are involved in a lesson. The more you learn that, the more you understand these things, these lessons, are not just things that are happening. The lesson is not, "Which product should I choose?" The lesson is, "These are my perceptions of the external world and how I interpret them."

You see, that's the lesson you're going through, and quite obviously that lesson is vitally important not only for your personal life and happiness but also for your career. Think about improving your ability to perceive all that is external and coming up with observations followed by action, if necessary, or adjustments in thinking that allow you to see the situation clearly. The idea of life becoming better than the previous tenant's would also be desirable, would it not?

So you see why your lesson is more important. This is to be expected in all walk-ins. That's the context it's in, and at some point, it will help others who are going through the experience to understand what can happen, how it can affect you, and how very pervasive it is in all aspects of your life, especially aspects that you might not consider would be affected.

People don't think about their ability to observe as associated with personality because they consider observation to utilize the senses as well as the analytical mind to gauge and reference what has been seen or observed — yes. But we're involved in training here that does not discard the analytical mind and also incorporates the feelings that provide you (when you know how to interpret them) with physical evidence that can corroborate or dispute what the analytical mind says therefore requiring other forms of means to establish how people can know what's what. That means it's always the result of what you do by strictly analytical application as compared to the result of what you do by strictly feeling the heat and so on. There is application in comparing the two in various decisions and waiting to see how it comes out. Over time, you get an idea of which is more reliable for you at your stage of personality.

When you come in initially and you know you're in as a walk-in, you're going to be able to make decisions based on feeling just as soon as the body and you become sufficiently assimilated to trust each other. But if you don't know that you're in as a walk-in (which will be the vast majority of people since they aren't privy at the moment to this interchange), you will tend to use the analytical.

Therefore, because you have been trained by the previous tenant to use the analytical, you are the best possible example in this situation to allow those who come in and use the analytical to identify with this experience and equally to allow those who come in and know they're in and can use feelings to gauge whether something is useful to them as well. You, in one person, are able to represent not only your own needs but their needs as well.

What we have, then, is an overview of what you as a walk-in are going through and an example in this case of perception: "What do I want." "The more I can work with this situation," you might say, "the more I have the opportunity to clearly perceive the difference between the previous tenant and me. I can, therefore, become much more aware not only on the feeling level but also on the analytical level. This is based on what appeals to me intellectually, comparing my intellectual observations to the previous tenant's intellectual observations according to the way I feel, according to my personality" (to the best of your recollection).

It is complex. It is intertwined and interweaved, and you will discover, going through this thing as consciously as you are, because of these interchanges, how much the walk-in phenomenon entirely permeates every aspect of your life.

Lesson in Feeling versus the Analytical Method

Now, perhaps there is some confusion when I'm speaking to you and ask, "Do you understand?" You hear, "Do you agree?" But what I am really asking is, "Can you feel that?" What I'm really saying is, "Do you understand what I am saying?" not, "Do you agree with me in this moment on all levels."

Yes.

Of course you understand what I'm saying. Now, that's an "aha!" is it not?

That's an "aha!"

So recognize that I know you understand what I say. I also know that it doesn't feel good at the moment. That is because you are not at the end of the lesson, eh? You are in the course of the lesson, and at the end of the lesson, you will be able to say, "Yes, I understand what you are saying. Yes, it feels good because I see why it is important for me to learn this with this homework and homework that will come up so that I can clearly define who I am and clearly understand how that differentiates from who was in my body before so that I can be me. I can clearly know when I am being me and when I am being the other person based on these clear understandings. Of course, I understand why this is so important not only for my happiness but for every single thing I do and every extension of what I do." This means you understand who you are, what you do, and how you do it. You understand who you affect, how others are affected by this, what they do and how they do it, and how it affects others in progression.

This is true for all people, but you are going through this, and you are being allowed to see it and to consider it mentally. You are being allowed to do that, eh? At the same time, you are experiencing it more and more on a feeling level since that is your nature. So I want you to understand mentally, and I want you to honor and appreciate the fact that I know (and you know too) that you're not comfortable with this. So you can say to me, "I understand," can you not?

Yes.

When I ask, "How do you feel?" I want you to tell me how you feel physically. Yes, you understand this? Now, how do you feel about what I said, that your lesson is more important? How do you feel about that?

I feel conflicted.

That's honest. I want you to recognize that that's where you are in the lesson now. For you, going back when you first came in, there wouldn't have been any conflict at all. It would have been entirely, "Let's do what the other person wants to do." Now that you feel conflicted, that is progress. Do you understand why?

It's an ability to recognize I want something that doesn't relate to the previous personality's way of thinking.

That's right. It means you are more present and you can honestly acknowledge — not only mentally, but also emotionally — that you are more present because you feel conflicted. This is something important for walk-ins to understand because the number one feeling that walk-ins are going to have, because they are not only, what? They are themselves *and* they have the residual of the other personality. The number one thing they might feel almost all the time about everything going on in their lives that they have inherited is conflicted.

You are now able to recognize that your feelings are important. Why have you had trouble in the past bringing up the heat [heart-warmth], all right? Because you have faith and trust in the analytical process based on the previous tenant. When you come in as a walk-in, you are unsure. It's like coming in as a baby, you know, you're unsure. You're going to grab what's there and hang on for dear life until you become more prominent as a personality. Then you will gradually let go of what was there and begin to express yourself as you build confidence. But if you don't build that confidence in yourself, you remain, what? Conflicted indefinitely! This book is intended to help walk-ins ease their process to be able to confront real, practical issues of daily life. It's not just for spiritual issues. This book is about a practical handbook for the walk-in to become a fulfilled and comfortable human being. So it can only be helpful that we can demonstrate *with* walk-ins *for* walk-ins what comes up, how it comes up, and how it shows itself.

I am not here to say, "This is how you should feel." You feel the way you feel. That's how far you've come, and now you recognize how you feel. As you become more yourself, you will feel less conflicted. You will recognize not only the validity of your lessons, which you intellectually recognize now, but also the value based on the evidence of what you feel and the results of what you can produce when you use the feeling method. "How does it feel?" you know. The feeling method can present you with absolute, irrefutable, undeniable proof of its value, whereas the analytical is always subject to further analysis.

The problem with spirituality in the past, even with religion, is that it often tended to be impractical, or there were conflicts between the spiritual and the practical world that were sometimes not easily cleared up. This book is not intended to be a religion. It is intended to support all philosophies and all practical applications of that which can be produced and evidentiary, meaning here's the evidence of how you feel as an individual using the heart-warmth method [see Appendix D]. Here's the results of your choice based on choosing that heart-warmth method, and here's the results of using the analytical method.

Sometimes the analytical method will be helpful. Sometimes it will work out all right. But at times you just don't know because, what? The analytical method depends on the information you have at your command. "It's available to me. The more information I have, the more I'm able to make my best guess based on this information," yes? But with the heart-warmth method, it doesn't make any difference whether you have information or not. You can have no information, and it will still work. In short, the heart-warmth method is simpler, it is faster, and it is universal. You know it's universal because the animals use it. You can interact with the animals using it.

You can relate back to the Shamanic Secrets books [Light Technology Publishing] on this, and it is also something that even the stones, the rain, the clouds — Mother Earth — use. It is typically in use by all planets, and the more you use it, the more likely you are to remember, acquire, and feel at home with your native (or natural) personality. By "native personality," I mean that which encompasses you and allows you to progress toward remembering your total being (reacquiring in gradual steps your native personality) while you are alive, while you are physical on Earth.

Your native personality allows you to be more, do more, and feel more comfortable, and just as important, it allows you to let others do what they are doing by making a choice, saying, "This is not for me. It feels uncomfortable to me." That means every time — not that it's bad, and not that it's evil. It is just for somebody else. It is perhaps something that is at times evil. Then if everyone decides it doesn't feel good, it's evil, then that part of the school is over. Until everyone decides that, some people are still in school with that issue.

I'm trying to put all these things in context so that you can see that what you have thought coming into this is just a simple decision, and with a snap of your fingers, you can go into self-denial and say, "Well, that's not important. What he does is more important." But how that fits into the bigger picture — is that not what I am doing here? Am I helping you understand how this relates to being a walk-in and why it is vitally important to honor your progress by informing you that feeling conflicted and knowing it is progress?

One and One Equal Three

At the end of this session, you won't feel much different. You'll still feel conflicted, but you might have time to think about these things, and you might have time to apply different solutions. You think back in your mind that I'm going to give you some clarity: "Has being entirely self-sacrificing in the past made me feel better?"

Okay, and "Has being entirely selfish in the past made me feel better?"

So you understand it's not about being self-sacrificing. It's not about being selfish. There's something else. It's about honoring through the union of feeling what has been said before: If one person feels the heart-warmth, it will tend to radiate on its own. If two or three or four people get together and can feel the heart-warmth at the same time, it will tend to radiate. You don't send it out. It tends to radiate and do a lot of good, yes? If two people are doing the heart-warmth regularly for themselves, their level of communication with each other increases exponentially. You like that word? But it increases in a fixed formula.

One is one — one person feeling the heart-warmth — but (and this homework is given out sometimes) two are three: Two doing this heart-warmth together produce more than the sum of their equal parts. They produce more than the sum of their parts producing the heat individually for themselves. One can produce the same amount of heart-warmth for him- or herself as one other, so they are equal. So one and one equal three because by coming together you produce not only your heart-warmth (for yourself that you normally produce) but both of you, by that simple coming together, produce more than you feel on your own. You feel that when doing that heart-warmth sitting in the same room, for instance. You feel that because your personal heart-warmth is much more obvious, much more prominent, and you can actually feel it flowing.

I bring this up because you are beginning to move toward being more yourself, and you are doing more heart-warmth — not discarding the analytical, but utilizing it, noticing it. After all, you have your senses. You don't discard them. It is the heart-warmth.

People have talked about the sixth sense, yes? What's the sixth sense? There's been confusion yes, thinking that the sixth sense is about knowing and perception and being psychic. It isn't! The sixth sense is the heart-warmth, and it allows people to access it because if the sixth sense is being psychic, how many people can do that? It is difficult. You are born to it, or you learn it after years and years of training. The heart-warmth is not as difficult for most people. It is accessible. If the sixth sense is real, why not make it something accessible to many people, such as sight, sound, taste, touch, and so on? That's the sixth sense. Do you think that's important?

That's why the walk-in experience you're having and this book is important. It's a practical primer for spiritual and physical union. Why separate them? You are moving beyond the capacity to perceive the external from the previous tenant. "So what am I moving beyond?" you might ask. You are moving to that. Describe what I'm doing.

Both hands are outstretched, firmly clasped together, and fingers intertwined.

That's right, and what way am I holding my hands? How am I holding them?

Horizontal, one on top of the other, left hand on top.

That's right. Earth — physical experience on ...

On the bottom. The left hand on top is spiritual.

Spiritual union, which allows you to experience your full and complete native personality. So you see why the things that seem to be simple distractions appear to be in the way but are not in the way. It is our continuing expedition through this book as represented by a walk-in. How else to pursue the book, to make it a practical primer, unless we're working with a walk-in who is experiencing on a day-to-day, practical, conscious level the difficulties and the conflicts of being a walk-in, eh?

So only in this instance, because it's the lesson and because the other person felt strongly that this defied everything he believed. We went to look at that thing. It felt good; therefore, we should have purchased it. The other person was upset about this because I had all these mental reasons why it wasn't a good choice. The other person said, "But it feels good."

We need to incorporate it beyond that, but I see you're trying to understand what has happened.

For him, the decision was clear, but we're talking about you. Put that in a frame of reference now that involves you. We're talking about your lesson today, thank you. Yes, his decision saying, "This is it," would have been correct for him. Now let's hear that question based on what is right for you. Ask it about you and your experience.

I need to get clarity because it did feel good, but there were so many things about it that did not seem — to my mind — to make it the best choice.

The reason that the analytical method felt more important is that you haven't established your new personality enough yet so that you can use your full capabilities of perception and have faith in that perception.

Had my capacities been more expanded, I would have ignored the mental doubts, then? I would not have paid any attention to them?

I'll give you the precise "what you would have done." You would have considered the mental, but you would have felt even more. You would have had a much stronger feeling that there would have been no comparison. The comparison, the analytical, tends to be expressed still based on what the previous personality felt was valid and could be trusted. She was trained that she couldn't trust her feelings. You understand all that. So the experience, you understand what I'm saying, would have been different.

If you were well established, then what would have happened is that you would have had a much stronger, warmer feeling, and (how can we say?) you would also have noted the analytical. But your decision would have been based on the strong feeling. You would have noted, "That's interesting that it's not really for me." You would say, "I don't feel like this is for me ..."

I have to expand. I'm going to expand a bit, okay? You would have been more present as you, yes? So you would have had a much stronger heart-warmth. I'm using this for an example, now.

We agreed yesterday that this is about your lesson, so that's it. I want you to get clear. I don't want you to be confused about that. Now, you would have noted the discrepancy in the mind; the feelings are different. As a result of progressing, becoming more the walk-in — and your own practical experience of applying the warmth, applying the analytical, considering the results, and so on — you would have said, "There is some reason to buy this beyond the obvious fact." What might be the case? Perhaps it is the people you will meet as a result of buying this product. Perhaps circumstances that are now unforeseen that will occur as a result of buying this product as compared to another.

You will have the faith in that. How will you give to that faith? By doing the comparison and making decisions based clearly on the warmth — which might be in your heart, might be in your solar plexus, wherever it comes up for you. You do something first. You discover that it's safe, and you discover that it's safe to pick "this" garment over "that" garment to wear during the day, something like that. That's how you build up your confidence and learn how it works and so on. After a while, you begin to try to make decisions that are a bit more important, and you build up slowly.

You Will Continue to Gain Confidence

You realize in the process of learning how to use the heart-warmth that many things occur. It has to be an accumulative experience, just like everything else, to build up not only the trust but also the awareness that when you choose the heart-warmth, other benevolent things happen. Perhaps it is not even the decision that you make is the result of using the heart-warmth. Whatever it's applied to might not have anything in particular to do with the actual decision you are making for yourself in that moment.

For example, you choose to go to the movies, "this" movie over "that" movie. Maybe you've been looking forward to seeing a certain movie and can't wait until it gets here. You move your finger across the pages where the movies are listed, and you get a tremendous heat to go to this other movie. You look at it and say, "Hey, it doesn't interest me to go to that movie." But because you are the spiritual student and strongly devoted to your spiritual progress, you say, "Okay, I know it's boring, but I'll go to this other movie," and you grit your teeth for the terrible duration of two hours.

You go to the movie, and it does or it doesn't interest you. But something wonderful happens on your way there, while you are there, or on your way back. Maybe the wonderful thing is the tree that crashed through the middle of the other auditorium doesn't hit you on the head. (That's an extreme example. Understand that this doesn't normally happen at the moving pictures.) Perhaps you meet someone, and you have a good experience. You have fun. In short, something happens at the other movie that didn't or wouldn't have happened if you'd gone to see the one you really wanted to see, which you can go to some other time.

It is not based on what I say that has the ability to resolve, what? The conflict within you. That's what we're talking about here. It's the accumulated evidence of making decisions based on the heart-warmth building up and trying different things — innocuous things at first, then more complex things. You discover in the process (if not in the immediate moment, later as you think about it over time or as a result of accumulated experiences of), "Look at all these things that happened. I just thought they happened because they happened. But if I'd made a different decision using a different method, they wouldn't have happened."

This helps you to build confidence in that method, which we're going to call the sixth sense because it's an actual sense. It involves the physical, just like eyesight or hearing. It's a physical thing in your body from which, when you know how to interpret it — warmth or a slight discomfort or no reaction — it allows you to make a decision. It is a means of perception just like the other senses. Therefore, it must be the next sense, the one that we haven't had available to us before. If you have five, it must be six.

As a result of going through these applied applications, you become less conflicted. You get to experience the heart-warmth, which is the union of the spiritual and the physical, to allow the smooth transition of becoming more of your native personality. Thus, you experience your total spiritual being from Creator — as anointed by Creator, given to you by Creator — who just sits back and says, "Okay, there it is. Now see how long it will take you to discover it." Creator has a sense of humor. It's not mean-spirited, you understand, but Creator respects you "I to I." If Creator had to wear the blindfold of ignorance that you wear to live a life here, the experience would be similar to: Creator respects you and says, "Okay, here it is. Here is what you can do, and I'm rooting for you."

You Create Your World from Your Solar Plexus

As you accumulate the evidence of your own experience, the conflict begins to ebb away because you have personal experience, not only mental experience. Mental experience can come from your own observations or things that other people tell you. This can create vast amounts of resistance or even blind obedience — everything from the existence of blind obedience and evidence of your own personal experience [points to the solar plexus]. The solar plexus is where you create your world on the physical level.

The whole point, my friend, is that you learn to develop confidence in what you are feeling as the walk-in as you begin to acquire and reacquire your native personality integrated into your Earth physical body, in your Earth physical world, on the practical, moment-to-moment level. You begin to have confidence; you know what is for you and what is for others. Then you are able to say, "This is for me. This is for others," and from that point, you're clear on what is for you. This doesn't mean that when you're interacting with others, you disregard what is for them; it means, "Okay, this is our compromise. This is for me. This is what I need to do for me."

Clarity and understanding. I have to insert here that I have memories as a child. I'm little and there's this big, big adult saying, "You understand?" waving a finger that meant, "By God, you agree with me, or else," you know?

That's right. That's why I had to create a differentiation between what I was saying and what the finger in the face meant. You can make this move to becoming more aware of your own personality as differentiated from the previous personality, thus able to be more, do more, have more, and provide more. In short, it is an opportunity to experience a lesson in a practical way while experiencing a degree of comfort in asking, "Hey, is this for me?" It's a way to learn and grow without suffering.

You can see that going on is a given because of the nature of the integration process of the walk-in. The walk-in integrates over time and, like everybody else in the practical world, bumps up against things. But how does the walk-in have the advantage, the capability, the enlightenment, the ability, and the practicality? In short, how does the walk-in expedite the process to learn and apply and experience in the practical world they find themselves in and still be good citizens? That's why the book is ongoing. It's perfect. We continue because you continue to experience life as a walk-in, and you're having lessons. You're in the middle of one now, and there'll be others. You'll say, "Oh, there'll be more 'ahas!' to come, eh?"

Yes. Wonderful.

CHAPTER FOURTEEN

You Are Here to Cocreate with Creator

Ont-say

May 8, 2006

I am Ont-say. I am a being who knows you in about eight hundred-some years, given that time is different, experiential time in the future.

Well, that's wonderful. Thank you. Welcome. Can you talk about the walk-in experience?

The physical body is your tether to the experience here. You know, the walk-in phenomenon is not unknown beyond this planet, for this experience of this planetary diorama, but it is gentle and has great ease. Perhaps you don't know this, but there are some civilizations and cultures in which the physical forms never die. You have heard these beings when they speak to you say that they are immortal, meaning that they have always existed. But what they don't say, because the query does not come from you (since you didn't know to ask) was that a different soul might have occupied that body from time to time. Therefore the body itself is immortal, but the actual personality comes and goes, since walk-ins are a well-established phenomenon on other planets in their cultures and one of the reasons these planets and cultures can live in absolute harmony.

The fixed so-called physical forms, meaning their fixed life forms on the planet, offer opportunities for souls to exist and be incarnated there in a very harmonic balance. For example, so many of "this," so many of "that," so many of "that." The souls simply come and go, but the forms themselves, the forms of this or that or the other, are all in a very fixed number and in complete balance. Because that exists in other places, the idea of being walk-ins on Earth is actually attractive to your souls because you have all done that in other places, in other existences.

The attraction, then, for walk-ins here is based entirely on something that you as souls have experienced and are used to. It is part of your normal experience as your actual, natural selves — as compared to the selves you must be here — because of the scholastic element of this planet and because the acculturization of you as beings on this planet is to be problem solvers. Even babies are not excused from this homework; they must solve problems entirely on their own when their parents or caretakers are not present. Granted, the parents and caretakers solve most of their problems but not all.

As a very young child, you will very often try to reach for something, try to get something and you can't reach it. You can't get it; it's beyond your grasp. Perhaps you don't have the physical mobility yet, or perhaps it is simply something that somebody put on a side table and didn't keep it in your reach. So your problem, then, as a being in this small body without its fuller capabilities, is to move past the frustration of being unable to acquire what you need in that moment.

That is just an example of how babies, the youngest ones, experience the educational foundations of this planetary culture, which is unlike anything that exists anywhere else. Beings come here and have come here for some time to stimulate the understanding within themselves and prepare themselves and their cultures, wherever they are in the universe, to stimulate and prepare themselves for growth.

All Existence Creates by Feeling

When you, as the Explorer Race (as has been discussed extensively in this book series), go out to explore the other planets, you're not going to arrive there cold and unannounced. Most of the planets and cultures that you encounter will have had souls who have come here and experienced, at the very least, a walk-in so that there was some stimulation for the experience of growth. Then the souls have eventually returned to their points of origin and have exposed others to the feeling of growth, if unable to expose them to a conditional thought pattern, and the feeling still emanates.

All beings and all existence create by feeling. Thought is strictly a function to understand the process that is happening, but thought does not create. This is a confusion in your time because of the great desire that has existed in the past on this planet to understand the mysteries of life, since life here is allowed to be a mystery because you are all here to learn how to be problem solvers. Therefore mystery must exist.

There has been a misunderstanding with this Explorer Race idea in your mind and in the minds of even others who are enamored with it. The Explorer Race is going to bring something to others. It's true, but you're not going to bring something consciously; there will be nothing mental. Get clear now that what you are bringing is something for which you have absolutely no conscious awareness and is based entirely on your physical feelings in your physical body, meaning something that radiates automatically and is exactly the same thing now that creates your culture. If you do not do that, if you are not aware of that, you will fall back into the same routine in which cultures achieve some pinnacle of existence and harmony, and they are promptly destroyed by some other culture.

It is vital to understand that the nature of your life right now is entirely about feeling, and thought cannot ever understand feeling; it can only analyze the aftereffects. If you analyze the aftereffects of something, you will always project your best guess on what happened. When you are guessing on what happened, many times you will be wrong. So no matter how much scientists attempt to guess on the basis of quantification and philosophers attempt to guess on the basis of their specific philosophy, there will always be at least 40 to 60 percent error built in. It often goes all the way up to 90 to 95 percent. Scientists, in their origin, completely understand this. So the missing key to science is that the individual human being body, as created by the Creator of this universe in its prototype in which you are now living (though the body is built in such a way as it will not last for too long so that no one has to struggle indefinitely on this planet) is perfect for a feeling being to create through feelings, to understand through feelings, not thought.

Thought is something that was generated into something beyond its ultimate purpose to create an understanding and to create an achievement of understanding in a world gone mad and chaotic. Think about the great philosophers who have spoken and who have left wisdom behind them. Every single one of them, toward the end of life, in whatever form that life took — its ending on this planet — spoke about the vital creation with feelings, and if you do not pay attention to physical feelings, you will completely flail around in the dark, only making your best guess. So these great teachers, these wise beings, found themselves attempting to commune with others in the model of understanding that was available to them, since the feeling beings they were living with were acting, interacting, and reacting on the basis of feelings they did not understand.

So the attempt was being made by these great philosophers and teachers to help human beings understand their feelings. When that could not take place very well, because the intellect was not as developed then as it is now, the eventual outcome of that was to educate people, to sharpen their intellect, so they could learn by intellectual means about their feelings. But as often happens, especially in cultures that are just building up to some point of perfection, the intellect became an end in itself. The missing key for those in science in any culture right now is to understand that the physical body of the human being has within it, by Creator's own design, the means to understand and to know it's all about feelings.

So when the Explorer Race understands that and applies it on a daily basis — experiences on a daily basis and enjoys on a moment-to-moment basis — their feelings and then interacts with others based on those feelings, then you will be welcomed. Other cultures exist in harmony because they understand that the creation of life has to do with what they feel. Since they feel complete harmony physically, their creation continues and perpetuates in harmony.

Harmony comes about because of harmonious feelings within yourself, and that comes about by exploring all the feelings within yourself. "We do not reject the feeling of anger. We do not reject the feeling of excitement. We explore it and discover all of its good elements that bring us happiness and enjoyment," you see (speaking as one of you). Thus you discover what feels good to you, and you emanate those feelings because, as a physical human being, Creator has made you in such a way that you will always broadcast what you are feeling all the time, whether you are mentally aware of it or not. That's how you can come here with things you want to solve or understand.

The creation of problems around things that you want to solve and understand is available for you. Whether it is a drama that you might not enjoy living or whether it is a series of friends, anything like that, what occurs is that the physical body, by emanating feelings, attracts to itself the complete experience of the function, the interaction, the application, and the existence of these feelings. It draws to you what you came here to learn.

You do not come here to learn only how to tie your shoelaces. [Chuckles.] You come here to learn what it is that you wanted to know. The beings who come here by the birth process as you know it and, these days, the walk-in process are (almost to a single being with very few exceptions) the exact souls who will meet the Explorer Race when you go out and interact with them on other planets. They will be in the perfect situation to understand what it is that they are looking for, for you to be emanating on your physical-feeling level. If they do not feel that — since they will know, they will remember — then they will not allow you to further interact with those cultures, no matter how curious you are, no matter how desirable that interaction might be, because they do not feel the code/key that unlocks the door that says, "Welcome."

Your Physical Feelings Create Your World

It's all about feelings. Now, is that possible, since I've just finished saying that it isn't about what you think? I'll tell you how it's possible. It's possible because you know very well that your feelings are affected by your thoughts. How many times have you, say, woken up from a nap or from a deep sleep and felt relaxed and comfortable, but then you started thinking about what you have to do, or you start worrying about things and immediately feel uncomfortable? Your feelings are affected by your thoughts.

You have to get to the point where you can do something physical that will allow you to welcome only thoughts that allow the free-flowing opportunity, the full interaction, with all other beings who can help you or wish to help you. There has to be a means that is physical, since you are physical beings, in order to allow it, to welcome it, and to experience it without worry getting in your way and without the demands of things that are over and beyond what one person can do, which many people are caught up in today.

What do parents do when they have many children who all have needs? They are constantly distracted with what to do and how to train the children to do for themselves. Being in the physical present moment is the way that allows, and has been established by Creator to allow and welcome, the solution to all the problems you came in with, to inquire what is possible, meaning your soul's challenges (that you set up as a soul, as an individual, who came in).

The soul comes in as a walk-in or as a baby being born. It comes in, welcoming and broadcasting the physical feelings to acquire that. Yet how do you help people come to that understanding in your now cultures? The way is to be in the physical moment. How do you understand the magnificent creation of the human being body, and how do you understand creation in the moment of creating? By being in your body — being conscious of your physical body and enjoying being in your body. That is why the love-heat/heart-warmth has been discussed in such great detail. Because when feeling that in your physical body, you want to be in your physical body.

You want to be inside your physical body. You want to feel it in a wonderful way. That always brings you into the present moment. Then you can literally experience life.

You will experience this love/warmth. You will attract beings who can help you and whom you can enjoy helping. You're not just going to attract beings you will struggle to help; you will attract the beings you can enjoy helping. Maybe it is just a kind word. Maybe it is a pat on the back. Maybe it is just sitting in silence and not adding more words to their confusion. It will be any number of things that will give you pleasure to help. And if they are experiencing that moment inside themselves, with that loving heat, which is the foundation — the glue that creates these wonderful, harmonious civilizations everywhere else in the universe — you will then understand that the attracting elements of this love experienced as heat in your physical body is you cocreating with Creator.

Think why you are here. You are here to learn. You are here to be able to solve problems beyond your own scope of existence. You are here, in short, to have moments when you cocreate with Creator. The best way to do that is to be in the physical present moment where you feel that heat, that wonderful existence, that is open to having all your problems solved by others who want to help you, because they are attracted to you either for something that you have or something that they have because they have pleasure in resolving it.

The life that you live here is intended to bring to your awareness the physical feelings in your physical body that are completely harmonious. These physical feelings create your world. They also, in moments of feeling this great and loving heat in this physical body right now are the foundational elements of creation. It is how Creator always feels — with that heat. It is how you will feel when you understand the nature and the purpose of your existence here. It is how you will feel as an astronaut going out and contacting other beings. It is the key that will unlock the door that says, "Welcome." It can be the key that will unlock the door of interacting between all your cultures here that will, in time, welcome cultures that have struggled with each other in the past and are still struggling today because they are trying to convince each other mentally that they have the truth. But the convincing can only happen when the other person feels a benevolent energy, a physical feeling, in harmony with them.

It will take a while to practice and learn, but that is why the Benevolent Magic Blog exists [http://www.benevolentmagic.blogspot.com], and other places exist, to teach you individually how to understand what you feel, learn how to have good feelings, recognize the creation point of being in the present, and appreciate the value of the moment-to-moment experience of being in the present re-creating civilization in Creator's most appreciated-by-you and natural feeling. You as Creator's offspring naturally have that feeling too. You have all been taught how to do this.

It will take some of you longer to learn that feeling [heart-warmth], but you cannot maintain that feeling in your physical body without being in the present moment. If it is difficult for you to create that feeling in your physical body, then focus on some internal part of your body, and maintain that focus. Just be focusing. That is how Buddha spent the retirement years of his life, focusing on being in his physical body, because he could feel the heat and he could feel the love, and he would know that this is creation, and this is cocreation with Creator.

About the Future

Now tell me about you!

I will say that I am a being in your future, and all beings at that time have these understandings. Nowadays your children learn facts about the culture in which you live, but in the future, we all have this knowledge and understanding that I am explaining to you today. You have that too because you have feelings. You just do not understand their value.

In my time, we all understand that, and I am simply a being like everybody else. I am no different. I am not special. I am not the reincarnation of some famous person in your culture. I am simply a citizen who understands these things and is, perhaps, more interested in helping you, in your time, to learn how to do that through such vessels as Robert.

CHAPTER FIFTEEN

The Walk-In Learns Material Mastery

Grandmother

April 30, 2006

Grandmother.

Welcome!

Greetings. Now, what would you like to talk about today?

How the Earth soul works in combination with the immortal personality soul to create the human being.

That's more than one question, but it's a well-spoken sequence. What you are referring to as the Earth soul is what I will call the body consciousness. This is a term that has been used by others. I will move to a different term at some point, but I want people to understand what we're talking about.

This is something that has to do with Earth. It contains your physical body, the entire experience of your conception, meaning when the sperm, as you say, and the egg come together and begin that creation of a different being, two beings, we could say. The egg and the sperm are each individual beings; they come together, and between them, they make a third. Doesn't this sound familiar? This is a theme in spiritual training as well as physical life on Earth. One or two things come together and make a third.

The training, perhaps you recall personally — have you done the training with the tree? You might not have yet, but some people who have been trained to feel the warmth are often encouraged to go out to a tree and once they feel the warmth for themselves, they say, "Good life," to the tree. Then they interact with the tree. When they find the right tree, meaning a tree that can engage with them, that feels the human being say, "Good life," it brings up the warmth in them. Then the tree, as far as the human beings know, also has its warmth, and the human beings know this because suddenly they feel greater warmth than they normally feel when they do this. That is an example of one and one coming together to make a third thing because the tree also feels greater warmth in that moment. The two of you make a third thing, meaning the extra warmth that you both feel, and the excess goes out into the world as love to serve the needs of whatever other beings might need it.

Now, I'm bringing this up as a point, because some of you who have read the Shamanic Secrets books [Light Technology Publishing] will have had this training already. It is important for you to see the analogy and the foundational elements of the sperm and the egg coming together to create a third thing, what becomes the baby. I want you also to understand that the Earth soul, or body consciousness, that we're talking about here begins the moment that sperm begins to enter the egg. It doesn't begin when the baby comes out of mother. It doesn't even begin when the baby seems to be something inside of mother, all right? It starts the moment that sperm begins to enter the egg, so when it actually penetrates the egg and goes in, that's when your body consciousness begins. The people who have experienced or been involved in the experiments done some years ago, I think, to trace back memory beyond birth, had the ability to recall not exactly memories but feelings that can be interpreted as visuals or even words that describe the feeling of inception, the duplication of cells, that goes on inside the egg as it becomes the nest to create the soul, the soul's vessel.

Very often portions of your immortal personality might be present. So what is the walk-in left with when the birth soul exits? The soul exiting cannot take Earth struggles, difficulties, or discomforts with it. It can only take itself because those discomforts can't go beyond that veil. They must be left here in this school, on this planet. Where? Of course they must be in the body of your physical self. So when your physical self, then, is conceived, that's when life begins. We have said before, you have heard from other spirit beings as well, saying that all life is sacred, and that's when that particular life of that particular person begins.

What occurs inside of mother, then, as that life begins to form (and eventually becomes something recognizable) is that your body, which is a portion like a foundation of the soul, will support and receive you. Your soul personality can only come in under very select circumstances. This is not just for walk-ins. It's for any soul coming in. Those select circumstances are that all must be in preparation to receive you, and during your time here on

Earth, that preparation must be maintained in some way so as to support you. It is like a vase, a vessel, yes? So your physical body receives you.

Incorporated within the physical body are all the things you need to not only carry on with your physical life on Earth but also all that your immortal personality needs as it comes to join your physical body and become one. Thus, your immortal personality, living life here on Earth for the duration of your physical time here, becomes one being with your physical body.

For the purpose of your question, we're breaking down the different parts here for clarity. I'm talking about a portion of your immortal personality, which joins your physical personality. Your physical body allows your immortal personality to demonstrate through a physical vehicle, which has been created as a direct reflection to interact with your immortal personality. The two of you, plus all the other things you bring to this life, the physical personality and the immortal personality, come together to create the physical means by which you can live your life here on Earth and learn things that are unavailable to learn on other planets and other realms of existence.

Those portions of you come together to create this temporal situation. The "temporal" means that you function in time and the physical personality, which is loaned by Mother Earth (for as long as Mother Earth is prepared to loan it to you). The duration of your time as the immortal personality is set to the duration of your physical personality in terms of your Earth life.

Now, as the birth soul exits, the physical personality remains alive and prepared to receive the walk-in soul, another immortal personality, and the physical personality also has terms. The new immortal personality to occupy it must have sufficient compatibility and similarity to the previous soul. All the basic physical things — your heartbeat, your breath rate, your basic willingness to eat and drink, the physical functions that support life — need to be acceptable to the new immortal personality or walk-in that comes in. Even though adjustments will be necessary, the basic life functions are able to continue. That is why the walk-in will have some similarity to the exiting soul, but they are entirely individual. They are, in fact, different. The similarity is required so that the physical personality can function as a vehicle to support that new soul.

At the time that the first personality walks out, it takes with it, I was told, 40 percent of all of the memories and attitudes and beliefs. So the other 60 percent of it stays in the physical personality of the birth soul's physical body? So when all the shamanic teachings say, "Listen to your body," you're talking about that physical personality?

Yes. Because the physical personality is an expert on living physical life in the most benevolent way, and the soul coming in is a novice at living physical life in the most benevolent way. The novice always learns from the teacher. Do you not agree?

Therefore, the key for the immortal personality is to determine how to learn from the physical personality in ways that feel safe and benevolent to both portions until they feel safe and comfortable with each other. Sometimes walk-ins don't feel comfortable for a while. It's awkward; it's unusual. You are used to the spirit form, yes? And you are not, as a walk-in, able to gradually get used to physical life the way a birth soul is able to. Portions of the immortal personality might come in and out of the mother while the baby is forming inside her, or portions might come straight into the baby and engage that physical personality as it's growing inside the mother and all kinds of variables in between. So there's a gradual experience of life forming up, and the interchanges between the immortal personality and the physical personality have a long time to get used to each other and to form a compatible engagement of cooperative life.

This is completely different for the walk-in. The walk-in comes in and just "bang!" right then and there, there is your physical personality, and you have to get familiar with it. You have to get used to each other. So that's why there's a period of adjustment for the walk-in. Sometimes it's fun; other times it's curious and uncomfortable. It depends on what the compatibility factors are, of course, between the immortal personality soul and the physical personality. Let's just call them the immortal personality and the physical personality, because we don't want to create a hierarchy in the minds of the reader. There is no hierarchy. The immortal personality and the physical personality are equal, and all life is equal with all other life. There is no hierarchy, period. You can ask Creator. You can ask any being.

Hierarchies are something that human beings have learned in various philosophies in order to understand how things work. That's it in the simplest possible form. From my experience and the experience of all other spirits I have spoken to, including Creator, there is no hierarchy. By that, I mean there are no bosses. [Chuckles.] So the joining of those portions in the walk-in situation is quite different, because the immortal personality comes in and finds the physical personality a fait accompli, yes? It doesn't have that gradual period of adjustment that the baby has.

Mother Earth Is a Material Master

Your physical body is in the moment; it is immediate. For you to get the most from your material-mastery teacher — your physical body is not just something that's an appendage, that you're dragging along. Your physical body is always your teacher — and by honoring your physical body's needs, you learn how to communicate with your physical body, learn its language. Once that's established, you will be able to more easily learn other things, and your physical body will be able to teach you with feelings, the language of feelings — for which you eventually can create a bridge, consciously, with the heart-warmth.

You will be able to learn all the wonderful things that your physical body can teach you about creation utilizing material mastery, which, as you know, is that everybody is harmonized. Everybody is happy with everybody else. Everybody, every being, is working with every other being in ways that feel completely harmonious to everyone. Material mastery is that which your physical body is prepared to teach you — how you can become a material master on Earth now.

You need to learn your physical body's language so that it can teach you. Once steps are taken, you're already capable. You are then able to learn more and more because your body is made up of Mother Earth's body, and Mother Earth is a material master. We know Mother Earth also has other capabilities, and you might be able to learn portions — even though you came in for material mastery on the physical realm, this particular type of physical realm. You came in for that, and that's what you're here to learn. That's why you came, but there are other things that Mother Earth can do as the teaching master, as the dimensional master, which we can change to the master of realms, if you like, or the quantum master, which is the master of consequences.

Quantum mastery is largely being accomplished by all the souls on Earth, the Explorer Race: "This person doing this." "This person doing that." Therefore, all consequences are known and understood by everyone. No one person has to learn all the consequences or circumstances of what Mother Earth has to offer you through your physical body, once you learn your physical body's language, and learning is not enough.

You know your physical body's language is feelings, some physical feelings, feeling here, feeling there. But the bridge, the means you can use, is the warmth, yes? Work toward the warmth, touch [heart-warmth], and even after you learn the warmth and can interpret it as, essentially, "This is love for me," or if there's discomfort and a question (you hold something up to you or ask a question, and there is discomfort), then you know there is no love for you to do that in that moment. So you don't do it; you do something else. This method can teach you, in a way. It's willing to respond to physical questions that you state, that are words, but first you must learn its language.

It is not only up to your physical body to respond to your language, your thoughts. It is up to you to learn your physical body's language, because that's part of material mastery. It is the way that Mother Earth speaks to all beings in your realm, this physical realm. Your Mother Earth speaks to you with feelings, and once you can interpret your own feelings and have the warmth to interact, which is a feeling you can interpret as yes or no (love for me, no love for me). Then you have the means to communicate and learn all these valuable, wonderful material-mastery lessons and perhaps others.

You can share your experience with those who wish to learn, thus allowing you, through their questions, to tap into some of what Mother Earth has to teach you through your physical-body feelings and the bridge of warmth. This allows you to respond to the needs of others and their questions, utilizing some forms of teaching mastery and learning how to teach in ways you are yet to know. But by the needs of others, you will learn.

Physical Language

You have to learn physical language. The people in some cultures might talk and move their arms around, stressing what they're saying. Even if they don't move their lips to say something, just moving their arms around denotes the urgency of what they're trying to communicate. So what you're learning with your physical body will prepare you to understand the physical-language implementation of various cultures, what they're attempting to communicate, which sometimes might seem so foreign as to be almost inconceivable, as you've seen perhaps studied in some foreign cultures. You might not actually come into contact with other cultures, but they are studied by anthropologists and other people, so you might have read about these things — people who speak with their hands and arms, you understand, waving their arms around to talk. You have probably met people like this. To a degree, you might do it yourself to make a point.

Your soul is highly sensitive, prepared to do highly spiritual work that requires great sensitivity. Therefore, you need to become familiar with physicality in general. So it's almost as if you have an infancy when you come in to become accustomed to that, during which time your physical body runs your life in the best way it can based on its prior conditioning, adaptation, and capabilities.

I see. So a good way to communicate is with the heart-warmth or with touch or by re-sponding to your physical needs?

That's right, and you will learn this. It's just shifting gears to understand that you don't have to learn a particular language; you can use your own words. You don't have to learn French or German or something like that.

By learning your physical language, you are putting your tools in place — how to learn a language, how to learn something that's really quite foreign. It's simple and uncomplicated, and it allows you to learn enough about feelings and feeling communication to communicate sufficiently and have plenty of time, in the future, to learn more when you and your body communicate and you are able to ask material-mastery questions. For example, "Would it be good for me to go 'here'? Would it be good for me to go 'there'?" That's material mastery, yes? You ask your body, and your body, by showing you the warmth that you can generate (if you practice it), responds, "Yes, this is a good time to go." So you get up and go to the store right now. You understand? Some of you have done some of this training.

Then that works. So you're learning. This is your primary education: to learn other languages. Then your wonderful, singular soul can interact with you once you learn how to interact with your physical body. At the most basic level it's, "Hungry!" "Eat!" "Bathroom!" "Go!" "Sleep!" "Now!" Things like that, that all beings must learn when they come in, and you as a spiritual student must react with immediacy if you can, "Bathroom! Now! Hungry! Eat!" because it acknowledges — it embraces — your physical body when you react in the immediate. Your physical body realizes that you want to establish this communication and that you are receptive to the communication because you are acting on it. That's how you know someone is receptive to you. You state a need to another human being, and because they act on it immediately, you know that they are receptive to you.

It's no different internally. Your physical body states a need, you act on it, and your physical body says, "Ah. He wishes to communicate, and I can perhaps have faith in him that he wants to learn how to communicate with me. I am perfectly happy to communicate with him, and I can be more receptive when he is trying to generate the feeling heat. I can produce the feeling heat much more easily, and he is still learning how to produce the heat (how to ask me to produce a feeling that he will feel and that he can interact with) in order to communicate with me in a way that is completely harmonious to me and him." Now, your physical consciousness does not think; I am interpreting its knowingness.

Ah, but you said something really important: The physical body produces the heat!

Well, of course.

One asks it to produce the heat.

Yes! However, you need to recognize that "I" means you, as you understand your personality, and I is your physical body as well. You do not produce external heat. Your physical body produces the heat just as your physical body produces all its other feelings.

How to Determine Your Body's Language

How does creation work, then, now that we know that we have these two parts, the soul and the body consciousness? How do we consciously create our lives?

What we are doing here essentially is teaching all of you the fundamental steps of how you can create in conscious, benevolent ways. We are teaching you only portions that will not in any way interfere with your body's creation mechanisms that interact with all of creation, all right? We don't want to interfere, or we don't want to put a bug in the system, eh? (Like computer talk.)

We don't want to interfere with what's working, but we do want to be able to give you the means to create in some benevolent way. To do that, you need to learn your physical body's language so that you can communicate physically, and your physical body can teach you what is benevolent for you in that moment. It can teach you what will work for you on the creative level in that moment, such as, "Would this be a good place for me to go? Would this garment be the best for me to wear?" The response being warmth, meaning yes, love for you to do that.

But if the response is discomfort, then no. There is no love for you to do that at that moment. That's how I'm interpreting it; your body doesn't use those words. Your body uses feeling, such as warmth means love. A little warmth means a little love. No warmth means, rephrase the question or ask it at another time — different garment, different place. A slight discomfort means, no, no love for that. You let that feeling go. Relax and get calm. You don't want to go into that discomfort and feel it, all right? Relax and get calm. Do something different, or do what you need to do in a different way, and ask about that.

So you're learning that language. You will simply put it into your life on the practical level, which you will do in order to build up personal trust and belief in the validity and value of doing this, which comes with practicing it and discovering its value. You will also, because of your particular interests, attempt to ask material-mastery questions utilizing that system. You will have to keep them personal. You (any student reading this who is able to do the warmth) might ask, "Is it valuable for me to learn material mastery techniques for my own well-being?" That's a material-mastery question. And you might get warmth for that, for instance. The feeling is the response. There is love. Warmth is the answer.

Then you might ask, "Are you, my body" (*my* body, not *the* body; it is always *my body*, because your body is part of you), "prepared to communicate to me in your language of feelings? Help me learn all these wonderful things you can teach me about material mastery. Are you prepared to do that in a way that is benevolent for me?" Then you will get warmth.

Perhaps if you don't get enough warmth, you might rephrase the question. You might say, "Would it be valuable and worthwhile for me to learn material-mastery lessons that you have to teach me, my body?" Then see how your body responds. Maybe over here there's some discomfort, and maybe over here there's comfort. So then you know that this part of your body says yes, but there's a problem over here. Is it that organ in your body, or is it that part of your body on the surface? You might ask that part of your body, "What are you trying to tell me?" Then you get a response.

For example, the pancreas produces the means by which you can digest food and so on, but also on the spiritual level, it regulates how much work you can do. It's the part of your body that says, "This far, no farther." So this part of your body might be saying, "If that's going to add to my work load, maybe it's too much." To use that information, ask your physical body about material mastery: "Are there ways you can teach me material mastery benevolently that will ease how I learn so that I can work in ways that are more benevolent for me?" Then, "whoosh!" a flood of warmth. Part of your body gets warm, so your physical body is saying that it can teach you how to do work in ways that are more benevolent for you. That's the process. When you can do portions of that consciously, then you can do more for others.

Help us understand. From the moment the sperm and the egg meet, there is a portion of the soul of Mother Earth helping to create this body? Is that what the Earth soul is?

Look at it in the bigger picture, yes? The sperm is coming from a physical body, and that physical body is made up of Mother Earth's body, yes? And it's going into another physical body, also made up of Mother Earth's body. So that tells you that Mother Earth's soul, the body consciousness of Mother Earth, is in anything that is physically manifested on Earth.

Oh! So it's not like a new piece comes in, it's ...

It's already present.

... already there. But it is a portion of Mother Earth's consciousness?

It's a portion of her personality. Her personality that you interact with on Earth as a spiritual student is her physical personality. Look what she can do! Look what she does with her body, the amazing things she can do. How often does a person admire a sunset? Is that not beautiful? The rain, all of the things she can do — amazing! Yet it is not always perceived that your physical body is made up of Mother Earth's physical body.

So there is not a reasoning consciousness but a feeling consciousness?

That's right. You're interacting with Mother Earth physically. And if you want to learn what she has to teach you through your physical body, which is a portion of her, you must learn her language, which is feeling. You have feelings that you might not know or understand right now, but you always have feelings. This is language from your physical body. When you can react and respond to that language — some discomfort here, some discomfort there — maybe you can say something that will help that to feel better, not just ignore it.

If you ignore it, the feeling will get more prominent or come up and reveal itself in some other way, because your physical body is communicating to you — initially in a gentle way with a physical feeling. But if it's an urgent thing that you must do, for your own desires as the immortal personality — and in the larger picture, since you came here to understand and practice material mastery, (everything that you do here including the physical and the mental and the immortal personality's desires, all of this stuff, is part of material mastery) — anything your physical body tries to communicate to you is not only something that you need to do but also something you need to understand so that you know how to do it.

Material mastery is everything working in compatibility with everything else, because it wants to, you know? "This" comes together with "that" because it wants to, that kind of thing, not just because you shove it together. All people in manufacturing know that you can put things together, but sometimes those things don't want to go together. So you need fasteners that work appropriately. But no matter how good those fasteners are, if those things don't want to go together, they're going to fall apart someday. That's why machinery becomes obsolete, not just because of new technology but because it falls apart; it wears out.

On the other hand, if that which was used to form the machinery — or let's say, the objects that produce other objects that you want, allowing the machinery to be simpler — comes together because of its own accord (it wants to come together based on your desires to produce something), it will never wear out.

How to Interpret Your Body's Response

Now, any human being on Earth can talk to his or her body in the language that it uses, and that body understands?

Yes. At the same time, any person on Earth can communicate with his or her physical body using the physical body's language of feelings. That's universal. It doesn't make any difference what language you use. Let's say that you are the material-mastery student learning and talking to your physical body. You say something, and you get warmth, but maybe part of your body feels warmth for that, but another part doesn't because it's concerned. It gives you a little pain (it passes, not permanent) to say, "Doesn't that just mean more work? And I'm already doing too much, and I don't feel good about that." Then you respond as the material-mastery student. You don't ignore the pain. You immediately respond to the part of you giving you the message of pain because you need to address something. In the case of the pancreas, the pancreas knows how much work you can do physically and how much rest you need, or how much you have to say, "This much and no more."

So you asked, "Can people on Earth speak to their bodies in their own language?" Yes, they can, because your body is going to understand your language, but you can also speak in your verbal language. However, your physical body will answer in its language, and you need to know how to interpret that. The simple way to do that, since it's not always easy to interpret every single feeling you have in your body, is to use the heart-warmth, which you can then interpret as yes or no. "The discomfort tells me that there is something here that needs to be addressed on one side of my body, and there is a warmth on the other side of my body, so I know the thing I stated is compatible with that side of my body. So the discomfort indicates that the request is not compatible with a particular part of my body."

If you as a physical spiritual student don't know what this is, then go through different questions, stating initially, "Is there something benevolent I can do to ease this discomfort in my physical body?" Notice any warmth. If you get some warmth, then there's something to do.

You might have to go through some steps. You might not even touch on it right away, but I have to remind you, especially people who work a lot (and maybe too much) that one of the first things you ask is, "Is this too much work for me to do now?" Then you ask, "Is there some easier way that you, my physical body, can teach me how to do my work that will be more benevolent and feel better to my physical body, my physical teacher, and still accomplish what I need to do?" You will feel warmth, perhaps. If it doesn't give you the warmth that you want or there is some suggestion of warmth, rephrase the question.

Ask, "Is there some means by which I can do my work more benevolently that will feel good to me in my physical body?" Maybe then you'll get the answer. You keep going around with different questions, rephrasing them until you get the heat. But you can't avoid the question. You might have to say, "Would it be better for me to do less work right now and rest, relax, eat, and generally get comfortable because this is enough work in this moment?" If you get that heat, then you know it's time to say good night.

Hmm. Are you saying good night?

[Chuckles.]

Excellent, thank you. Thank you very much.

CHAPTER SIXTEEN

You Chose to Incarnate on Earth

Creator

March 15, 2008

There is a time coming when elements of life will be incorporated in a completely different manner from what you have seen in the past. Individuality was explored in the past, so [there were] birds of various types and forms, animals (this one, that one), and human beings — different varieties, men and women, of course, but also different colors of skin, slightly different features, and so on. What is occurring is a blending of sorts, not the sort of blending that is being done by science for various reasons, albeit controversial, in genetic combinations, but a blending of spirit.

Many beings on the planet, and you are all equal, you understand, in my eyes — animals, plants, humans, and so on — are coming to the end of their time here, and they are moving off the planet in traditional ways, dying off. Yet they have wisdom and knowledge for the human being. Some can be demonstrated physically in places where the human being can see, or come to know, that there is some action needed by the human being to help animals, or other life forms, but sometimes the human being might not be conscious of species moving off the planet because contact is not typical.

To have the knowledge and wisdom needed, the keys to unlock your own knowing, you have to find a way to incorporate your instincts and connect with these beings so that communication can take place, whether verbal or nonverbal (sometimes visions, messages, or simply knowing occurs). This might happen for any person, a dream, some coordination of life, meaning you have always done something one way and suddenly you are doing it a new way, or the new way blends with the old way, and it feels even more natural than the old way.

These kinds of actions in general are taking place now so that those who have been carrying knowledge and wisdom for the human being will not be required to stay here as a form of life. This makes more room for the human being to live on the planet, although the loss of a species is unfortunate. Still, there will be ways to remember that species, and as the human being learns to welcome him- or herself (meaning other human beings) into the flow or stream of life, there will be a capability to achieve the knowledge and wisdom, the knowingness, that you so desire.

Everyone wants to know something that he or she does not know. Sometimes it is something simple, something that would improve the quality of life. Other times, it is something greater that might improve the quality of your life and the lives of others you hear about, but this knowledge is held from you so that you can desire to know it consciously. It's not so much the desire to know little things, meaning what someone is thinking, "What does she really think of me?" "What does he really want of me?" It is not that so much, though that might be a desire. It is more how it is done, how the knowingness takes place, and it is so simple.

It requires, however, that you do not in any way desire to know something if others lose by it. It has to be the desire to know for the sake of all beings. This might not be a thought. It would more likely be felt, so once you have the feeling, it will feel as something completely relaxing, comforting. It will be the general feeling of continuity but a continuity that is completely immersed in the feeling of safety and ease. It will be along those lines for everyone, physically.

This interspecies combination of spirits is how you are going to know things that need to be known, even if animal types or plant types are no longer on Earth. This will enable you to feel a sense of relief and of being well cared for. What most adults miss is that feeling. That's why love between human beings often is about that feeling, less about sexuality, though sexuality is a component. That feeling of being loved and cared for is something that is largely absent for many adults and has created many problems. It is hard to believe, but true, that a simple blending of spirits — not something you go for, so to speak, meaning "I am going to blend with the spirit of my dog or cat," but something that just occurs even for a moment — can create this feeling. You feel after that, for quite some time, that sense of being cared for, even though there wouldn't have been someone to hug you or reassure you that you are loved individually.

You Are the Future Guides

What you are into now — the totality of humanity — after having passed through that gate, is an exploration of union of species, not physically through consumption, but in the spirit world. Your total being, the true you, is not the physical person you are, though your physical shell is a loving portion of Earth that encapsulates you while you are on Earth so that you can perform and do and be as a human being to learn what you are learning here. Overall, your total being is a spirit, immortal then, and it is typical for spirits to blend in all forms in all ways in other circumstances of life — not just in other planets, but in other realms of being.

Here on Earth, to learn compassion and patience universally for all human beings and, to a more individualistic sense, lessons, you might each wish to learn on your own. You have this physical form, your bodies, to help you to learn. You are all learning for the sake of what you will do for others beyond this planet.

You are learning things that you are unable to learn elsewhere, because elsewhere in other forms of life that you exist in, you already know these things. But knowing them and understanding them are not the same. You can know something, but if you are not conscious of that knowledge because it's a portion of your day-to-day life and so integrated with the way you are, you might not think about it. It might not be conscious. It is just a portion of the creation in which you live.

But if you are training and learning something specific, as in patience and compassion, then you must have a physical form to learn that. In a world that is more individualized (meaning you live moment to moment), you are conscious of time, and you experience lessons repeatedly so as to learn that. You might experience pain not because you are being punished but so that you can someday, in some other form of life, have compassion for others who are experiencing pain and are able to help them as someone who knows rather than as someone who lectures about something for which you have no knowledge. You know that the best teachers for you are those who have knowledge of that which they teach, even though their solution might not be your solution for whatever issue.

Still, there is a feeling that passes between teacher and student — isn't there? — if the teacher knows what the student is talking about. "The teacher understands my pain," says the student. Some day you will teach just as these guides/teachers, and you will be able to help others in the universe who have not been able to receive the help, no matter how lovingly offered from others, because they are waiting to have teachers or guides who understand them. This is so important, so often unspoken by adult human beings in your now cultures but so important as a reality.

Young people understand these things, and one often hears as a parent, "Mom, you don't understand me," or "Dad, don't try to tell me; you don't understand." Parents have heard this and know it, and younger people know it too, but imagine the gulf between a teacher and a being of another form entirely, and you will teach these beings some day. While they will have a form such as you have a form now, a physical form, you will not have that form. You will be in spirit, and they will be able to hear you, but hearing is not enough. They have to feel, and you have to be able to feel as a spirit.

It is not typical on the planet now for spirits in communion with human beings to broadcast feelings, but that is exactly what is needed to communicate with these beings. You will be able to broadcast not something that will cause the human being to be uncomfortable but something that humans will recognize as a feeling they have, or have had, because of their pain, physical or emotional. Thus, that's how the connection will be made, and those beings who have been unable to hear, unable to react, no matter how loving the teacher, no matter how patient, will be able to hear or feel. Thus, as the teaching continues, they will act and react in ways benevolent for themselves and others. This has been done over and over in similar situations, places, and times. You are in training for this on this planet, now on Earth.

Much of your lives on this planet have to do with teaching or learning. Sometimes it happens on your own. You have an experience with something, and uh-oh, you can't do it that way anymore. You trip over something, "Ouch, I have to watch where I am going." Other times, people teach you about things, or you teach others on the basis of the experience. I am here today to remind you of this, to give you something to think about as you live your life.

I am not speaking of dreams so much, where you are seeing yourself swimming in the ocean with dolphins or whales, for example. I am speaking of something that is universal in nonhuman life on this Earth, meaning those feelings I indicated, knowing you are loved, knowing you are needed, and knowing you belong. That kind of feeling usually welcomes babies when they are born and loved by mother and father, but that almost universally in your now human cultures evaporates the older you get. You need those specific feelings now more than at any other time.

Animals and plants have those feelings all the time. Thus, your connection on a spirit level with these beings is essential. I have come here today — you know me as Creator — to remind you of these things so that you can understand your lives more.

It's good for you to be able to see animals in the wild, but if you don't have that opportunity often, then you might have to see whatever presents itself. You might see a bird fly by. It might be momentary. You might see a beetle crawl across a wall. You might see a fly zoom across the room. Why do they linger? Don't assume that just because they crawl or fly, that which you call insects, are there to bother you. They might be there bravely to remind you of those feelings missing in the human being. So welcome them, if you can.

If you are living near water, be more conscious of water life, fish, and so on. They are not simply there to be food for you. They are there to remind you of those feelings you are missing because they have them. They are not missing them. You might be able to just go out on the lake, paddle out, and if there are fish there, don't bring a fishing rod. It will make them nervous. They will just paddle out on the lake and sit there quietly. After a while, they might come to the surface.

If they don't, then talk to them. Don't use the term "fish." Just speak out loud and look at the water, and say, "Would you come up to the surface" (or would you be close to the surface) "so that I can feel your feelings?" It is not their job to feel your feelings as human beings, but it is your job to be able to feel their feelings, if possible. If you are unable to be where animals are or even where plants are, then try to remember animals and plants, or ask someone to bring a potted plant for you. Even plants that are potted and raised by human beings have this feeling. However, a plant in the wild growing on its own will have more feelings because of the freedom of its being as well as the welcoming the land has tended, that it can grow there and be supported by Earth's offerings of rain and so on.

Act and React Benevolently

It is a time for you to encompass the true qualities you have. You have the opportunity to solve the world's problems now, but you must incorporate those feelings so that you do not turn a blind eye to the sufferings of others — plants, animals, earth, or your fellow human beings (not in that order, but in a consistency, meaning to feel, to know, to care) — because you sometimes feel uncomfortable. Some of you might think that this means you are becoming sick, but very often, you are being reminded that other human beings near you are feeling uncomfortable for some reason. Say a prayer for them to feel better. Ask not only that you be relieved of your momentary uncomfortable feelings but also that all who have those feelings be relieved of them as well, and it will help.

You can be many things on this planet, but it is very important that you be able to act and react toward your fellow human beings benevolently. You will not be able to do this strictly because you have a moment of altruism. You might have to have all forms of life other than human beings, but even human beings, when you are very young and sometimes when you are very old, will have to have those feelings replenished on a moment-to-moment basis.

The animals and the plants have volunteered to replenish those feelings with you on the spirit level. Ask them to share those feelings with you. Talk to a tree. Talk to a bird. Talk to ants as they move across the ground. Don't expect them to stop and stare at you, though one or more might. Keep your distance from them. Do not interfere with their lives, but ask them, "Would you mind if I feel some of those feelings?" and then just pause. Try not to think. You can sit down if you like, and if you feel something, it might be calming. It might make you happy. They might cause a tear, but it will be like food, the food that has been missing from your lives.

When you come to the end of this, or even now as you are reading, lay back, rest, and remember, if you can, those feelings. Then seek out a plant or an animal, especially animals that are free, that are living their own lives. Pets might not always be able to do this because they are engaged so much with you or with other human beings.

Pick a plant that grows on its own. A weed, as you call it, is best because weeds are free and not cultured and tended by human beings, such as your lawn. Or choose an animal that happens to be going by. If you are in the country, try to pick a deer that you happen to see.

The animals don't have to be close. They can be at a distance. It can be a mountain lion or a bear, though many people do not see those in nature. But many of you will see animals, maybe a coyote, at a distance as long as they are free. They don't have to stop, but just talk to them, even if you see them for a moment — hawks, eagles, whatever you see in the country. Try not to pick so-called domesticated animals — cows, chickens, and so on. They are not living the natural life they would live if they were not associated so directly with the human being and your activities. This is what to do. This is what I recommend. Good night!

Oh, no questions?

✳ ✳ ✳

Beings Who Volunteered for the Earth Project
Creator's Emissary

Greetings! I am a being who works with Creator. You can ask me questions. Creator is otherwise occupied. But keep them only to this, okay?

There has been this consistent phenomenon in all of the animals and plants that we have talked to through Robert's channeling, that an emissary of Creator came to them, in a way that they could see and hear and understand, and asked them to participate in this experiment on Earth [see the Explorer Race series, Plant Souls Speak and Animal Souls Speak, Light Technology Publishing 2007 and 2011]. Are you one such emissary?

Yes.

Did you go to any of these beings and ask them to inhabit, or embody, these creations on Earth as animals or plants?

Yes. Something else that might interest you is that I went to certain cultures, not all, on other planets and asked them in their travels, of human beings, you understand? There is human life beyond earth though it might not always be exactly the same, not precisely, as your own physical makeup. I did go to a certain culture and ask them that in their travels — if they felt drawn to being a portion of the Earth project, would they consider being volunteers to establish life on Earth as the human sort of being.

Oh, that's how we got all these different ... ? Go on! Go on!

That's right, exactly as your enthusiastic response. That's how you got all of the different types of human beings for which a certain minor degree of biology creates a difference, yet you are all quite clearly human beings, because the mix of human beings is what is required for Earth to be able to assimilate the knowledge and wisdom and, in time, blend into one form of being that would not normally have come into being as a human. These cultures and races of human beings from other planets would not normally come into contact with each other, and even if they had initially when they populated Earth, they would not have felt drawn to each other. They would not have wanted to create a hybrid human being that would eventually come about as a result of there simply being many types of human beings on Earth now. But you can see it happening now.

"This" race is attracted to "that" race, or "this" culture or nationality is attracted to "that," and that will be an ongoing situation, which Creator desires. It has taken this long because everyone had to learn basic lessons that the human being is learning on Earth. Volunteers also needed to assimilate as much of their individual spirit's lessons, so that they would be on Earth but essentially have a feeling of anticipation, meaning, they are on Earth, but why? You very often find with people interested in spirituality the number one question is, "Why am I here?" So that feeling of anticipation is entirely about the blending of humanity to become ultimately one form, not one race.

Not that everybody is going to be white or black, not that, but a homogenization, so to speak, where everyone gradually blends on the basis of mutual attraction, one to another. Gradually you will see an emergence of forms of life that become predominant on Earth, not through struggle and strife, but through love. This form of life will begin to take place in certain unique ways, giving signals that something new and different is occurring.

Right now, you are seeing one of the signals that is happening with children who are considered to be different to the point of discomfort. These children, while they don't speak much (do not seem to communicate well) seem to be able to communicate with each other without speaking. They have developed ways of communicating with each other that appear to be telepathic or through certain hand motions.

Also, their brains are different. They actually function differently.

Yes, and one sees this. This is one of the signals that the blending of human beings is ongoing and intentional. It's not intended to be done scientifically but rather through natural love, people falling in love with each other, wanting to be together, wanting to be committed together, and raising their families naturally. So it will be a process that will take place over the next three or four generations. Certain types of beings will, as human beings, begin to emerge, and they will have capabilities that are more in alignment with your natural spiritual personalities.

That is absolutely wonderful. We are creating something totally new.

For Earth, this is actually more of what you would see on the personality level visiting human cultures in other places.

We'll only meet humans for the first couple hundred years?

You will probably only meet humans, or beings who remind you of humans, for the first few years, however long it might be, until you get to the point that you realize everything and everyone you are meeting is a form of life that you are meant to meet. The irony of this, of course, is that after this space exploration goes on, you will look at the animals on Earth in an entirely different way. You will realize that they are truly forms of life on other planets, which is why Creator looks at animals and plants and human beings as equals. You are all forms of life that live in other places on other planets, and as the astronauts or cosmonauts discover this, they will report back to their civilizations and cultures, and it will come to be common knowledge in time. Thus, when you see a bird fly by, you will begin to say, "Oh, I wonder whether they're from this planet." [Laughs.]

[Laughs.] Yes.

You will no longer say, "Oh, it's a robin" or "It's a bluebird."

Creator Blends with the Immortal Personality

Now, you can clear up another thing. When immortal personalities come to this planet, they inhabit physical bodies, but within those bodies, they are "ensleeved" — or please give me a better word if there is one — by a portion of the Creator.

"Sleeved?" I am not sure what you mean by that.

An immortal personality comes into Earth and inhabits a body. But around that is a portion of the Creator in some way. How does that work?

It's not unlike coffee or tea. In that sense, when you pour the coffee or tea into the cup, you might add cream or sugar, and there is a blending. You don't wrap the cream around the coffee. You don't insert the sugar inside the center of the coffee. It blends like that. That's how it works.

Okay. When that immortal personality leaves and the body is no longer functional, then what happens? Does the portion that belongs to the Creator separate from the immortal personality?

The only way that would occur is if you left the universe.

Oh, as long as you are in this universe.

Oh yes, because Creator created this universe, and in order for you to no longer be associated with the creator of this universe, you would have to move to another universe.

So this blending doesn't just happen when incarnating on Earth. It happens when incarnating anywhere in the universe.

Yes, just imagine the universe as a cup of coffee with cream and sugar, eh? [Laughs.]

Ah! So then what happens when we leave the universe at some point to go play somewhere else? Then what?

If you do, and that's a big *if*, then you either take some of that with you, as it is allowed, or you simply move from one creation to another, meaning like a bridge. You might go out of this creation and create yourself, meaning start something on your own. When you do that, you usually take some of the energy of the creation in which you had been, but if for some reason (and this happens rarely but [does occur] now and then) you move beyond this universe to some other universe created by another creator, then the same process takes place. You shed what you had been a portion of and move, if we can continue my analogy, from coffee to tea.

I see. So some of the beings that we've talked to who have been invited into this universe by the Creator for the purpose of coming to Earth and incarnating as animals or plants will go back to their original homes when this is done, won't they?

If they're from another universe, yes. It does not mean that, say, a pine tree would go to another universe, meaning as an individual pine tree. It would, after ceasing its existence on Earth, return to its home planet (if it cared to) as a spirit. It would be somewhere in this universe. That might be a long way off, but it would be somewhere in this universe.

Most of the beings who came from other creations have sort of a second home here in this universe somewhere as a stopping point before they came to Earth, right?

If they had some other home. Most of them did not come from other universes.

Oh, I thought a lot of them did. A lot of them seem ...

If they say they do, then they do, but the bulk of them are associated with life in this universe.

So you are part of the Creator. Do you have your own individual, well, nobody is individual, but ... ?

The difference between us is I remember who I am, and I am not in form, such as you. That's really the only difference. If you are not in form, you remember who you are and that you are also a portion of the Creator. Even so, you are still a portion of the Creator now, but you don't remember who you are in totality so that you can be the human being on Earth.

All right. What would you like to tell the people reading this?

Only this. You understand I am here exclusively because you said "questions." So I didn't come here to tell the readers anything.

Well then, whatever you want to say.

As an emissary, I have personally been involved in inviting certain groups of humans to Earth. You reading this now are in the lives you are in associated with extraterrestrial life. It might be hard to imagine, since some of you can trace your families back for a few hundred years, but going back many, many thousands of years and beyond, those ancient ancestors all came from other planets.

I personally was involved in inviting some of the most ancient explorers who were in human form to Earth. I can recall going to the Sirius star system and speaking to people with dark skin. These peoples like to travel in their own galaxy, and most of them did not have an interest in traveling beyond that galaxy. Still, there were a few volunteers. As is often found in any culture, there are always a few adventurers who are prepared to go over the crest of the sea, so to speak, and explore worlds beyond. Those beings chose to do that on the basis of my request, speaking for Creator.

I also spoke to another group of people, loosely referred to, as you say in the West, the Asian people. These people came from another star system far away, Arcturus, and some from Andromeda. As a result, they also had some adventurers who came to Earth and settled here and there.

Other emissaries invited other human beings. All the emissaries from Creator and all the beings —adventurers who chose to come to Earth and are your ancestors — know that there is no human being on Earth who cannot trace their roots back to other star systems as well as other planets. If you know that, you will recognize that your coming together was brought about by those adventurers from the past who chose to say, "Yes, I will. I will do this, because this project, this Explorer Race, this genetic experiment on Earth, thrills and excites me. I feel welcome to join, and I am enthusiastic to build a new society."

Good life!

Thank you very, very much. Good night!

CHAPTER SEVENTEEN

The Soul Is a Student of Life Experiences

Zoosh

April 16, 2008

What's happening?

Well, I want to make a brief comment about souls and their passage from one life to another. It is true that when the soul leaves the body, the essence of the personality goes with the soul, meaning that the soul doesn't leave without the personality. But the accumulation that helped to define and change that personality in the physical life of that person — meaning the body, and so on, everything that the person has gone through, all of that — stays with the physical body. In this way, when the walk-in takes place and the new soul arrives, it doesn't arrive completely disoriented. The new soul would not bring anything other than the essence of its own personality and soul. Without there being some essence of the exiting soul left for the new soul, the new soul wouldn't have any means to cope with the world it finds itself in.

The new soul wouldn't be able to tie its shoelaces or know which end of the pencil to hold. In short, the new soul has to have that knowledge and experience in the physical body in order to function. The fact that the physical personality is totally colorized by the life experience of that person, that birth soul, just happens to go with the package. So it is not surprising that the soul that comes in — while it is very clear that it is completely different — for a short time the experience of the personality in the body, the life experience, immediately looks for, "What is this new thing? What is it about?" It starts thinking and starts adapting, and before you know it, that new soul, the walk-in soul, is caught up in attempting to figure out who it is.

So in some ways, this is a good thing. The soul comes in not only to discover who it is in relation to this world but also in the course of looking for who it is to identify and to apply the characteristics that it brings in, in terms of talents and propensities and so on. The search to discover who you are is not a bad thing, because that's how the accumulated personality and the new soul align to discover the new talents of that new soul (walk-in), meaning new to the old physical personality.

This is important to walk-ins, especially for those people who don't know they're walk-ins but just know that something radical has changed. Their personalities have changed, and they suddenly discover (1) they can do things that they could never do before, and (2) they have interests that don't compare to anything that they've had before and a lot of subtleties around that, meaning nuances. Also, there will likely be some interests that they used to have that they don't feel as strongly about, and those things tend to fade in terms of holding their attention. You know, for instance, a person might have been an avid golfer, and after the walk-in comes in, the person is still interested in golf, but it's not quite as a major influence in the life. Just use that sport as an example.

The Soul Knows Who It Is

Now, the confusion comes when the new soul does not know how to resolve something. The new soul comes in and has a great deal of knowledge and wisdom and talents and so on, but of course, it doesn't have any Earth-type street smarts. So the walk-in soul must rely on the accumulated knowledge of the physical personality's street smarts in order to know how to get along or to know which end of the pencil to grab, so to speak. This, of course, comes with the whole package of everything the previous personality was. Also, the sense of your personal self, your personal identity — who you see yourself to be — isn't quite as urgent as it used to be.

Most people have an urgent sense to know, "Who am I? Why am I here? What am I supposed to be doing?" Now, I grant that there are times when this is not of particular interest, but there are other times when it comes up. There's also a tendency to just shrug it off and say, "I don't know" or "God knows" or "That's enough for me." And while that might be so, God has also placed you here, allowed you to come, so it's okay to look. Given that, the difference is that when those moments come up — the feeling of finding out who you are, the need to know who you are — they will not be as strong as they once were.

That is because that new soul and the essence of that new soul's personality knows who it is. This is a fine point, but it's an important one.

So the walk-in needs to keep the basic talents of how to be a human — how to tie one's shoes, use the computer, whatever ... ?

Yes.

The struggle, then, is to assert one's own personality when the personality traits that you inherited are particularly strong. What are some ways to do that?

No. I don't agree with you. You are saying that it would be good to assert your personality over the other personality. No. When you come in as the walk-in, you are the student, the Accumulated Personality — let's use that as a term, capital A, capital P — of the exiting soul's physical body is the teacher. Don't try to assert it with authority, which you don't have when you come in, because you come in with the idea of being a student. "What can I discover?" That would be your number one question, if you had words in your head — if you, the walk-in soul — had a head. [Laughs.]

Your number one question would be, "What can I discover?" Of course, the first thing you're looking for is a teacher, and the Accumulated Personality is your first teacher. So, no, don't try to assert your authority, when, in fact, you know almost nothing about living on Earth, wherever you are. Rather, the important thing to do is be observant, and when the Accumulated Personality (the personality you've inherited) begins to do something that it doesn't really feel — maybe it's to do something or to change something, or maybe it's to do something that is innocuous, something mundane, something ordinary — like it wants to do that anymore, maybe you want to do that differently, or maybe you want to do something else entirely.

When you catch yourself in those moments, say, "Well, I'm open to doing that differently." That's all, but it isn't your job to say, "No, don't do it that way anymore! Now I'm going to do it this way." Authoritarianism is something you do not come in with, and while the old personality might have that, the old personality will very likely feel the truth of that, the physical truth of that, like it really doesn't feel like something it wants to do anymore. "Okay, I'll try it this way." No matter how rigid a person with that Accumulated Personality is, no matter how rigid the traits have become, which I am not saying they do, but in some cases, that feeling would predominate in time. "Well, okay, I'm not interested in that anymore. I'm going to do it 'this' way." You see, that's the better way. Don't try to come in and be the boss.

Well, after several years, do some of the Accumulated Personality traits fall away and one can express one's own self more?

They don't fall away on their own. They fall away when you have something that you do that works better than what you used to do, not necessarily that the outcome is better. For instance, you're a carpenter, and you decide to cut to the inside of the line as compared to the outside of the line; carpenters know what I'm talking about. I'm sure they do. Regardless of that, regardless of the precision, it's not that so much; rather, it's little things you do in your day-to-day life.

Maybe you never went to the greengrocer's before, all right? Maybe you asked somebody else to do that because you were too busy. Suddenly the idea of going to the greengrocer's is wonderful, and you see your friends and neighbors there. They're surprised to see you, and before you know it, you have friends you see when you go to the grocer's. In short, what happens is that the new things that you're doing feel better, and even though the way you did it in the past might not have been wrong, the new way feels better, and that's how those traits fall away.

Ah! As you create new ones.

As you use them. You're interested, you know, "What can I discover?" Then, "I discovered that I love going to the greengrocer's" and "Hey, it's fun to see most of my neighbors. Wow, this is wonderful!" In short, those old rationales that kept you from going to the grocer's (using this example here, nothing about grocery stores, but just as an example of something people often do), those old rationales that kept you from going there just don't seem very important anymore. And while you might have wanted to go to the grocer's in the past, because you had built up certain traits and people knew you a certain way, you felt again, another reluctance. "Well, I don't want to break my habits, or people are going to ask me why. And I don't want to deal with that."

So people get caught up in personality traits that they've had for a long time simply because they don't want people to question them about their personality traits. But when a walk-in comes in, you don't care about that anymore. It's like, "Oh, you're at the greengrocer's. What's going on?" Then you just simply say, "Wow, I just discovered this is fun," and then they accept that. You don't need to give them a twenty-page essay on the answer to their question. It's like, "Oh! I'm not going to say why." The end. On you go! Be open to doing things differently, but be alert to your impulses. "How do I want to do this?"

Now, it's also possible that the new soul coming in might be naive. So it's the Accumulated Personality's job to keep you from doing something that would be an error, but not so much to the point where you stop yourself from doing things that are new simply because, you know, "What would people think?" Even that whole idea of "what will people think?" which is a powerful motivation for a lot of people, just falls away. The desire to do things in a new way, even though they might seem naive to some people, will often lead to something that is benevolent for you.

But you know, you're not going to jump off a cliff and say, "Hey, I can fly." The new soul is not going to do anything like that. For the most part, the things that will change will be your interaction with life forms, meaning how you interact with plants, animals, and human beings — not necessarily in that order.

So that's the main thing that's going to go on. For example, the old soul is a terrible driver, and then the new soul comes in and is a cautious driver. Most likely you will start driving cautiously. People will ask, "What happened?" You'll say, "I want to notice my surroundings more." You'll come up with a perfectly reasonable answer. You slow down. "I want to see where I am going. When I see a beautiful tree, I want to stop." You don't have to have a camera along to rationalize that. "I want to stop and enjoy the beauty" or "I saw my friend by the side of the road, and he was carrying these bags of groceries. I stopped to give him a ride. I used to whiz right by him and not think about it. I don't do that anymore." Like that! Don't make it too hard.

That explains what you said before, that it's easier to do new things than try to change old things.

That's right. It all fits, doesn't it?

It fits.

Good night!

Good night!

Good Life

Reveals the Mysteries

Date Unknown

Now that you have read this book (some of you having read more than others) and have had a chance to think about it and consider it, over the next few years, the application of what is offered here will be invaluable for some of you. For those of you who do not identify with it yet, know that it is offered as a support system should you find you personally need it or that it is at least helpful to advise you in terms of what is going on.

The realities of life, as you have noticed simply by living in these modern times, are becoming increasingly complicated. Most of your souls were not born for such complications. Rather, they were born to function on a planet in societies, cultures, families, and communities, if you like, that are changing, transitioning.

On a practical level, many of you can look around and count off ten, fifteen, or more points that represent radical change from how things were when you were young to how they are now. Some of those changes might be considered good; others might simply be considered to have so much complication with them that you find yourself full of overwhelming emotion all the time. Just because you have that feeling does not mean you will become a walk-in, but it is one of the important signs to let you know that you *might* find that you will depart as the exiting soul, and another soul who is more prepared to live in such complicated times will come in. It will be a benevolent process for you personally and all others associated with it.

It is important to note this not only because there are going to be terrible things or complicated things happening in the future but also that an adjustment to the times sometimes becomes so complicated that there needs to be a means, spiritually from love and Creator, to allow such an adjustment to happen in the most benevolent and loving way possible. So don't think this suggests that you have somehow failed or that some invasion of strange ETs are taking over, not that at all. Rather, Creator loves you all, wants you to have fulfilling lives, and does not want you to be overwhelmed by life on Earth. As a result, Creator always provides for you to have the most loving and fulfilling lives wherever you are living — with your loved ones or with loved ones who are waiting for you.

Don't worry about it. Just live your life as well as possible, and Creator will look after you. This has always been the way, and now as these days go by and life seems to turn into something that is not what you expected years ago when you were born or when you were raised, there is more waiting for you elsewhere.

Your departure as a soul can be simple. Perhaps you'll just go to sleep at night (your body, you understand, will be asleep), and you'll just move on. Perhaps the soul will come in and life will go on for that family, that culture, or that community, of which you are a part. Know this: As these changes come, they are all intended by Creator, and the motion through these changes sometimes will require the walk-in process to create smoothness for all beings and for the planet herself.

I hope you enjoyed this book. Have a good life wherever you may go.

Appendixes

Excerpts from other Light Technology Publishing books or monthly metaphysical magazine
Sedona Journal of Emergence! *articles by beings who spoke through Robert Shapiro that relate to and may be helpful to walk-ins.*

Long Touch - A Beginning

Robert Shapiro

October 31 2005

There are many reasons to include Benevolent Magic and Living Prayer in your life. They're also other capacities you have, and I'd like to give you a little training on that now. Many of you have indicated your interest.

I'd like you to lie down, if you can, someplace comfortable for you and look up at your ceiling. This needs to be a ceiling that you cannot reach, so if you have a bed that sits up high, it's better to lie down on something where you cannot reach the ceiling.

Now I want you to relax as best you can, but to stay alert, and once you feel relaxed, then look up at the ceiling. I would recommend that light fixtures be off unless it is at night (then the light can be on). Look up either into a corner of the ceiling or if there is some object on the ceiling, say a ceiling fan or something (but the electricity is not on and the fan is not moving) that can be the object you look at. If you are not sure, just look at a corner of the ceiling.

Then I'd like you to reach up with your right hand — obviously you will not be able to touch the ceiling, but I'd like you to follow the contours of the ceiling or the object on the ceiling by just keeping your eyes open and imagining that you are touching that area. Now reach — don't stretch your arm, but reach as if it were possible to touch that part of the ceiling and move your fingers along the contours of the shape. Imagine what it would be like to touch that — you can imagine that and see if you can get to the point where you almost feel — it will be like an imagination and a touch, so it will be an almost feeling eh of touching that thing.

That's all the homework on that for today. I'm giving you your beginnings of long touch homework and long touch capability. I know many of you would like to explore and see beyond your world. The purpose for this long touch is to be able to create a basis for seeing beyond your world, and in order to enjoy that feeling, you will have to have other capabilities. This is one of them. There is more that goes with this, and this is a foundational element of a much broader application of your capabilities. There are spiritual safeguards built into this. One, however, you must make the effort on yourself. That is, I do not recommend that you reach for a human being or even an animal at this point because they will have personal energies that will probably not be compatible with you as you open up a bit spiritually to develop this capability that you have.

I will give you more in these lessons as time goes on. Thank you for your interest. Goodlife to you all and goodnight. For more on this topic, go to http://benevolentmagic.blogspot.com.

A Lesson in Benevolent Magic

Zoosh

All right, Zoosh speaking. Let's start off with benevolent magic. It is time to take a conscious, aware step toward changing your reality. It has been useful in the past to experience what exists, then unconsciously change it or work with it. Now one cannot wait any longer for changes to occur.

I'm going to suggest what to do about changing your reality. If you are around children, this will be easier. If you are not around children, then you will have to wait for your opportunities. Your opportunities are as follows.

When people around you are laughing, cheerful, happy or joyful, simply take note of it and observe from a distance. If you are involved, note your cheerfulness, your laughter, and be that quite sincerely. If you are observing, however, look at the happy people, especially if they are laughing just for fun or because they heard an amusing story or because, being children, they are having a good time. Focus on it, then turn away and look at something else. Try to look at a neutral scene such as trees, the sidewalk, cars — whatever is available — and stay in that feeling of joy.

What is going on in your society all the time are moments of joy and happiness, but these moments of joy and happiness are bursts of happiness, yes? They are not sufficient to sustain benevolence for you all anymore, so I'd like you to begin to spread it around. After you have glanced quickly at it, notice that it cheers you up. It is especially important to smile at it if it cheers you up. Then look at something neutral, and if you can, glance back to the cheerful scene and again look at something neutral. Hopefully, it will be something in your environment that you see every day. Now, this will not work if you are looking at a movie or a television program. The emotion has to be demonstrated by *living people.*

If you can, then look at something that is either unpleasant or that usually annoys you, and you will notice that it doesn't annoy you as much. This is not a profound revelation. You all know that if you look at something that annoys you while you are laughing, it usually doesn't annoy you as much. This is a way of becoming consciously involved in that process so that you are like a farmer — you are reaping the excess happiness. You are not draining it from people; you are just an observer. It's just like picking an apple off a tree that has many apples; one will not be missed.

Look at something that might be annoying or is usually annoying for a moment, and don't dwell on it. Notice that it doesn't annoy you as much. When you can do this around your home, ultimately things that annoy you — even if people aren't around laughing — will not annoy you so much.

This is really a way of seeing your world and making it different. It is simple. You will not remember to do it all the time, but when you do, it might be something to experiment with. Consider it an experiment, because we will build on this later. It is interesting to note that the electronic media (such as television) are not something you can draw energy from. It has to be people. It can be people laughing at the television, but it must be people. It can be people laughing at something on the radio, but it cannot be pulled *from* the TV or the radio. If you do that, you will simply pull the electromagnetic radiation and not feel very good.

It is not that there is an immediate crisis, but there is a tendency now to become overinvolved in the dramatic. The dramatic is there to catch your attention, to relieve you of the need to create dramas of your own. But it is necessary to begin making an effort to change your reality, not through your will, but through a conscious effort to utilize the excess joy. There is not a crisis. I just want you to begin to do this.

Benevolent Magic for Walk-Ins

Grandfather

All right, this is Grandfather. Now, I need to make something clear in case it hasn't been said before. For those of you who've been involved in saying and performing benevolent magic or living prayer for yourselves, if you find that you've had a walk-in, you will discover that anything you've said in the line of benevolent magic or living prayer that effects you will still be in effect as long as it has to do with your physical body and your physical surroundings — your physical interactions with your world.

Now, the only thing that will change after the walk-in has to do with your soul — what your soul came in to do, what your soul wants to do — but that's all. To discover what your soul wants to do, you can say a living prayer or benevolent magic to encourage that to happen.

Please never say a benevolent magic or living prayer to encourage something for your soul with the term "speedy" or "as fast as you can" or anything like that. You want it to take as long as possible. After all, your soul comes in to experience life here on Earth with all that it has to offer, and there's no point in starting your soul off by giving it the rush act.

All right, good life.

The Love-Heat
(Heart-Warmth) Exercise

Robert Shapiro

I am giving what we're calling the love-heat exercise in a way that Speaks of Many Truths taught me how to do it. Take your thumb and rub it very gently across your fingertips for about half a minute or a minute. And while you do that, don't do anything else. Just put your attention on your fingertips. Close your eyes and feel your thumb rubbing slowly across your fingertips. Notice that when you do that, it brings your *physical* attention into that part of your body. Now you can relax and bring that same physical attention anywhere inside your chest — not just where your heart is, but anywhere across your chest, your solar plexus area or abdomen — and either generate or look for a physical warmth that you can actually feel.

Take a minute or two or as long as you need to find that warmth. When you find it, go into that feeling of warmth and feel it more, just stay with it. Stay with that feeling of warmth. Feel it for a few minutes so you can memorize the method, and most importantly, so your body can create a recollection, a physical recollection of how it feels and how it needs to feel for you. The heat might come up in different parts of your body — maybe one time in the left of your chest, maybe another time in the right of your abdomen or other places around there. Wherever you feel it, just let it be there. Don't try to move it around — that's where it's showing up in that moment. Always when it comes up and you feel the warmth, go into it and feel it more.

Make sure you do this when you are alone and quiet, not when you are driving a car or doing anything that requires your full attention. After you do the warmth for five minutes or so (if you can) or for as long as you can do it, then relax. And afterward, think about this: The warmth is the physical evidence of loving yourself. Many of you have read for years about how we need to love ourselves, but in fact, the method is not just saying, "I love myself," or doing other mental exercises that are helpful to give you permission to love yourself. Rather, the actual physical experience of loving yourself is in this manner, and there are things you can do that are supportive of it. But in my experience and the way I was taught, this is the method you can most easily do.

The heat will tend to push everything out of you that is not of you or that is not supporting you, because the heat, as the physical experience of loving yourself, also unites you with Creator. It unites you with the harmony of all beings, and it will tend to create a greater sense of harmony with all things. You might notice as you get better at this and can do it longer that should you be around your friends or other people, they might feel more relaxed around you, or situations might become more harmonious. Things that used to bother or upset you don't bother you very much because the heat creates an energy not only of self-love but of harmony. Remember that the harmony part is so important. You might also notice that animals will react differently to you — maybe they'll be more friendly, perhaps they'll be more relaxed, or maybe they'll look at you in a different way. Sometimes you'll be surprised at what animals, even the smallest — such as a grasshopper, a beetle, a butterfly, a bird — might do because you're feeling this heat.

Because it is love energy, it naturally radiates just as light comes out of a light bulb. Remember, you don't throw the heat out, even with the best of intentions. You don't send it to people. If other people are interested in what you are doing or why they feel better around you, you can teach them how to do this love-heat exercise in the way you learned or the way that works best for you. And the most important thing to remember is that this method of loving yourself and generating harmony for yourself creates harmony for others, because you are in harmony. Remember that this works well and will provide you with a greater sense of ease and comfort in your life no matter who you are, where you are, what you are doing or how you're living your life. It can only improve your experience. The love-heat exercise is something that is intended to benefit all life, and in my experience, it does benefit my life.

One Way to Know You're a Walk-In

Robert: I noticed I was having a memory. I don't remember what of right now. When I have a memory, I get pictures sometimes; usually I get pictures. And I noticed that the picture was in a particular location. I think it was, you know, in front of me or to the side of me or something. I don't remember exactly, but it goes into that here, briefly.

Then I purposely tried to remember something that I know was in the distant past, and that picture showed up in a different place, a different location from my perspective of the moment, the physical direction that I was looking. I wondered whether that was a way of telling that someone was a walk-in or not. Then this channeling proceeded.

✳ ✳ ✳

"Time" Travel
Grandfather

Here is more on how to know whether you are a walk-in. Now, generally speaking, when you have recollections and there are pictures associated with them in your mind — when those pictures are localized, when you see the image localized physically in front of you — that would suggest that you are looking at something that is not your own physical memory. Rather, it is a memory associated with the physical impact on your body of seeing it.

You would have looked at it, perhaps, with one of your guides or teachers

239

present when you were in observation. It also, of course, means that you would have gone back in time to do that. That might seem to be a Herculean possibility, living in the world of time as one knows it here, but in reality, this would take place before you had walked in, as a soul with your guides and teachers and so on. Time is no longer a physical attraction, and one can move from one point of it to another with ease.

Now, on the other hand, if the recollection you are having involves an image that seems to show up on your left, generally speaking, this refers to an image associated with your soul in your now body. So this is just an opening remark (Robby having a memory of himself as a child, noting that the memory was in front of him, and then trying to have a memory in which he was certain he was present, meaning it was something in recent times). This is something I'm adding so that you can try it for yourself.

Good life. This is Grandfather.

Chocolate and Walk-Ins

Grandfather

There is an element in chocolate that calms a soul. The reason I bring it up is that it is the ideal thing for walk-ins to consume for at least the first six weeks. After that, it is a matter of personal taste.

Grandfather.

Welcome!

Greetings! Now, this is particularly relevant to people who are aware of being walk-ins, and even for those who are going through a spiritual crisis, who can feel (if they are spiritually aware) their souls, or their personalities, trying to get out of their bodies. "Get me out of here! End the experience!" Chocolate is a calming agent.

It's not unknown, certainly, to candymakers, but it is also not unknown to people who have looked into this. Scientists have looked into this, social scientists as well, and it's been discussed quite widely. But what hasn't been discussed much is the fact that there is something in chocolate, not something that can be chemically classified, that has the effect of calming the soul. Now, there is some confusion about that, even off Earth.

There is a belief off Earth in some communities that chocolate interferes in the spiritual process, and to put that to rest, I will simply say that's true on other planets but not on Earth. So it's really important to understand that those of you who might have read that Pleiadians in contact with Earth people in the past have suggested that they avoid "this" or "that" food, one of them being chocolate, this is true on the Pleiades and other places but not on Earth, because what it does on Earth is to calm the soul in the soul's grounding in Earth. So it doesn't just ground you. You have to ground yourself as a result of being on Earth when you are just born on Earth. But it is particularly useful when you are a walk-in.

Now, some of you might come in from the Pleiades or some place where it is well known (or even philosophically understood) that "this and that" food or "this and that" intake might interfere with connecting spiritually. If you think that way, believe that, or are associated with that, then you might come in with an abhorrence to chocolate as a consumable and even wince in its presence. But if you know (and it's my intention to make this clear to you now) that the consumption of chocolate in any form now (not artificial, all right) — the reason I say "in any form" is it can be dark chocolate or it can be milk chocolate, okay, that kind of thing; it can be chocolate with nuts, but I recommend just chocolate on its own, meaning as a candy — then you will be able to eat a piece or two and feel comforted.

You will feel comfort within the first two to three minutes at the most, and you will notice it. You will calm down. Now, I know if you eat more of it, it has that stimulating aspect to it, and you will become less calm. But if you eat just one or two pieces (small bits you understand, not tiny amounts, but little squares maybe), then you will feel better.

Are there any other foods that have that effect?

I believe the only food is chocolate. It is the only one that has that effect.

Chocolate and the Soul

How does chocolate, which is a physical substance, affect the soul? What's the connection? What is the interaction?

It is hard to describe it, because you are looking for something mechanical. You want a chemical answer, perhaps.

Would a vibration lead to that?

You know when you add fertilizer to the soil of plants? I am not talking about the liquid you might spray on or near the roots or something but rather when you mix it into the soil. It's like that. It is a combination of qualities and experiences that welcomes the soul, calms the soul, allowing it to relax and experience the process in the case of a walk-in or experience the process in the case of a natural birth or even, to a lesser degree, a hospital birth. That will allow the soul to relax, let go, and allow the process of assimilating into the life form in which you are contained as compared to your previous experience being in spirit or being in some other world. It allows and supports that process. That is why I say it calms the soul, but it is a combination of factors. So chocolate in that sense is like a catalyst. You understand the meaning of that, "catalyst"? It forms a "catalytic" act, if that's a word. There's a catalytic action whereas it simply, by its presence, eases your way.

So as a walk-in for the first five to six weeks, if you can, eat chocolate. Try. And for a child, if the child is having a hard time with physical life, check with your doctor, but if the doctor says it's okay, give the child a little bit of chocolate. Just break off a tiny piece, put it on the child's tongue, and see what happens. I am not trying to be a doctor here, but I am saying that it could benefit the child. This is particularly important if children are colicky, as it is called, meaning the child cries all the time, and there is no apparent reason.

Often colic is a spiritual discomfort. It doesn't mean the child doesn't love Mom or Dad, but it is a spiritual discomfort if you are certain that everything else is all right, okay? Of course, there are other things that could be done, but I am allowing for your own spiritual practices. That's something I recommend, unless the doctor says no, and that must be honored.

Don't eat chocolate if you are on a diet [laughs] or you've decided you are on a diet. It's not about food allergies or food sensitivities or anything like that. Utilize chocolate for its medicinal purposes. Do you know that the people who are aware how the cocoa bean naturally grows, especially the older ones who know about these things, knew that the cocoa bean was always intended to be medicinal? So understand that, and you can appreciate its value in these kinds of circumstances.

Seriously speaking though, the chocolate, having it around in just little packages of small squares, as one might find in a bag of things like that, for example, a candy with caramel inside or a nut, would be okay. But no more than that. It is the chocolate on its own.

I think I have little Hershey bars here.

That might work just fine. Just take one, and don't eat it fast. Eat it slowly. I don't mean nibble it, just pop it into your mouth, if it is little, and eat it slowly. Let it melt in your mouth, and lean back and relax. That is the idea.

Okay, is there anything else that you want to say or start or finish?

Already there are people who are sensitives but who do not consider themselves candidates for this kind of thing, not that anybody does the first time, who are having the experience.

What percentage are ... ?

I cannot give you that detail. I will just say that it is beginning.

Thank you.

The Significance of Astrology for Walk-Ins

Astrological Historian

May 29, 2004

Does the astrology for the walk-in stay mostly with the soul who built the body?

Let's not say the soul who built the body. Let's say the soul whose intentions inspired the form of the body. Generally speaking, and I am not just splitting a hair here, the fundamentals of how the body looks, unless there are obvious anomalies — say, nine fingers instead of ten — is meant to be a certain way, the way most people look, all right. Other than that, there might not be that much influence of the individual soul on the physical body, which is why souls might tend to come and go. While the child is growing in its mother, a soul that is going to be in the body on a full-time basis might not always be there. In that sense, also being the personality, or sometimes called the immortal personality, it might tend to come and go. When it is there more often, it tends to get more active, as all mothers know, moving one's arms and legs.

You are saying that the birth soul comes and goes, and then what?

Then when it occupies the body, there is some adaptation by the body to that soul, but it is more the other way. The soul has to adapt to the body and to the physical world that body and soul are in. The purpose is so that the soul learns to adapt and acquire the various interactions of the lessons that it desires to learn, or study, in its Earth life. So when a walk-in takes place and that soul exits without a physical death, the walk-in will simply inherit a body that has not been programmed by the soul, no, no. Rather, that soul had to utilize the body to acquire its lessons, and it had to accept the body as is to do that, the original soul. If there is a walk-in, the walk-in has to do the same thing. It has to accept the body as is and then interact, study its lessons, and so on, based on what is found. So the system is almost identical in terms of acquisition of ones experiences as for the original soul in form.

So does there come a point when the walk-in is in the body long enough that the date it came in has any relevance?

I would say that if you can tell when you came in — it is very difficult, if there is no cognizance of the walk-in experience — within a day or even two or three days, just make a note of it. The chances of your being able to get the exact time are unlikely, but if it was possible or if in some time it is possible, then write that down. It can be considered by a good astrologer the way, say, the rising sign might be considered or the Moon. It doesn't replace them, but it is considered ...

Another influence.

... in equality with those signs, as compared to, say, the Sun sign. But if it is not known, then one accepts wholly and completely the astrology from the point of physical birth, right?

Yes. Well, most people don't ever know. Is there anything that astrologers should look for, or is it irrelevant? Should the astrologer be concerned about whether the person was a walk-in or not?

I wouldn't say so, unless the people bring up the subject on their own. "What about walk-ins?" "Could I be a walk-in?" Then astrologers, if the personality of the person is known, might have accumulated enough information about walk-ins by that time, their time, to be able to make the best guess utilizing their inspiration. But if they are not able to get it on the basis of their information and they have not been able to observe on the basis of simply talking to the person over time, then I would say that it would be best for the astrologers to put that aside.

Generally speaking for the walk-in, though, you would use the astrology based on the physical birth of your body because, as I say, both souls — the original and then in the case of the walk-in — have to accept the physical body as is, so that is the same for both souls, you see.

I always thought from what I read that the soul created the body in a way that would be best for what it wanted to do in its life.

Well, this is possible if the physical body has any specific identifiable anomalies such as, for instance, a condition that one might be born with. As I say, some unusual body thing, a handicap, or maybe something just the opposite. Maybe the body is born with a tremendous capacity for understanding the relationship of one thing to another, as in a high IQ, for example, which is not the best method of understanding mental capacity. However, it is something you perhaps still use. Or the person might have physical capabilities, being born, say, stronger than other youngsters as he or she develops or might even have other talents and abilities physically that are not readily apparent on examination of the baby.

In short, one might be born with extended capabilities as well as difficulties or challenges that might be known or observable. In that case, the soul must adapt. The original soul must adapt to that body, even though there might be something associated with that soul's desire to learn something, or develop compassion, for example, just as one possibility. The walk-in must accept that body as is, even though it also has desires or lessons or something it is here to study or learn in correlation to that physical body. Both souls, in the case of the original and the walk-in, must have certain similarities in their intentions for physical life so that the body as is, is not a burden, something that works in detriment to the soul being here physically.

The body has to work with your soul. There has to be some bias so that you as a walk-in might have some significant similarities on the soul level to the being who was originally in there. But there would be significant differences as well, which is why, for example, after a walk-in, it might be possible for that persona, the new soul in the physical body, to suddenly be able to resolve something that the previous had never been able to do.

Equally, it might be that something that the previous soul had been able to do is suddenly no longer of interest to the new soul in the body, and the person stops doing it or suddenly doesn't know how to do it. It would seem to others that this person has suddenly forgotten to do something. The new soul might be able to pick it up quickly, or it might be something that the new soul simply won't have interest in. Usually, it will not be something that has to do with vital family relationships or anything like that. It might be something simple. Maybe the previous soul liked to listen to old music, and the new soul is more interested in modern music, something like that.

※　※　※

Walk-Ins Express Different Traits of the Same Sign
Astrology Expert

Does a walk-in continue to be influenced by the point of birth of the body it walks into?

Yes, the walk-in brings with it — and of course, you rarely know the moment you walked in, as a doctor or nurse might write down the moment (to the best of their ability) you were birthed from mother — only a slightly different version of the influence. You have your Sun sign, you have your rising sign, and you have your Moon sign. Astrologers understand this. As a walk-in, you might have that as a distant influence with a personality that you bring with you. This can be noticed in a walk-in, some subtle differences in the personality of the individual. You see how the person was before the walk-in, how the person was after the walk-in.

In this situation, the subtle influence of personality change can be understood by an expert astrologer's observation. Of course, it would be helpful if the astrologer had known the person beforehand. But another way to factor it is — this only works if you have noticed you are or believe you might be a walk-in, based on the criteria that you have for that — anytime within a week or two is sufficient to grasp a subtle influence.

You cannot, really (I am trying to talk around this carefully so as not to reveal too much at this time) use your own systems, your own astrology. Generally speaking, walk-ins never come from systems that are their own. They will come from entirely different systems. That is why they stumble through the first year or two of life here — because they are learning new systems.

※　※　※

Physical Compatibility
Saturn

Walk-ins come in with different purposes, different personalities, different everything. How do they work with astrology?

Now, for a walk-in, of course, you find yourself in something that was prepared for someone else. However, anytime the preparation takes place, there is not just the initializing of the body (preparing it for your arrival as a soul) but also — and this cannot be ignored — preparation for the potential for a walk-in to take place. The walk-in can only take place if the initial soul chooses, for a reason, to exit or to go somewhere else, to continue life some place else.

The new soul coming in, in benevolent ways supported by Creator, must be comfortable with the creation of the previous soul. So you might say, and this is not an unreasonable observation, that the soul that left and the soul that came in must resemble each other. It might not necessarily equal a physical resemblance, of course, but if you were able to see the exiting and walk-in souls in their energetic states, you would see something that is profoundly similar. So you might say — and how can we say this in a not entirely joking manner? — that there's a family resemblance.

Therefore, the physical body that the walk-in finds him- or herself in is adequate to his or her expression. It might not be as ideal as it would have been had it been the initialized physical body, but it's as ideal as it can be given this manner of creation expressed in this form. It would be in that sense if you had, say, a twin brother or twin sister, and twins often do this, especially if they're identical. They sort of pretend to be each other sometimes, just for fun, and then that's okay so long as it's done just for fun, for a short time. Then you tell the other person, and no one gets hurt. It is not that difficult for a twin to maintain that for a short time because there is not only a physical resemblance but also some similarity in personality — not exactly the same, but some similarity. It is not unlike that in the walk-in situation.

So everything about the birth chart is still applicable to the walk-in?

No, not everything. That's why the walk-in often finds the physical body not to be particularly expressive of him- or herself. It is not at all unusual for the first one or two or three years of the walk-in to try to change the physical body in some way. Some people become more athletic, especially if they're younger. Some people put on weight, especially if they're older. There is a desire to allow the physical body to be more of the creation of the soul that walked in. So what is usually the case, say, seven or eight times out of ten, is some weight is put on, if only temporarily. This allows the new soul coming in to experience the simultaneity of creation that goes with the existence of being in a physical body that is normally experienced in the case of birthing, yes, to your mother, as the soul is inside mother and the physical body is forming in and around you.

Don't automatically assume, if I might be humorous for a moment, that if your friend or neighbor or lover is putting on weight, that he or she is a walk-in. On the other hand, it is not unusual for a walk-in to do this. It does not have to be permanent. It's almost like the feeling that you missed something. You can't be in mom, so you grow, you might say, as an adult. Then when you feel more comfortable and compatible in your physical body and are familiar with it, you can, if you choose, reform the physical body if you have reasonable physical health. You can perhaps reform it in some other way. You can do some activity; you can change your habits. In short, don't feel that you have to be big to be a walk-in.

How to Determine Time of "Birth"

What method does a walk-in use in astrology to get the information that he or she is looking for, since the walk-in ... ?

It's that it is good, but it is very difficult, all right. It is good to know the exact time of your birth. I do not know of any walk-in who knows that. So the next best thing is to know the exact day. It is very rare for a walk-in to know that. The next best thing is to consult with an astrologer, one who is very experienced — who has worked with many clients and who can (on the basis of your birth astrology), by simply being with you for a time, observe you well and thoroughly (conversation, going to lunch, something like that). Take an astrologer to lunch, okay? [Chuckles.]

You can ask him or her whether your personality traits (you know, sometime after he or she gets to know you) indicate a time of your entry as a walk-in. You might have to go to lunch or dinner so that the astrologer can take time to get to know you, and he or she might be able to catch it right away. It depends. Ask whether your personality traits follow in the astrologer's experience with the birth chart or whether it might be an expression the astrologer would normally find, in his or her experience, with some other sign in the chart.

This might also be a nice way to make a friend. It could be a way to discover more about yourself. Remember, this is a planet where people do not only serve one another all the time but also come here to meet others, to have experiences with beings who are having experiences similar to yours — not always, but very often.

There is another application for this. There are some of you who are adopted or perhaps not aware of what time you were born or even what place you were born in. You can use this same method. You can talk to an experienced astrologer who might be able to tell you, according to the birth chart, if not the exact time of birth and perhaps not even the exact day, your basic signs on the basis of their perception of human personalities as applied to their chosen fields.

Humor

There's another thing, if I might bring up something on my own, that is really important for walk-ins, for people who know they are walk-ins, to do. Try to become familiar with the humor of the person in the culture you find yourself in. Read books, be with friends as you make them, and enjoy your family to the extent that you can. Try to discover humor and how to react to it. Sometimes it will be obvious and easy, but at other times, it will be difficult.

Humor is a profound thread that will connect you to other human beings through shared experience and will often help you over the difficult times when you are feeling very strange in a place that does not have any landmarks familiar to you. This is a typical experience for walk-ins (and even those born naturally) when they do not have a great deal of experience on Earth in your times.

✳   ✳   ✳

The Body's Zodiac Sign Is Relevant
Virgo
July 28, 2007

How does a walk-in approach coming into the body of a previous soul who had chosen a particular sign to work in? Is there always a connection? Do the walk-ins come in wanting that sign for their growth, or is it just an accident of the bodies available or what?

There are no accidents, period. The soul who comes in will have similar desires as compared to the previous, so the astrology associated with the physical being's birth cycle will very closely encompass the desires of the walk-in personality. It may not be exactly the same, however. It might be some other aspect of Virgo in that sense. So if you are close to such a person who has had a walk-in, you might notice some perceptible change in personality and perhaps different expressions of Virgo qualities, but you will not notice anything that resembles a change of personality so drastic that they are no longer the Virgo.

So is it safe to say that if the walk-in had had a physical birth, he or she would have chosen that sign also?

Yes. It is essential in the walk-in world (as much as I know about this) that there be a very significant compatibility between the exiting soul and the walk-in soul. It would be so much of a compatibility that if they could meet as two individuals they would become very close friends almost immediately. This is why there must be a slight intermission, so to speak: One has to walk out, and there has to be a gap — usually a few seconds, sometimes a little longer — before the walk-in takes place. Otherwise, if they are both there, there is a tendency to become attached to each other.

Sometimes when, for one reason or another, a walk-in takes longer, it is because there is a certain attraction from one to the other. This is rare, but it happens sometimes. If you suspect this is the case for you as a walk-in, it is best to practice just letting go. If you can practice letting go, then those parts of you that need to move on and that are confusing you and causing you to feel hazy or strange will simply move on. Practice that, and you will feel better soon.

All right. That's very good advice. One of the reasons I have stayed away from astrology after I became a walk-in is that I felt it wasn't relevant to me. I felt it had nothing to do with me, and my astrology sign had to do with the previous occupant.

No, that is not true. What it means is that you are approaching your sign from a different direction. If you read as much as you can about those influences in your chart as it formerly was, you will be able to see clearly how the previous version of you matches you now. The more you can read about innuendos and details and so on, the more you will discover how you still match that sign but are expressing a different face. Picture yourself looking in the mirror, but then you turn and your reflection in the mirror is still you, and from that angle, you do not see the mirror well, but the mirror sees you well.

In short, others still see you that way, but you do not see yourself that way. It pays you to read about what you might have been physically, and it also helps you to understand why you might have certain drives and tendencies, even though it has nothing to do with who you are in your present personality. It would help you to identify what is you and what is not you, but it is not good to resist these drives and tendencies if your personal being, who you are now, is attracted to that. Look at how you've changed and where your energy is specifically expressing itself in that sign but in a different way, and then you will appreciate that sign more. You will appreciate the vast subtlety the astrologic world is all about. It seems, on the surface, to be very blunt, but in fact, it has many, many fine points that require a considerable amount of reading, and you are not afraid of that, so try it.

Thank you.

You are very welcome. Astrological pursuits are a great deal about fine lines. Think of it this way: You walk into an art museum and look at some fine old painting. And the museum people don't want you to get too close to the picture, so you look at the picture in some other way, perhaps in a photograph, a blowup of tiny portions, and you can see the brushwork. You can examine the picture's details in certain ways (in books, for example), and you can see different aspects of the picture that you hadn't seen before, even subtle messages that are not obvious from a distance. As you examine the details more closely, what the artist is attempting to reveal might be very fine details indeed.

Sometimes the direction of the brush stroke is intended to influence those who look at it. Do you know that when the artist uses a longitudinal brush stroke, the tendency is for the viewer of that artwork to relax, but when the artist uses a vertical brush stroke, the tendency is for the viewer to become aroused or stimulated? Did you know that?

Absolutely not. That's wonderful.

That's an example of the value of examining the detail that Virgo is known for. Look at a painting like that some time. You will notice that the direction of the brush stroke has an impact as well as the image. This kind of thing is usually studied in more esoteric circles in art, but you artists out there, if you're reading this, incorporate this (if you don't already know about it). Put this into your painting or even in other forms of expressive artwork, and it might surprise you and even delight you how your audience reacts.

It is important to recognize the qualities of personality associated with a sign, and I believe the planets have made this clear, trusting astrologers to recognize and interpret those planetary personalities and add that interpretation into their knowledge base. It is my intention and, I believe, the intention of the other signs to reveal such qualities as per the planets so that astrologers can apply, learn, know, and interpret for themselves and others.

Thank you very much.

Living Prayer

Speaks of Many Truths

Living prayer allows you as an individual to give to the Earth. So many of you ask, "What can I do for the Earth? What can I do for the animals? What can I do for people suffering in other parts of the world or in my own town or family? What can I do?"

If people are suffering on the other side of the Earth, you can say, "May the people be nurtured and know they are loved. May their hearts be healed and may they find what they need, or may it be brought to them in a benevolent, beneficial way for all beings."

Say this key phrase — "I will ask," or "I am asking" — out loud, though perhaps softly. This way it is understood that what you are asking is about physical things. In the case of a war on the other side of the world, you might say, "I ask that everyone's heart be healed and that people find peace together in the most benevolent and beneficial way for them."

Let's say you are driving [in the forest] and there is no one else around. Suddenly your heart hurts. It is a dull ache. When you get used to this living prayer, you will look around and say, "I will ask." The moment you say that key phrase, Creator knows that you are saying a living prayer. "May the heart of the forest be healed. May the hearts of all the trees, plants, rocks, animals and spirits who like to be here be healed. May they enjoy their time in the forest and feel welcome."

Then go on. Your heart will probably feel better. If you get the feeling again farther up the road, say it again without looking at them, "May their hearts be healed. May they feel welcome wherever they go or where they are."

Always say these things out loud, although you can say these things softly if you need to.

Remember, you have to say these blessings only once for each place, person or group of people. You are more sensitive now, and the plants and the animals and the stone and maybe even other people are more sensitive, too. You all need each other now more than ever, and here is something you can do to help others and feel better yourself.

Try not to look directly at people who cause your heart to hurt. Some other part of your body may hurt sometimes when you are near people who are suffering in some way. First ask that their hearts be healed, then add other parts of them according to what hurts on you. You don't have to name the organ unless you feel sure; just say the place on the body.

It is intended now that many people begin giving and asking for such prayers. As Mother Earth and her rocks, trees, plants and animals come under more strain in your time due to so many people and their needs, these natural forms of life may no longer be able to give you the healings and blessings they have been giving simply by being and radiating their good health. So you can now give to them in return for all their generations of benevolence. These prayers are all they ask.

Cellular Tissues and Walk-Ins

Mars

Are there opportunities determined by the energies affecting the soul at birth?

Yes. We are talking about physicality here. The soul's desires are actually in the cellular structure of baby at birth. The memory of that — if not necessarily every single one of those cells, though some of them remain — is infused, at the very least, as an echo in the cellular tissue, even up to the point of death by age. So that soul, and this also affects walk-ins, has those opportunities to continue to come up.

A sidelight here for walk-ins: Even if the walk-in experience takes place, there will be those opportunities that continue to come up that the new soul simply doesn't take advantage of because the new soul does not have that same desire. But those experiences continue to come up. They might not, however, cause you to trip over something, as it were. The previous soul might have gone straight for that, whereas you will simply take notice of it, "Oh," and go on and do something else. But the opportunity presents itself, nevertheless, because of the memory of that original intent.

So where are the desires of the walk-in soul, then? They are not included in the cells?

It becomes an overlay. It's very much like, oh, you spread peanut butter and jelly on a piece of bread, and it doesn't necessarily soak in. It is there for a while, but walk-ins don't necessarily say, "Okay, here is where I am, and here is where I am going to stay." That is why, if you have a walk-in experience, there is no guarantee that you are going to be there forever. Maybe somebody else will walk in. So it is kind of like peanut butter and jelly, if you don't mind my epicurean reference.

APPENDIX J

The Changing Human Perspective

Isis

All right, this is Isis. It is a real challenge for most walk-ins when they come in. As souls, they don't have an opportunity to adapt in the usual way in which their souls can be nurtured and given that bridge to life. The bridge begins inside mother. You are in the water. You are insulated and protected up to a point. You feel a sense that perhaps life could be done here in some way. You are cheered and nurtured.

Also, because you start to hear sounds inside of your mother, you get interested. You want to see what's going on out there. In short, there's an opportunity to get used to and to anticipate life as you know it here. Then there is the time of childhood that also prepares you for life. The walk-in does not have any of these things.

The walk-in might be an old soul, a wise being, but he or she has no buffer for life beyond Earth, which is, for the most part, totally benevolent to life on Earth in an adult body, usually. This lack of buffer creates an urgent desire within a walk-in's soul to hang on to something that he or she can use as a bridge just the same way that new soul is a bridge growing in baby. And the thing that the new soul, the walk-in soul, hangs on to is whatever the old personality, or the soul who has departed, hasn't completely taken with him or her.

Generally speaking, the old soul is a little reluctant to migrate out of the body. You might think that the old soul would be happy to get out with no pain, "Yay! Let me outta here." But because the walk-in soul's departure is happening in a way that is not a portion of the natural cycle of life on Earth, there is kind of a slow release from the physical body.

Initially, when that soul departs, it feels very much like the sleep state — when one goes out and travels but remains tethered to the physical body, you understand, at the deep sleep state. That is actually something that soul will do. He or she will hang on to the physical body on a tether for a time. And that is exactly what the new soul often, not always, grabs on to. This does not hold the exiting soul because the tether itself is not part of the soul. It has to do with an umbilical cord that Creator provides so that souls in deep sleep can connect with guides and teachers and life beyond Earth to be reminded that life in general is benevolent.

The new soul comes in with no bridge and immediately grabs on to that tether. When that grab takes place, the exiting soul is like, "Oh okay, they're there. I can go now," and away they go. So the challenge is that when a new soul comes in and grabs on to that tether, there's a tendency to hang on to habits, personality quirks, and other adaptations to the physical life that the previous soul made to how the new soul, the walk-in soul, will adapt to life.

This creates, at least temporarily, a situation where the new soul has some greater element of instantaneous ways of coping, so for a couple days, that's fine. It's not a problem. The problem exists when the walk-in soul won't release that tether, and then the walk-in personality experiences dread, literally, a physical feeling of dread, of letting go of something. The walk-in soul just doesn't know what it is.

An Exercise for Letting Go

I want to give an exercise here so that it isn't just gloom and doom. I want to suggest that if you have determined that you might be a walk-in, the first thing to do is to lie down somewhere or sit down in a comfortable chair alone if you can. Turn the phone ringer off. Try to do this at a time of day or night when there will be the fewest disturbances. If there's a lot of noise, especially coming in from outside your house or your apartment or your dwelling, feel free to use earplugs or some other means to quiet that noise. But do not use a so-called white noise–maker. This will be a distraction. Also do not use music; you need to be able to focus and concentrate here.

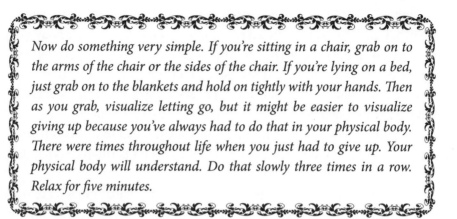

Now do something very simple. If you're sitting in a chair, grab on to the arms of the chair or the sides of the chair. If you're lying on a bed, just grab on to the blankets and hold on tightly with your hands. Then as you grab, visualize letting go, but it might be easier to visualize giving up because you've always had to do that in your physical body. There were times throughout life when you just had to give up. Your physical body will understand. Do that slowly three times in a row. Relax for five minutes.

This will most likely let go of that tether, and you can get on with life. You'll wake up feeling refreshed.

Disentangle from Your Discomforts and Pains

Become Your True Self

Ssjoooo

The Disentanglement Basic Process

Lie on a flat surface on your back, hands by your side, palms down and slightly away from your body — preferably three hours after eating and before you go to sleep, but it works anywhere, anytime. Do not cross your legs or feet. This position allows you to get used to being vulnerable in your most receptive area.

Say out loud (if possible), "I ask gold lightbeings to disentangle me from my pains and discomforts. If other teachers or guides or lightbeings of other colors want to help, I ask them to assist the gold lightbeings."

Squeeze your eyelids shut and then focus on the light patterns — don't think. If you catch yourself thinking, gently bring your attention back to the light patterns and continue. Do this for an hour or as long as you feel like doing it or until you fall asleep. This can be done twice a day.

After a few weeks, make a list of every person and event in your life that makes you feel uncomfortable. Say the above statement and add, "I am asking to be disentangled from the discomfort and pain of _____," reading one or two names or events from the list. Do each name for two to three days or until you feel clear with the person.

Speaks of Many Truths Adds:

"You may notice that if you say those specific words or names during the course of your day, after you've done disentanglement on them three to five times, you no longer feel as physically uncomfortable about them as you once did.

"This means the disentanglement is working. The objective is to feel physically calm. Keep saying those specific words or names in your disentanglement process until you feel physically calm. When you do, move on to other words or names, never more than one or two at a time."

About the Author

ROBERT SHAPIRO is largely known as a professional trance channel who has channeled several series of published books. As he is now, he is a mystical man with shamanic capabilities that are well and thoroughly infused into him. He also has many unusual skills that he teaches through blogs, the *Sedona Journal of Emergence!*, and books. It is his intention to bring about the most benevolent change available on the planet through sharing his personal inspirations as well as his channeling. Learn more about Robert and his work at google.com/+BenevolentMagic.

His great contributions to a better understanding of the history, purpose, and future of humanity on Earth are his epochal works:

- The Explorer Race Series
- The Shining the Light Series
- The Shamanic Secrets Series
- The Ultimate UFO Series
- The Secrets of Feminine Science Series
  (All are available as print books and ebooks.)

♀ **Light Technology** PUBLISHING **Presents**

THE EXPLORER RACE SERIES

ZOOSH AND OTHERS THROUGH ROBERT SHAPIRO

Superchannel Robert Shapiro can communicate with any personality anywhere and anywhen. He has been a professional channel for over twenty-five years and channels with an exceptionally clear and profound connection.

The Origin... The Purpose...The Future...of Humanity

If you have ever questioned about **who you really are, why you are here** as part of humanity on this miraculous planet, and **what it all means**, these books in the Explorer Race series can begin to supply the answers — the answers to these and other questions about the mystery and enigma of physical life on Earth.

These answers come from beings who speak through superchannel Robert Shapiro, beings who range from particle personalities to the Mother of All Beings and the thirteen Ssjooo, from advisors to the Creator of our universe to the generators of precreation energies. **The scope, the immensity, the mind-boggling infinitude of these chronicles by beings who live in realms beyond our imagination will hold you enthralled.** Nothing even close to the magnitude of the depth and power of this all-encompassing, expanded picture of reality has ever been published.

This amazing story of the greatest adventure of all time and creation is the story of the Explorer Race, all of humanity on Earth and those who came before us who are waiting for us. The Explorer Race is a group of souls whose journeys resulted in incarnations in this loop of time on planet Earth, where, bereft of any memory of their immortal selves and most of their heart energy, they came to learn compassion, to learn to take responsibility for the consequences of their actions, and to solve creation's previously unsolvable dilemma of negativity. We humans have found a use for negativity: We use it for lust for life and adventure, curiosity and creativity, and doing the undoable. And in a few years, we will go out to the stars with our insatiable drive and ability to respond to change and begin to inspire the benign but stagnant civilizations out there to expand and change and grow, which will eventually result in the change and expansion of all creation.

Once you understand the saga of the Explorer Race and what the success of the Explorer Race Experiment means to the totality of creation, **you will be proud to be a human and to know that you are a vital component of the greatest story ever told** — a continuing drama whose adventure continues far into the future.

THROUGH ROBERT SHAPIRO

The Explorer Race
Book 1

gives you the foundational understanding of who you are, why you are on Earth, and where you are going.

Zoosh, End-Time Historian
through Robert Shapiro

"Welcome to the Explorer Race — of which you are a portion. What you are about to embark on now is a way to understand the entirety of your being as well as all that is around you.

"The Explorer Race series — what I like to call the Explorer Race history books — is intended to give you all the background you need to understand the value, purpose, and greater vision of what you are doing here on Earth. The information contained within is intended to remind you of your true capabilities and your true capacities. Don't let anybody tell you that you have to give up God or religion to do this. You don't. These books don't take that away from you.

"These books will give you the background you need to understand why you are here and help you to appreciate your true value. The Explorer Race books are intended — literally — to change your life, to put meaning where there wasn't meaning before, and to provide you with the insight and wisdom you need to improve the quality of your life and the lives of those all around you, maybe even on other planets.

"That's why you exist. That's why you're here. So enjoy the liberation you feel from the wonderful insights of Book 1 — and the others in the series you read. Welcome to the Explorer Race!"

— Zoosh

$25.00 • Softcover • 608 PP.
978-0-9293853-8-9

CHAPTERS INCLUDE:
- Origin of the Species: a Sirian Perspective
- Conversation with a Zeta
- The ET in You: Physical Body
- Coming of Age in the Fourth Dimension
- The True Purpose of Negative Energy
- The White Brotherhood, Illuminati, New Dawn, and Shadow Government
- Fulfilling the Creator's Destiny
- Etheric Gene Splicing and the Neutral Particle
- The Third Sex: the Neutral Binding Energy
- The Goddess Energy: the Soul of Creation
- The Heritage from Early Civilizations ꝗ

THROUGH ROBERT SHAPIRO

ETs and the EXPLORER RACE
Book 2

Joopah, Zoosh and others
through Robert Shapiro

The purpose of this book is to guide you toward acceptance of the differences among you all, as well as acceptance of the wide variety of life that the universe has in store for you.

Know that we will look forward to meeting you explorers as you come out to the stars, and we will help you in every way we can. Please enjoy the book.

— Joopah

$14.95 • Softcover • 240 PP.
978-0-929385-79-2

CHAPTERS INCLUDE

- The Great Experiment: Earth Humanity
- ETs Talk to Contactees
- Becoming One with Your Future Self
- ET Interaction with Humanity
- UFOs and Abductions
- The True Nature of the Grays
- Answering Questions in Las Vegas
- UFO Encounters in Sedona
- Joopah, in Transit, Gives an Overview and Helpful Tools
- We Must Embrace the Zetas
- Roswell, ETs, and the Shadow Government
- ETs: Friends or Foes?

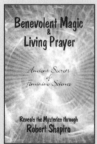

Benevolent Magic
&
Living Prayer

*Ancient Secrets
of
Feminine Science*

Reveals the Mysteries through
Robert Shapiro

Benevolent Magic & Living Prayer
$9.95 • 3.75 x 5 • Softcover • 96 PP. • 978-1-891824-49-4

This book is intended to cover, at least in a beginning way, manners and methods by which you can create for yourselves benevolently and create for others benevolently. This book is intended to teach you the ancient wisdom of gentle methods of feminine creation.

I want to remind you, to let you know immediately, that the purpose of these little books, what these books are intended to do, is to nurture, to support and—by their very titles, as well as how the books read—to serve you, to improve the quality of your lives and to support you in supporting yourselves and others. —Isis

Light Technology PUBLISHING Presents

265

TO ORDER PRINT BOOKS
Visit LightTechnology.com, Call 928-526-1345 or 1-800-450-0985,
or Check Amazon.com or Your Favorite Bookstore

THROUGH ROBERT SHAPIRO

ORIGINS and the NEXT 50 YEARS
Book 3

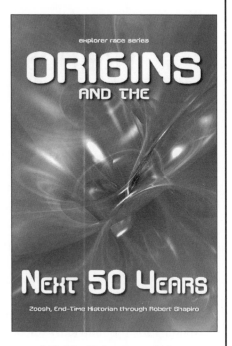

explorer race series

ORIGINS AND THE NEXT 50 YEARS

Zoosh, End-Time Historian through Robert Shapiro

This volume has so much information about who we are and where we came from — the source of male and female beings, the war of the sexes, the beginning of the linear mind, feelings, the origin of souls — it is a treasure trove. In addition there is a section that relates to our near future — how the rise of global corporations and politics affects our future, how to use benevolent magic as a force of creation, and then how we will go out to the stars and affect other civilizations. Astounding information!

$14.95 • Softcover • 384 PP.
978-0-929385-95-2

CHAPTERS INCLUDE

- Our Creator and Its Creation
- The White Race and the Andromedan Linear Mind
- The Asian Race, the Keepers of Zeta Vertical Thought
- The African Race and Its Sirius/Orion Heritage
- The Fairy Race and the Native Peoples of the North
- The Australian Aborigines, Advisors of the Sirius System
- The Return of the Lost Tribe of Israel
- The Body of the Child, a Pleiadian Heritage
- Creating Sexual Balance for Growth
- The Origin of Souls
- The New Corporate Model
- The Practice of Feeling
- Benevolent Magic
- Future Politics
- A Visit to the Creator of All Creators
- Approaching the One

THROUGH ROBERT SHAPIRO

CREATORS and FRIENDS:
The Mechanics of Creation Book 4

Now that you have a greater understanding of who you are in the larger sense, it is necessary to remind you of where you came from, the true magnificence of your being, to have some of your true peers talk to you. You must understand that you are creators in training, and you were once a portion of Creator. One could certainly say, without being magnanimous, that you are still a portion of Creator, yet you are training for the individual responsibility of being a creator to give your Creator a coffee break.

This book will give you peer consultation. It will allow you to understand the vaster qualities and help you remember the nature of the desires that drive any creator, the responsibilities to which that creator must answer, the reaction any creator must have to consequences, and the ultimate reward of any creator. This book will help you appreciate all of the above and more. I hope you will enjoy it and understand that maybe more will follow.

$19.95 • Softcover • 480 PP.
978-1-891824-01-2

CHAPTERS INCLUDE
- Andastinn, Prototype of Insect Beings
- Kazant, a Timekeeper
- Founders of Sirius, Creators of Humanoid Forms
- A Teacher of Buddha and Time Master's Assistant
- Designers of Human Physiology
- Avatar of Sea Creatures; and Quatsika, Messenger for the Dimension Makers
- The Empath Creator of Seventeen Planets
- Shapemaker of Portals
- Creator of the Inverse Universe, Our Creator's Creator

☥ *Light Technology* PUBLISHING **Presents**   267

TO ORDER PRINT BOOKS
Visit LightTechnology.com, Call 928-526-1345 or 1-800-450-0985,
or Check Amazon.com or Your Favorite Bookstore

THROUGH ROBERT SHAPIRO

PARTICLE PERSONALITIES
Book 5

All around you in every moment you are surrounded by the most magical and mystical beings. They are too small for you to see as single individuals. But in groups, they form all of your physical life as you know it.

Particles — who might be considered either atoms or portions of atoms — consciously view the vast spectrum of reality yet also have a sense of personal memory like your own linear memory. Unlike your linear memory, where you remember the order of events you have lived, these particles remember where they have been and what they have done in their long, long lives and can access the higher strains associated with their experiences as well.

For instance, perhaps at one time a particle might have been a portion of a tree, when it had access to all the tree's higher wisdom and knowledge, what it had been before or might be in the future. Or perhaps it might have been in the ocean. The knowledge of anything swimming past it or growing or simply existing nearby would also be available to it. So a particle has not only its own personal wisdom but anything or anyone it has ever passed through.

Particles, then, have a unique and unusual perspective. In reading this book, understand that some of them will have similar points of view. But others will have quite extraordinary and unexpected points of view. Expect the unexpected!

$14.95 • Softcover • 256 PP.
978-0-929385-97-6

CHAPTERS INCLUDE
- A Particle of Gold
- The Model Maker: the Clerk
- The Clerk, a Mountain Lion Particle, a Particle of Liquid Light, and an Ice Particle
- A Particle of Rose Quartz from a Floating Crystal City
- A Particle of Uranium, Earth's Mind
- A Particle of the Great Pyramid's Capstone
- A Particle of the Dimensional Boundary between Orbs
- A Particle of Healing Energy

Light Technology PUBLISHING Presents

269

TO ORDER PRINT BOOKS
Visit LightTechnology.com, Call 928-526-1345 or 1-800-450-0985,
or Check Amazon.com or Your Favorite Bookstore

THROUGH ROBERT SHAPIRO

COUNCIL of CREATORS
Book 7

The thirteen core members of the Council of Creators discuss their adventures in coming to awareness of themselves and their journeys on the way to the Council on this level. They discuss the advice and oversight they offer to all creators, including the creator of this local universe. These beings are wise, witty, and joyous, and their stories of love's creation create an expansion of our concepts as we realize that we live in an expanded, multiple-level reality.

THE EXPLORER RACE
COUNCIL OF CREATORS
AND ZOOSH THROUGH
ROBERT SHAPIRO

$14.95 • Softcover • 288 PP.
978-1-891824-13-5

CHAPTERS INCLUDE

- Specialist in Colors, Sounds, and Consequences of Actions
- Specialist in Membranes that Separate and Auditory Mechanics
- Specialist in Sound Duration
- Explanation from Unknown Member of Council
- Specialist in Spatial Reference
- Specialist in Gaps and Spaces
- Specialist in Divine Intervention
- Specialist in Synchronicity and Timing

- Specialist in Hope
- Specialist in Honor
- Specialist in Mystical Connection between Animals and Humans
- Specialist in Change and the Velocity of Change
- Specialist in the Present Moment
- Council Spokesperson and Specialist in Auxiliary Life Forms

THROUGH ROBERT SHAPIRO

The EXPLORER RACE and ISIS
Book 8

This book will address the Creator in all of you and speak directly to stimulate the benevolence of that energy you are all built upon. Creator School is the place where the energy that precedes creators comes from in order that creators might create their ability, their energy, and their capacity to manifest. It is my intention to speak not only about the seen and the unseen, but also, from time to time, the unimagined.

— Isis

This is an amazing book. It has priestess training, shamanic training, Isis adventures with Explorer Race beings — before Earth and on Earth — and an incredibly expanded explanation of the dynamics of the Explorer Race. Isis is the prototypal loving, nurturing, guiding feminine being, the focus of feminine energy. She has the ability to expand limited thinking without making people with limited beliefs feel uncomfortable.

She is a fantastic storyteller, and all her stories are teaching stories. If you care about who you are, why you are here, where you are going, and what life is all about — pick up this book. You won't lay it down until you are through, and then you will want more.

THE EXPLORER RACE AND
ISIS

THROUGH
ROBERT SHAPIRO

$14.95 • Softcover • 352 PP.
978-1-891824-11-1

CHAPTERS INCLUDE

- Isis and Your Creator
- The Biography of Isis
- The Planetary Influence of Isis
- The Adventurer
- Soul Colors and Shapes
- Creation Mechanics
- The Insect Form and Fairies
- Orion's Transition and Its Application to Earth
- The Veil and the Blue Portal
- The Goddess and the Natural Feminine
- Self-Violence and Self-Love
- The Concept of Mutual Benefit
- "The Vast You" and Other Realities
- Priestess/ Feminine Mysteries
- Levels of Being
- Who Is Isis?

🕯 *Light Technology* PUBLISHING **Presents** 271

TO ORDER PRINT BOOKS
Visit LightTechnology.com, Call 928-526-1345 or 1-800-450-0985,
or Check Amazon.com or Your Favorite Bookstore

THROUGH ROBERT SHAPIRO

The Explorer Race and Jesus Book 9

THE EXPLORER RACE AND **JESUS**

through ROBERT SHAPIRO

In this book, I will make an effort to speak of who I really am, where I'm from, what I'm doing now, why I went to Earth, what I hoped to accomplish, what I really did accomplish, and perhaps other things. I want to try to explain why things happened, why people did "this" or "that" during my lifetime. I will try to fill in details.

— Jesus

The immortal personality who lived the life we know as Jesus, along with his students and friends, describes with clarity and love his life and teaching on Earth 2,000 years ago.

These beings lovingly offer their experiences of the events that happened then and of Jesus's time-traveling adventures, especially to other planets and to the nineteenth and twentieth centuries, which he called the time of the machines — the time of troubles.

It is so heartwarming and interesting that you won't want to put it down.

$16.95 • Softcover • 352 PP.
978-1-891824-14-2

- The Teachings and Travels
- A Student's Time with Jesus and His Tales of Jesus's Time Travels
- The Shamanic Use of the Senses
- Many Journeys, Many Disguises
- The Child Student Who Became a Traveling Singer-Healer
- Learning to Invite Matter to Transform Itself
- Inviting Water, Singing Colors
- Learning about Different Cultures and People
- The Role of Mary Magdalene, a Romany
- Jesus's Autonomous Parts, His Bloodline, and His Plans

CHAPTERS INCLUDE
- Jesus's Core Being, His People, and the Interest of Four of Them in the Earth
- Jesus's Home World, Their Love Creations, and the Four Who Visited Earth
- The "Facts" of Jesus's Life Here, His Future Return

THROUGH ROBERT SHAPIRO

Earth History and Lost Civilizations
Book 10

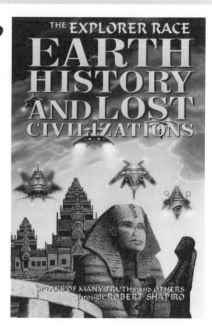

Speaks of Many Truths and Zoosh, through Robert Shapiro, explain that Planet Earth, the only water planet in this solar system, is on loan from Sirius as a home and school for humanity, the Explorer Race.

Earth's recorded history goes back only a few thousand years, its archaelogical history a few thousand more. Now this book opens up the past as if a light was turned on in the darkness, and we see the incredible panorama of brave souls coming from other planets to settle on different parts of Earth. We watch the origins of tribal groups and the rise and fall of civilizations, and we can begin to understand the source of the wonderous diversity of plants, animals, and humans that we enjoy here on beautiful Mother Earth.

$14.95 • Softcover • 320 PP.
978-1-891824-20-3

- The Academy of All Peoples: Cave Paintings, Symbols, and Crop Circles
- Sumer, an Art Colony from Sirius
- Nazca Lines Radiate Enthusiasm for Life
- Easter Island Statues: a Gift for the Future
- Lucy and her Laetoli Footprints
- Egypt and Cats as Teachers of Humans
- The Electrical Beings
- The Andromedan Origins of Stone Medicine Wheels
- Carnac in Brittany
- Egypt
- China
- Tibet and Japan
- Siberia

CHAPTERS INCLUDE
- When Earth was Sirius
- Ancient Artifacts Explained
- Fire and Ice People and Multidimensional Lightbeings
- Early Civilizations on Earth: Mongollians and Desert People
- The Long Journey of Jehovah's Ship, from Orion to Sirius to Earth
- Andazi Teach Jehovah How to Create Human Beings

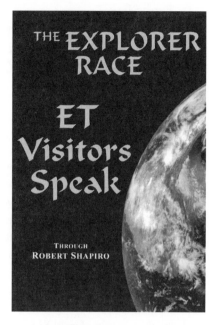

THROUGH ROBERT SHAPIRO

Animal Souls Speak Book 13

"The animal world will speak, if you prefer, through elders. This has certain advantages, since that way they can include knowledge and wisdom to a degree — not to a vast degree, but to a degree — about their home planets."

— Grandfather

Each animal brings a wondrous gift to share with humanity — enjoy it!

"Welcome to the footsteps of the loving beings who support you, who wish to reveal more about themselves to you, and who welcome you not only to planet Earth but, more specifically, to the pathway of self-discovery. Take note as you read this book of what resonates, what stimulates your own memories.

Use it to inspire you and to encourage you, to support you along your path toward inevitable self-discovery — ultimately to support self-discovery in others that results in revealing the true and most benevolent heart of all beings. Good life."

— Creator's Emissary

$29.95 • Softcover • 640 PP.
978-1-891824-50-0

THROUGH ROBERT SHAPIRO

Plant Souls Speak
Book 16

Planet Energies Available to You:
Live Plant 100% • Dead Plant 10%

"What we intend to speak about — if I may speak in general for all plants — is how you can interact with plants in a more benevolent way for you as the human species. For a long time, you have been clear on medicinal uses of leaves and stems and seeds and flower petals and so on, but you are only getting about one-tenth of the energy available to you that way. It is always better to interact with the plant and its energies in its live form, but you need to know how.

"The intention of this book is to reveal that formula so that you can stop searching, as a human race, for the magical cures to diseases by exhausting the supply of life forms around you when a much simpler process is available. The beings in this book will not just comment on things you know about but show you what you are missing in your interaction with plants."

— Dandelion

$24.95 • Softcover • 576 PP.
978-1-891824-74-6

In this book, the plant world will speak through elders. This has certain advantages, allowing them to include knowledge and wisdom about their home planets. In this way, you will learn some of the old wisdom again, shared so that you can discover how to interact with the plants while they are alive, while they are a portion of the Creator of All Things.

With this, you will learn the beginnings, the reminders, and for many of you, the fulfillment of the transformation of that which does not work in your body, in your life, in your community, and in your world: the transformation of what you call dis-ease or disharmony into harmony and ease.

— Zoosh, Isis, and Grandfather

**Each plant brings a wondrous gift to
share with humanity — enjoy it!**

CHAPTERS INCLUDE

- Cherry Tree
- Maple Tree
- Palm Tree
- Peach Tree
- Pine Tree
- Redwood
- Walnut Tree
- Brown Rice
- Crabgrass
- Oat Grass
- Wetland Grass
- Angelica
- Bamboo
- Corn
- Daffodil
- Dandelion
- Hibiscus
- Holly
- Ivy
- Kelp
- Marijuana
- Orchid
- Rose
- Sage
- Soy Bean
- White Rose

🜚 *Light Technology* PUBLISHING **Presents**   279

TO ORDER PRINT BOOKS
Visit LightTechnology.com, Call 928-526-1345 or 1-800-450-0985,
or Check Amazon.com or Your Favorite Bookstore

THROUGH ROBERT SHAPIRO

TIME and the Transition to Natural Time
Book 17

THE EXPLORER RACE

TIME
AND THE **Transition to Natural Time**

THROUGH ROBERT SHAPIRO

"The purpose of this book is to provide a context for your lives in the sequence you find yourselves in now. This explanation of time — and, to a degree, its variables — is being provided for you so that you will understand more about your true, natural, native personalities and so that you will be reminded that you are, as you know, in a school and that this school is purely temporary.

"You don't come here very often to this place of linear time; like in your own human lives, you are in school for only so long, and then you live your lives. When you exist beyond this school, you will find all those lives infinitely easier. And even as the Creator, your lives will be easier than they are in the single, linear existences you're living now, because you will have all your components."

— Founder of Time

$16.95 • Softcover • 352 pp.
978-1-891824-85-2

CHAPTERS INCLUDE
- Time Is Now Available for Your Personal Flexibility
- Your Blinders Are Coming Off
- You Live in a Stream Hosted by Planet Earth
- Time Is an Application for Expansion
- You Are Moving toward Complete Safety and Benevolence
- You Can Transition to the Future in Warmth and Safety
- The Gift of Time
- Your Future Selves Are Linking to You
- You Are Here to Learn about Your Personal Physicality
- You are Making the Transition through Deep Sleep
- You Will Let Go of Conflict in the Next Focus
- There Are Many Expressions of Time

THROUGH ROBERT SHAPIRO

ETs on Earth, Volume 1 Book 18

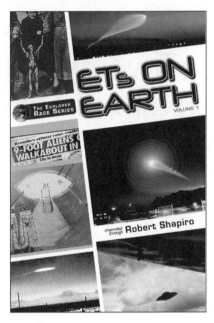

$16.95 • Softcover • 352 PP.
978-1-891824-91-3

Greetings. This is Zoosh.

In the beginning of the Explorer Race adventure — that means you, all humans on Earth — way back, ETs on Earth were a normal thing. In fact, you were ETs who came from many different planets those thousands of years ago, and you felt that Earth was a wonderful place where you could thrive.

I want you to keep that in mind when you read about these ETs that happen to be still visiting Earth. In this book, as well as in other books that have material like this, if you can keep that in mind, it will not be too surprising or shocking. In fact, for most of you, you will be ETs again in another life, and your youngsters just might be ETs from Earth visiting other planets in the future.

This should be a fun read and a gentle reminder that ETs are just friends from some place — you might say from another neighborhood.

Good life.

Chapters Include
- ET Beings Use Green Light to Support Earth Beings
- Humans Are Going through Rapid Changes on Earth
- Update on ETs and UFOs
- Blue Spiral Light over Norway
- A Glimpse Beyond the Explorer Race
- Will There Be a Phony ET Invasion on Earth? Orbs Are Lightbeings Visiting Benevolent Spaces
- You Traverse to Your Home Planet in Deep Sleep
- The "Little People" Are Humans from Alpha Centauri
- Beware of a Staged ET Invasion
- Crop Circles: Origins, Purposes, and Mysteries

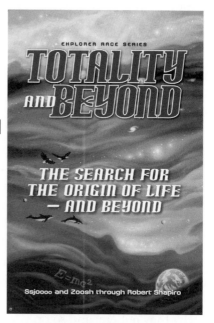

☽ *Light Technology* PUBLISHING *Presents*

TO ORDER PRINT BOOKS
Visit LightTechnology.com, Call 928-526-1345 or 1-800-450-0985,
or Check Amazon.com or Your Favorite Bookstore

THROUGH ROBERT SHAPIRO

Shamanic Secrets Series

Speaks of Many Truths, Zoosh and Reveals the Mysteries through Robert Shapiro

Shamanic Secrets for Material Mastery

This book explores the heart and soul connection between humans and Earth. Through that intimacy, miracles of healing and expanded awareness can flourish. To heal the planet and be healed as well, you can lovingly extend your energy self out to the mountains and rivers and intimately bond with Earth. Gestures and vision can activate your heart to return you to a healthy, caring relationship with the land you live on. The character of some of Earth's most powerful features is explored and understood with exercises given to connect you with those places. As you project your love and healing energy there, you help Earth to heal from human destruction of the planet and its atmosphere. Dozens of photographs, maps, and drawings assist the process in twenty-five chapters, which cover Earth's more critical locations.

SOFTCOVER • 512 PP. • $19.95 • ISBN 978-1-891824-12-8

Shamanic Secrets for Physical Mastery

Learn to understand the sacred nature of your physical body and some of the magnificent gifts it offers you. When you work with your physical body in these new ways, you will discover not only its sacredness but also how it is compatible with Mother Earth, the animals, the plants, and even the nearby planets, all of which you now recognize as being sacred in nature. It is important to feel the value of oneself physically before you can have any lasting physical impact on the world. If a physical energy does not feel good about itself, it will usually be resolved; other physical or spiritual energies will dissolve it because they are unnatural. The better you feel about your physical self when you do the work in the first book, as well as this one and the one to follow, the greater and more lasting the benevolent effect will be on your life, on the lives of those around you, and ultimately on your planet and universe.

SOFTCOVER • 608 PP. • $25.00 • ISBN 978-1-891824-29-6

Shamanic Secrets for Spiritual Mastery

Spiritual mastery encompasses many different means to assimilate and be assimilated by the wisdom, feelings, flow, warmth, function, and application of all beings in your world that you will actually contact in some way. A lot of spiritual mastery has been covered in different bits and pieces throughout all the books we've done. My approach to spiritual mastery, though, will be as grounded as possible in things that people on Earth can use — but it won't include the broad spectrum of spiritual mastery, like levitation and invisibility. My life is basically going to represent your needs, and in a storylike fashion it gets out the secrets that have been held back."

— Speaks of Many Truths

SOFTCOVER • 528 PP. • $29.95 • ISBN 978-1-891824-58-6

✲ Light Technology PUBLISHING

ANDROMEDA

The Andromedans and Zoosh through Robert Shapiro

The Andromedans who originally contacted the Professor speak through superchannel Robert Shapiro and again give instructions that will allow trained scientists to construct a shield around existing Earth planes so that Earth astronauts can fly to Mars or to the stars.

The Andromedans also tell what really happened on their journeys and on Earth, and they clear up questions one would have after reading the English or Spanish version of the previous book — the text of which follows the channeling in this book.

In addition, they supply a lively account of their lives on their home planet in the Andromedan constellation of our galaxy.

The eight-foot-tall, highly mental crew members of the ship who speak include

- Leia, the beautiful cultural specialist and social diplomat who so intrigued the Professor
- Cheswa, the cultural liason
- G-dansa, Leia's daughter, equivalent to an eight-year-old ET Eloise
- Duszan, the Junior Scientist
- Onzo, the Senior Scientist and Crew Leader, the youngest yet genetically modified to be the most brilliant of the crew
- Playmate, a two-foot-tall, roly-poly Andromedan who teaches communion of heart and mind

Ultimate UFO Series:
ANDROMEDA
Channeled Commentary by
ANDROMEDANS & ZOOSH THROUGH
Robert Shapiro

Includes the Text of UFO CONTACT FROM ANDROMEDA
EXTRATERRESTRIAL PROPHECY
UFO Books: Rodriguez • Hernandez • Stevens

$16⁹⁵

464 PP. • SOFTCOVER
ISBN 978-1-891824-35-7

Chapters Include

- Our Ancestors Came from Space
- Extraterrestrial Concepts of Energy
- Reviewing the Past and Feelings
- Early Visits to Earth
- Antimatter
- Our Explosive Atmosphere
- On Space Travel
- ET View of Our Religion
- Life and Death of Planets
- Changes Overcome Me
- The Extraterrestrial Photographed

ULTIMATE UFO SERIES

The ZETAS

History, Hybrids, and Human Contacts
THROUGH Robert Shapiro

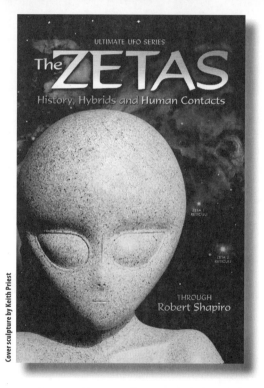

Cover sculpture by Keith Priest

The Zetas Speak About

- Betty Andreasson, the Hills, and the Ceremony of Renewal
- Children of Isis: Path of the Zeta
- Zetas Describe their Lives
- The Zetas in Human History
- The Truth of Travis Walton's Case, Among Others, and the Planet of Cats
- Gifted Spacecraft, Crashed Spacecraft, and the Test of Technology
- Roswell and the Case of Billy Meier
- The Effects of Time Travel
- Parent Race of the Zetas
- Creation of the Zetas
- Earth's Work with Quantum Mastery and the Loop of Time
- Joao and the Andromedans
- The Pascagoula Affair

$24⁹⁵
Plus Shipping

ISBN 978-1-891824-36-4
Softcover • 480 PP.
6 X 9 Perfect Bound

"The beings on Zeta Reticuli are the future selves — granted, several million years into the future — of the beings on Earth right now. On the soul line, this has to do with your evolution to become more, to be more established benevolently on a creative level. By the time your souls become those Zeta Reticulan beings several million years into the future, you will be able to interact with all life in the most benevolent way while being strongly intellectual and scientific.

"In this way, your science will have a complete balance with heart and soul. This is one of the greatest aspects of significance between you and the Zeta Reticulan beings as of this time. So to them you are their past lives — that's why they're so fascinated with you — but for you, when you interact with these beings, you are truly meeting, in many senses, your future."

— Zoosh through Robert Shapiro ❦